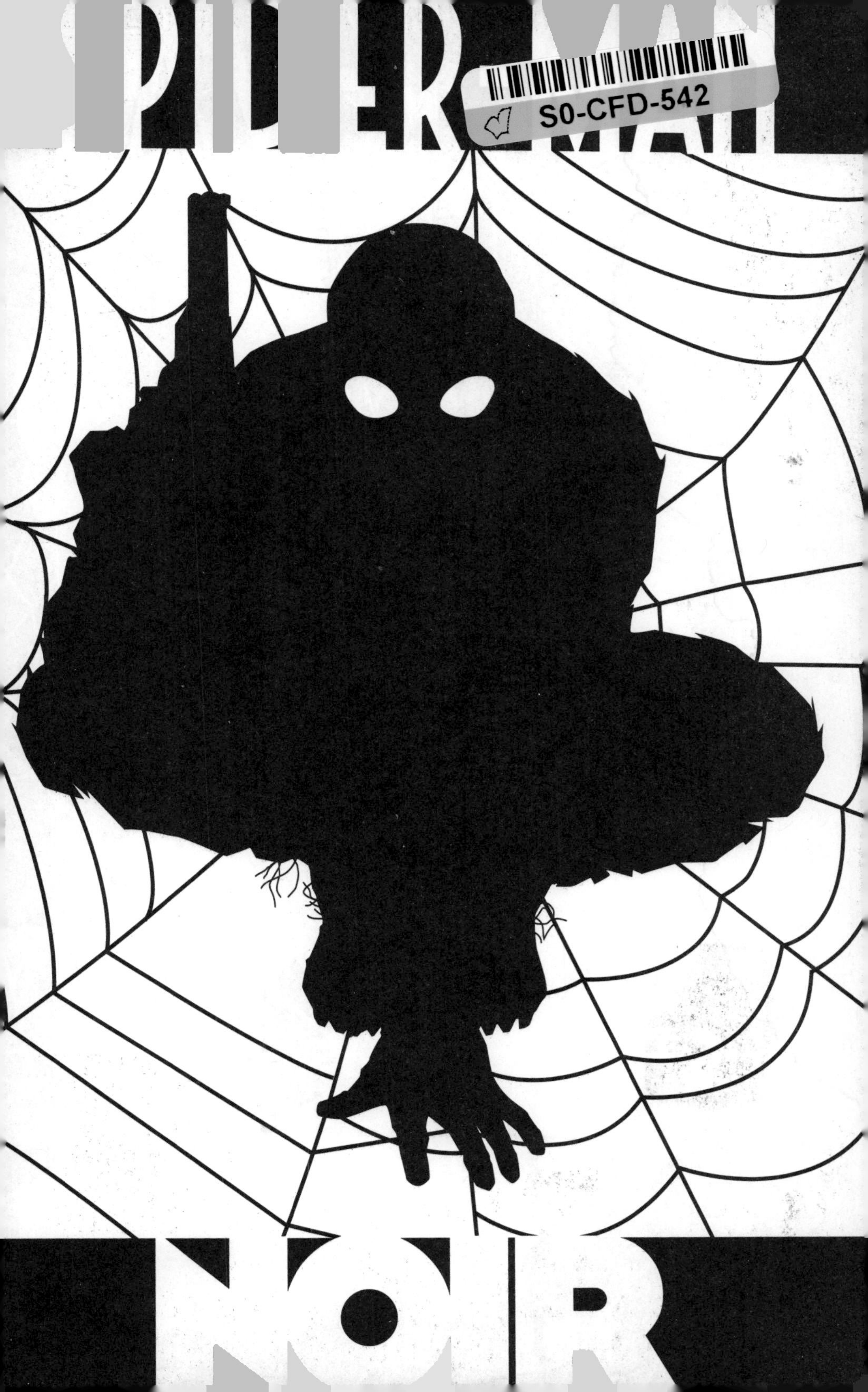
SPIDER-MAN
NOIR

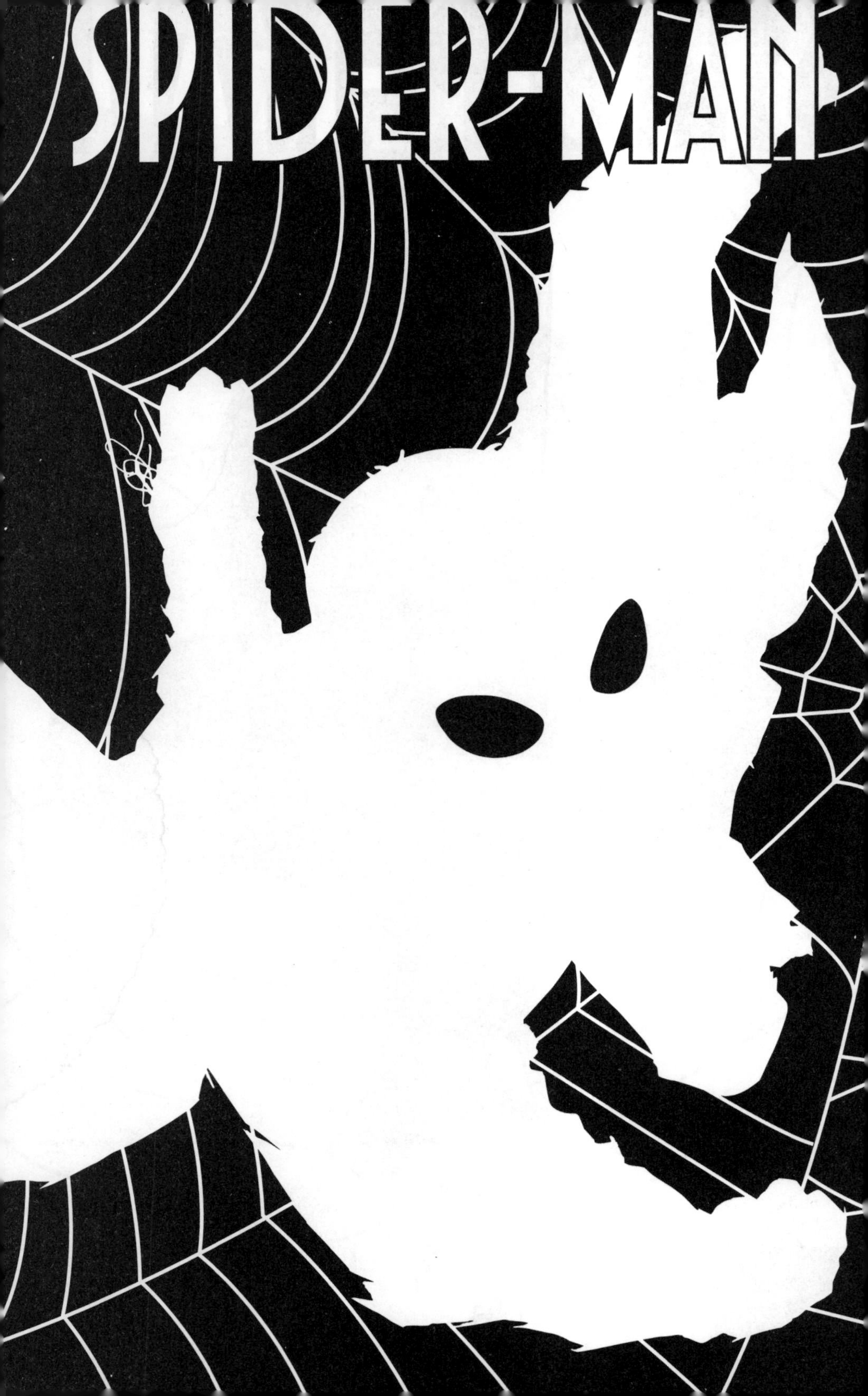
SPIDER-MAN

WRITERS
DAVID HINE
WITH
FABRICE SAPOLSKY

ART
CARMINE
DI GIANDOMENICO

LETTERS
ARTMONKEYS STUDIOS

COVER ART
PATRICK ZIRCHER

EDITOR
ALEJANDRO ARBONA

SUPERVISING EDITOR
WARREN SIMONS

COLLECTION EDITOR
JENNIFER GRÜNWALD
ASSISTANT EDITORS
ALEX STARBUCK & JOHN DENNING
EDITOR, SPECIAL PROJECTS
MARK D. BEAZLEY
SENIOR EDITOR, SPECIAL PROJECTS
JEFF YOUNGQUIST
SENIOR VICE PRESIDENT OF SALES
DAVID GABRIEL
BOOK DESIGNER
JEFF POWELL

EDITOR IN CHIEF
JOE QUESADA
PUBLISHER
DAN BUCKLEY
EXECUTIVE PRODUCER
ALAN FINE

SPIDER-MAN NOIR. Contains material originally published in magazine form as SPIDER-MAN NOIR #1-4. First printing 2009. ISBN# 978-0-7851-2923-3. Published by MARVEL PUBLISHING, INC., a subsidiary of MARVEL ENTERTAINMENT, INC. OFFICE OF PUBLICATION: 417 5th Avenue, New York, NY 10016. Copyright © 2009 Marvel Characters, Inc. All rights reserved. $14.99 per copy in the U.S. (GST #R127032852); Canadian Agreement #40668537. All characters featured in this issue and the distinctive names and likenesses thereof, and all related indicia are trademarks of Marvel Characters, Inc. No similarity between any of the names, characters, persons, and/or institutions in this magazine with those of any living or dead person or institution is intended, and any such similarity which may exist is purely coincidental. **Printed in the U.S.A.** ALAN FINE, EVP - Office Of The Chief Executive Marvel Entertainment, Inc. & CMO Marvel Characters B.V.; DAN BUCKLEY, Chief Executive Officer and Publisher - Print, Animation & Digital Media; JIM SOKOLOWSKI, Chief Operating Officer; DAVID GABRIEL, SVP of Publishing Sales & Circulation; DAVID BOGART, SVP of Business Affairs & Talent Management; MICHAEL PASCIULLO, VP Merchandising & Communications; JIM O'KEEFE, VP of Operations & Logistics; DAN CARR, Executive Director of Publishing Technology; JUSTIN F. GABRIE, Director of Publishing & Editorial Operations; SUSAN CRESPI, Editorial Operations Manager; ALEX MORALES, Publishing Operations Manager; STAN LEE, Chairman Emeritus. For information regarding advertising in Marvel Comics or on Marvel.com, please contact Mitch Dane, Advertising Director, at mdane@marvel.com. For Marvel subscription inquiries, please call 800-217-9158. **Manufactured between 8/7/09 and 8/26/09 by R. R. DONNELLEY, CRAWFORDSVILLE, IN, USA.**

10 9 8 7 6 5 4 3 2 1

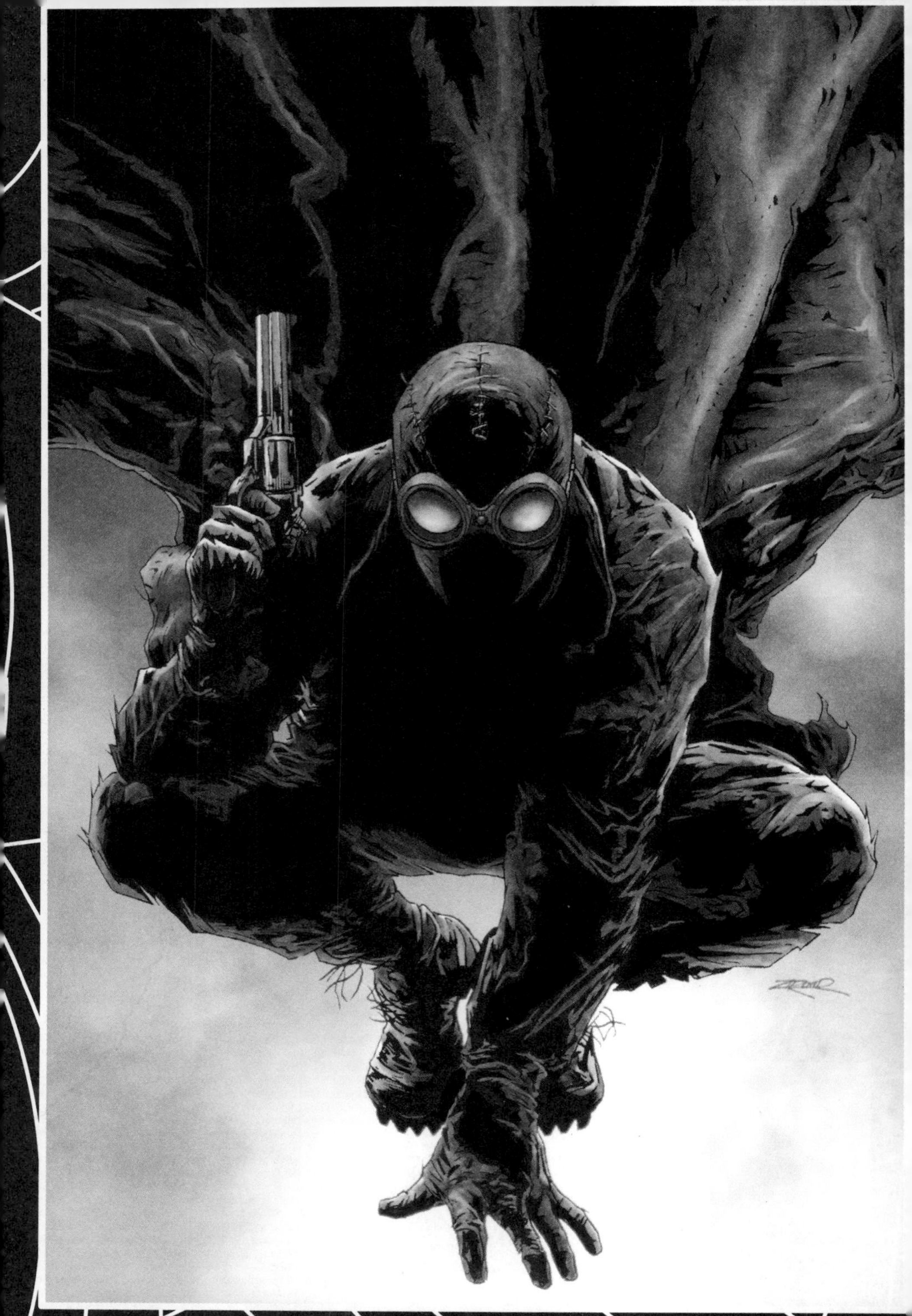

ONE

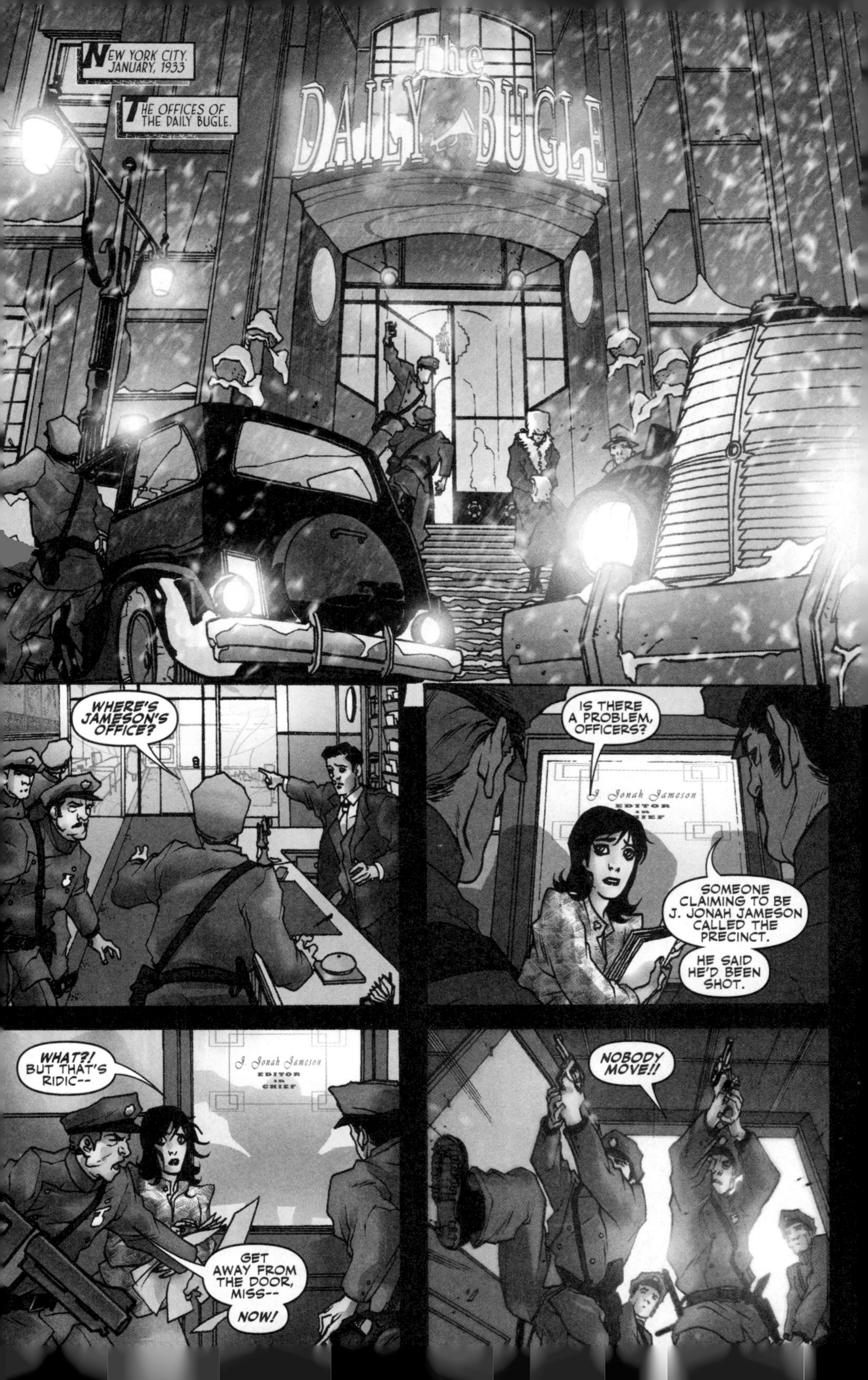
NEW YORK CITY. JANUARY, 1933
THE OFFICES OF THE DAILY BUGLE.
The DAILY BUGLE
WHERE'S JAMESON'S OFFICE?
IS THERE A PROBLEM, OFFICERS?
J. Jonah Jameson EDITOR in CHIEF
SOMEONE CLAIMING TO BE J. JONAH JAMESON CALLED THE PRECINCT.
HE SAID HE'D BEEN SHOT.
WHAT?! BUT THAT'S RIDIC--
J. Jonah Jameson EDITOR in CHIEF
GET AWAY FROM THE DOOR, MISS--
NOW!
NOBODY MOVE!!

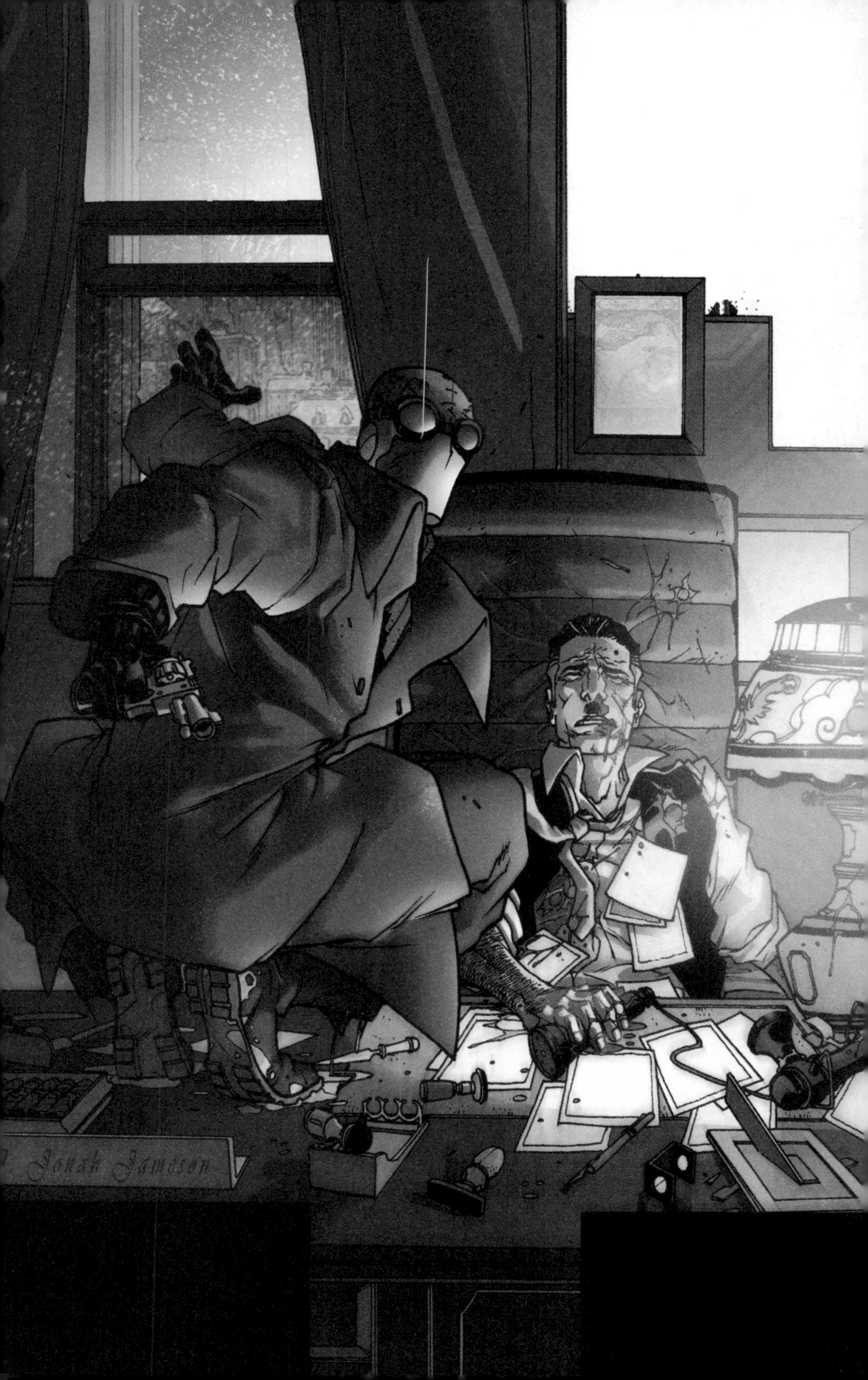
Jonah Jameson

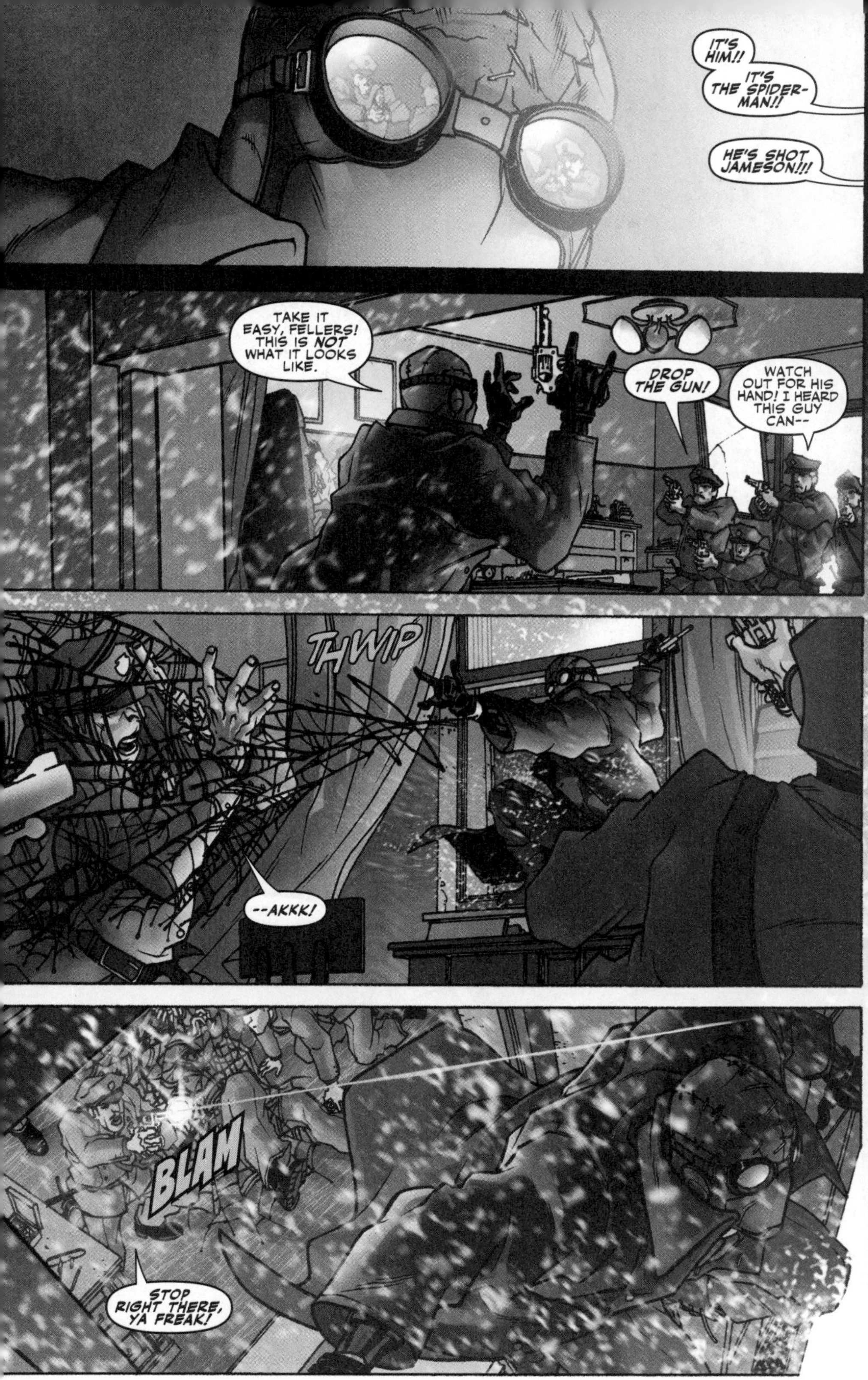
IT'S HIM!!
IT'S THE SPIDER-MAN!!
HE'S SHOT JAMESON!!!
TAKE IT EASY, FELLERS! THIS IS NOT WHAT IT LOOKS LIKE.
DROP THE GUN!
WATCH OUT FOR HIS HAND! I HEARD THIS GUY CAN--
THWIP
--AKKK!
BLAM
STOP RIGHT THERE, YA FREAK!

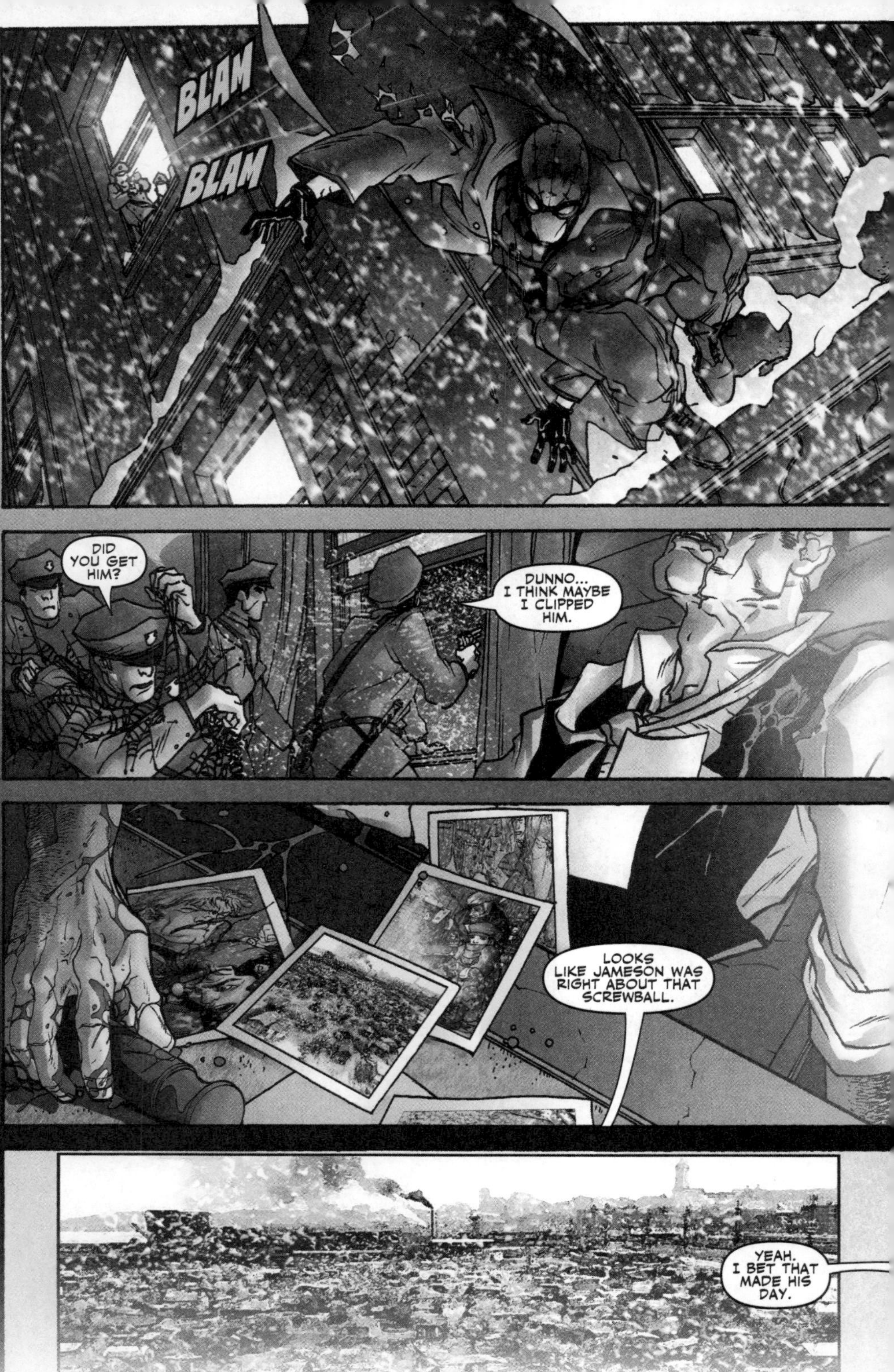
BLAM
BLAM
DID YOU GET HIM?
DUNNO... I THINK MAYBE I CLIPPED HIM.
LOOKS LIKE JAMESON WAS RIGHT ABOUT THAT SCREWBALL.
YEAH. I BET THAT MADE HIS DAY.

Three weeks ago... is that all it was? Winter was setting in hard. Down below Riverside Drive, squatters had put up a shantytown along the Hudson from 72nd Street to 110th.

"Get me pictures, Urich," JJJ told me. "We're going to show the public what's really happening out there."

I want broken men and hopeless women. I want snot-nosed kids in rags. I want to see the hunger in their eyes. I want pictures that'll make 'em **weep!**"

YOU FROM THE PAPERS, PAL? WHAT RAG YOU REPRESENTING?

THE BUGLE.

YOU MIND IF I TAKE YOUR PICTURE?

SURE, THE BUGLE'S A GOOD PAPER. I'VE GOT THE FRONT PAGES RIGHT HERE...

...SPORTS PAGES IN MY SHOES...

...AND I SAVE THE FINANCIAL SECTION TO WIPE MY KEISTER!

WHAT'S GOING ON OVER THERE?

THAT'S MAY PARKER ROUSING THE COMRADES.

"LET THE RULING CLASSES TREMBLE...THE PROLETARIANS HAVE NOTHING TO LOSE BUT THEIR CHAINS..."

≶P-TOOO≶

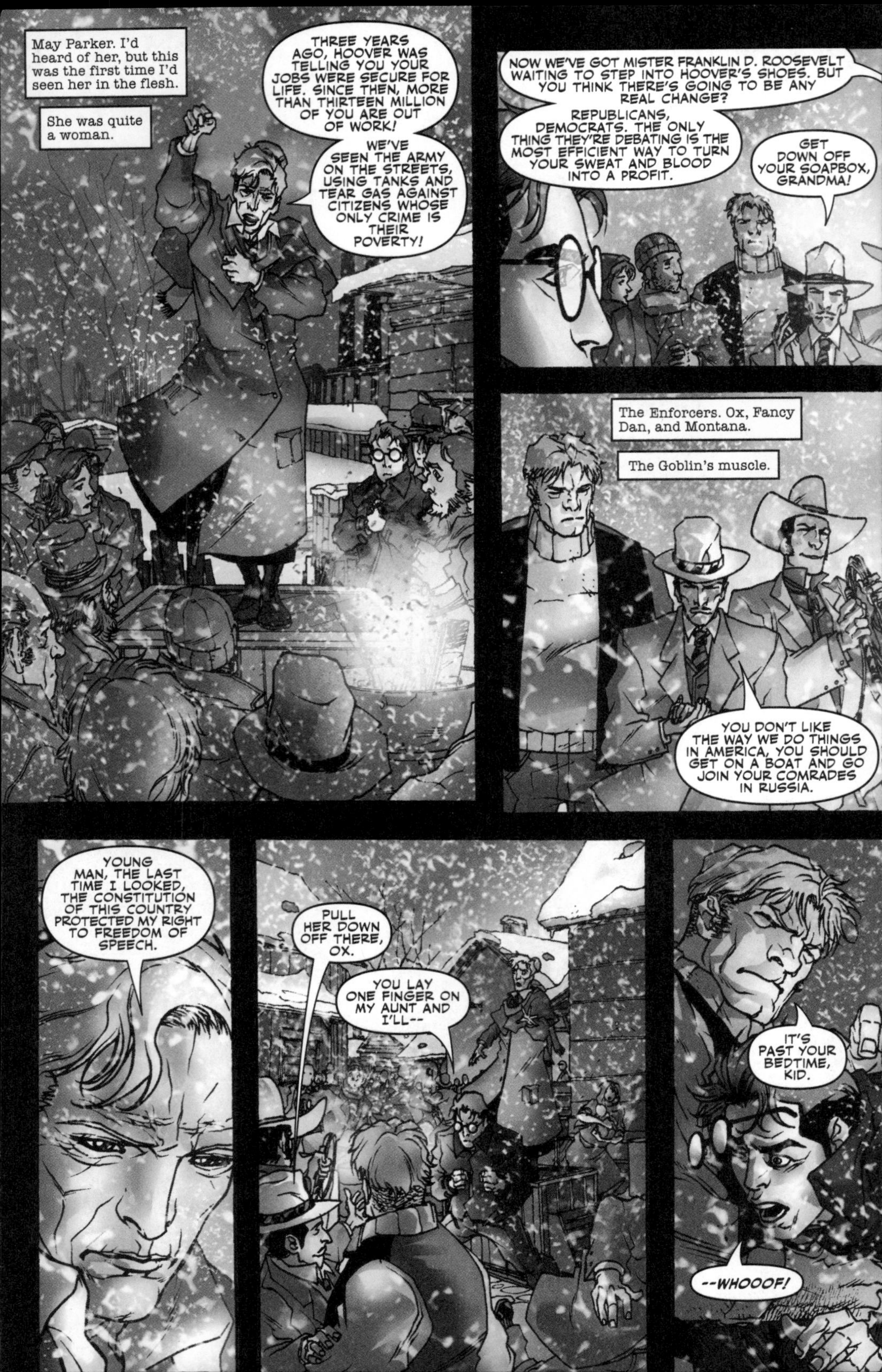

May Parker. I'd heard of her, but this was the first time I'd seen her in the flesh.
She was quite a woman.
THREE YEARS AGO, HOOVER WAS TELLING YOU YOUR JOBS WERE SECURE FOR LIFE. SINCE THEN, MORE THAN THIRTEEN MILLION OF YOU ARE OUT OF WORK!
WE'VE SEEN THE ARMY ON THE STREETS, USING TANKS AND TEAR GAS AGAINST CITIZENS WHOSE ONLY CRIME IS THEIR POVERTY!
NOW WE'VE GOT MISTER FRANKLIN D. ROOSEVELT WAITING TO STEP INTO HOOVER'S SHOES. BUT YOU THINK THERE'S GOING TO BE ANY REAL CHANGE?
REPUBLICANS, DEMOCRATS. THE ONLY THING THEY'RE DEBATING IS THE MOST EFFICIENT WAY TO TURN YOUR SWEAT AND BLOOD INTO A PROFIT.
GET DOWN OFF YOUR SOAPBOX, GRANDMA!
The Enforcers. Ox, Fancy Dan, and Montana.
The Goblin's muscle.
YOU DON'T LIKE THE WAY WE DO THINGS IN AMERICA, YOU SHOULD GET ON A BOAT AND GO JOIN YOUR COMRADES IN RUSSIA.
YOUNG MAN, THE LAST TIME I LOOKED, THE CONSTITUTION OF THIS COUNTRY PROTECTED MY RIGHT TO FREEDOM OF SPEECH.
PULL HER DOWN OFF THERE, OX.
YOU LAY ONE FINGER ON MY AUNT AND I'LL--
IT'S PAST YOUR BEDTIME, KID.
--WHOOOF!

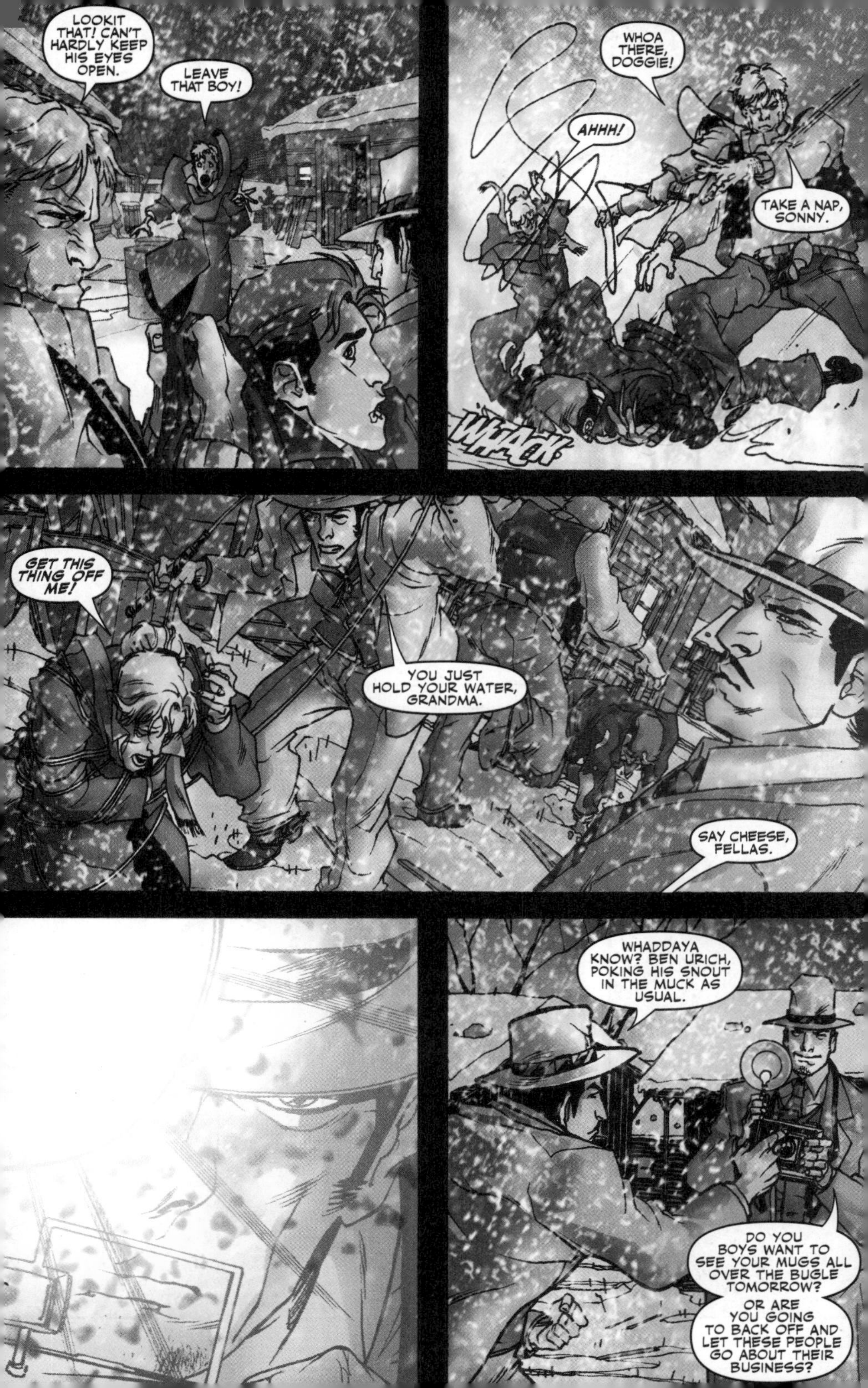
LOOKIT THAT! CAN'T HARDLY KEEP HIS EYES OPEN.
LEAVE THAT BOY!
WHOA THERE, DOGGIE!
AHHH!
TAKE A NAP, SONNY.
WHACK
GET THIS THING OFF ME!
YOU JUST HOLD YOUR WATER, GRANDMA.
SAY CHEESE, FELLAS.
WHADDAYA KNOW? BEN URICH, POKING HIS SNOUT IN THE MUCK AS USUAL.
DO YOU BOYS WANT TO SEE YOUR MUGS ALL OVER THE BUGLE TOMORROW?
OR ARE YOU GOING TO BACK OFF AND LET THESE PEOPLE GO ABOUT THEIR BUSINESS?

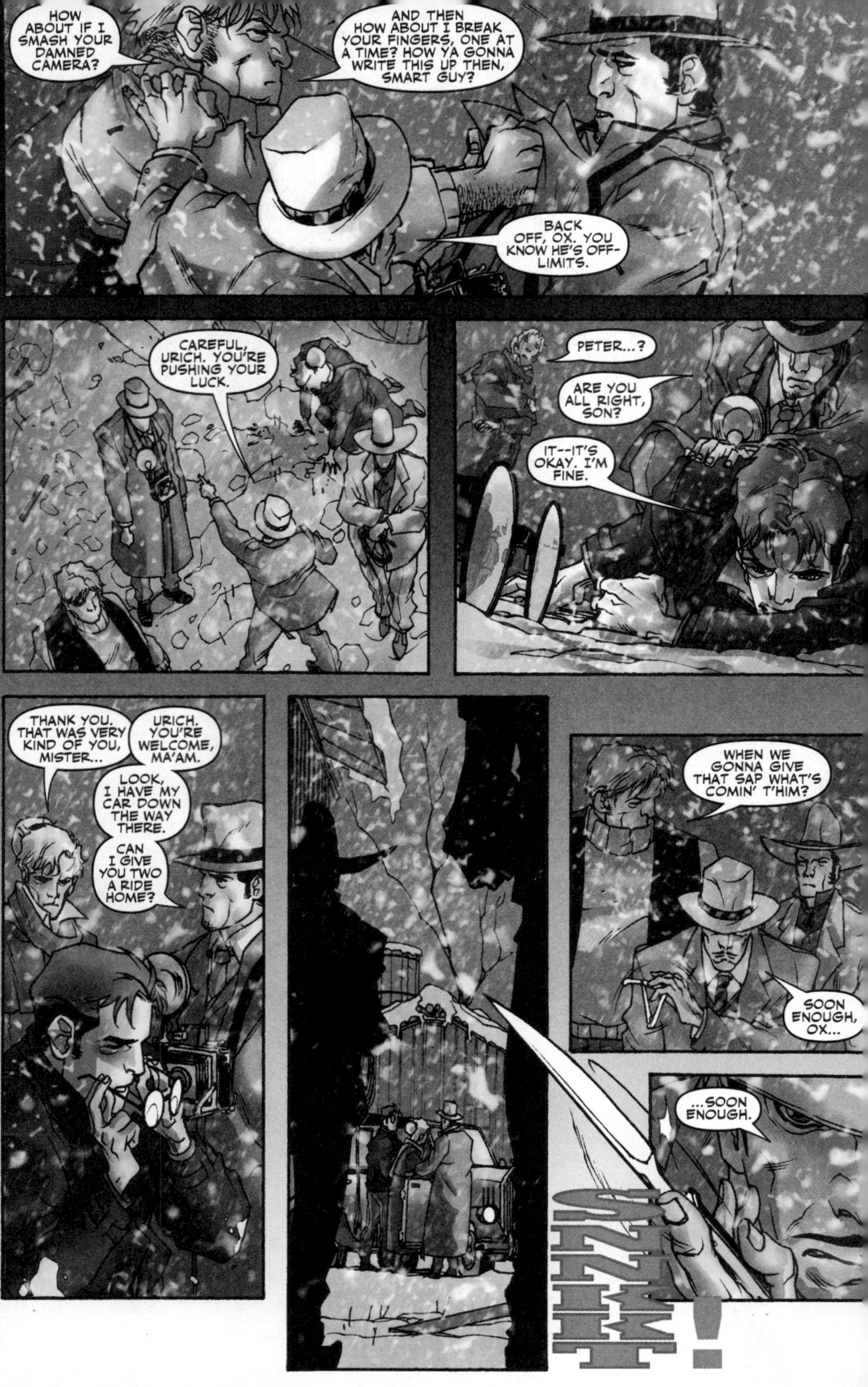
HOW ABOUT IF I SMASH YOUR DAMNED CAMERA?
AND THEN HOW ABOUT I BREAK YOUR FINGERS, ONE AT A TIME? HOW YA GONNA WRITE THIS UP THEN, SMART GUY?
BACK OFF, OX. YOU KNOW HE'S OFF-LIMITS.
CAREFUL, URICH. YOU'RE PUSHING YOUR LUCK.
PETER...?
ARE YOU ALL RIGHT, SON?
IT--IT'S OKAY. I'M FINE.
THANK YOU. THAT WAS VERY KIND OF YOU, MISTER...
URICH. YOU'RE WELCOME, MA'AM.
LOOK, I HAVE MY CAR DOWN THE WAY THERE.
CAN I GIVE YOU TWO A RIDE HOME?
WHEN WE GONNA GIVE THAT SAP WHAT'S COMIN' T'HIM?
SOON ENOUGH, OX...
...SOON ENOUGH.
SNIKT!

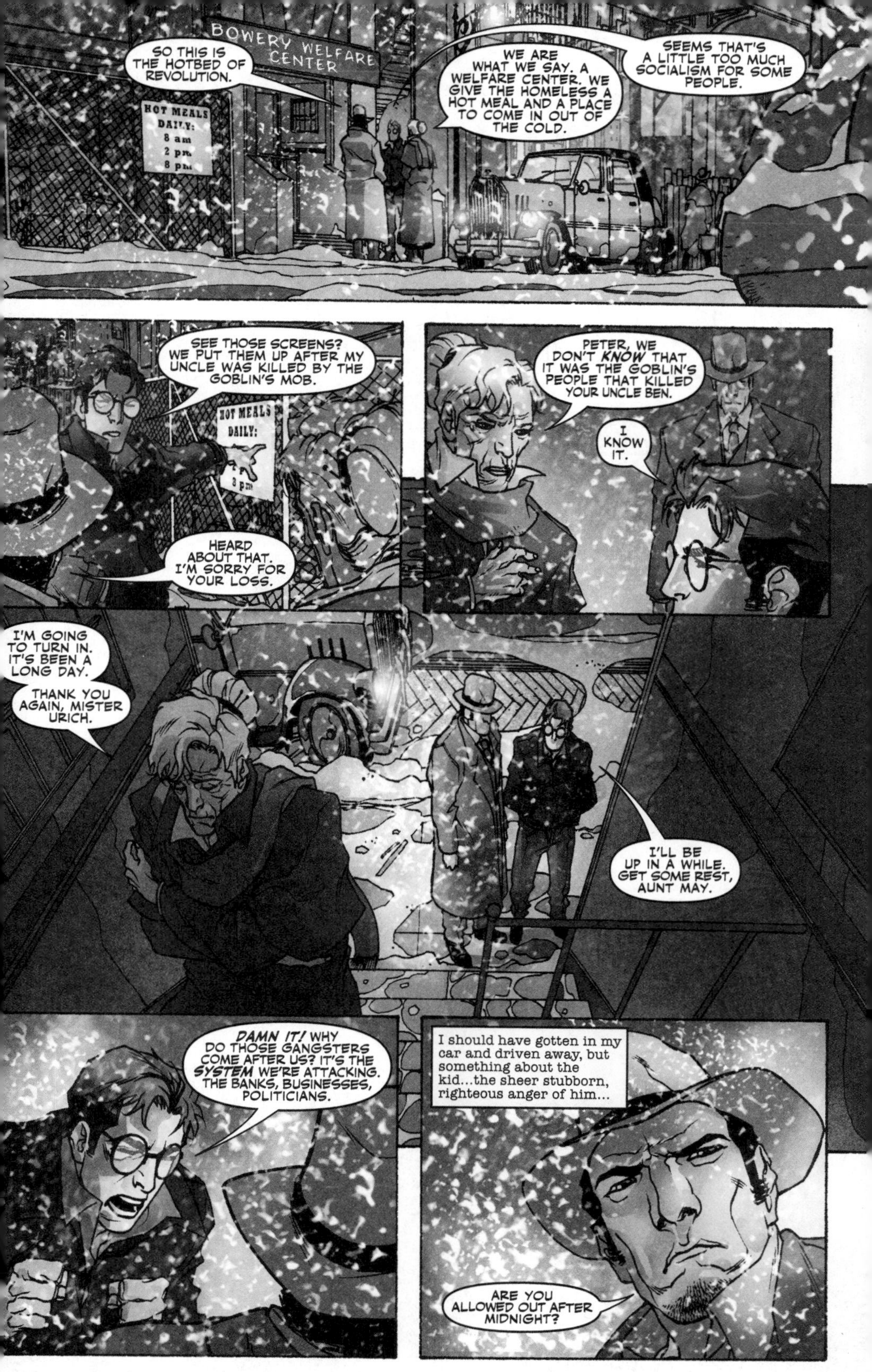
BOWERY WELFARE CENTER
SO THIS IS THE HOTBED OF REVOLUTION.
HOT MEALS DAILY: 8 am 2 pm 8 pm
WE ARE WHAT WE SAY. A WELFARE CENTER. WE GIVE THE HOMELESS A HOT MEAL AND A PLACE TO COME IN OUT OF THE COLD.
SEEMS THAT'S A LITTLE TOO MUCH SOCIALISM FOR SOME PEOPLE.
SEE THOSE SCREENS? WE PUT THEM UP AFTER MY UNCLE WAS KILLED BY THE GOBLIN'S MOB.
HOT MEALS DAILY:
HEARD ABOUT THAT. I'M SORRY FOR YOUR LOSS.
PETER, WE DON'T KNOW THAT IT WAS THE GOBLIN'S PEOPLE THAT KILLED YOUR UNCLE BEN.
I KNOW IT.
I'M GOING TO TURN IN. IT'S BEEN A LONG DAY.
THANK YOU AGAIN, MISTER URICH.
I'LL BE UP IN A WHILE. GET SOME REST, AUNT MAY.
DAMN IT! WHY DO THOSE GANGSTERS COME AFTER US? IT'S THE SYSTEM WE'RE ATTACKING. THE BANKS, BUSINESSES, POLITICIANS.
I should have gotten in my car and driven away, but something about the kid…the sheer stubborn, righteous anger of him…
ARE YOU ALLOWED OUT AFTER MIDNIGHT?

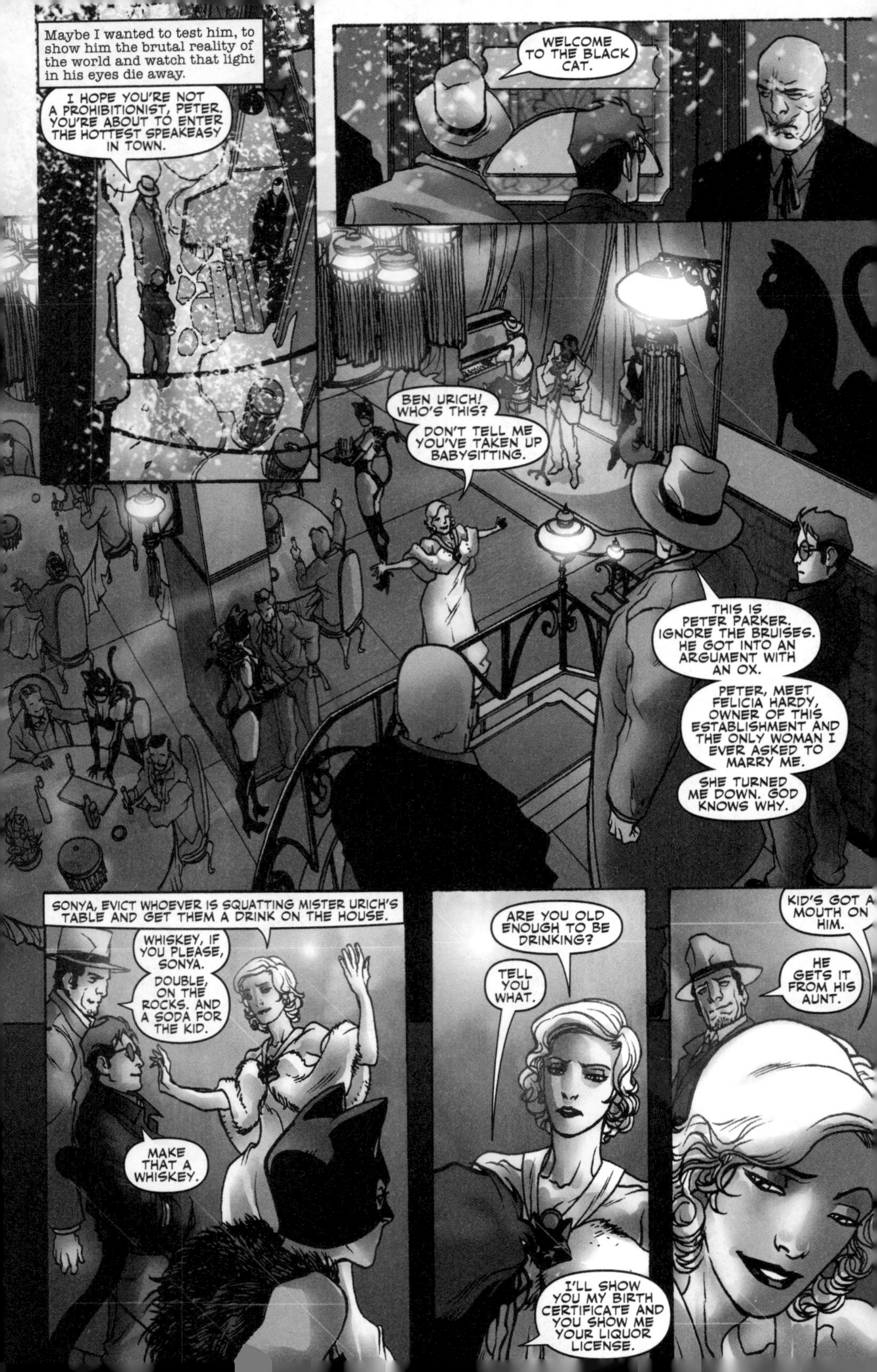

Maybe I wanted to test him, to show him the brutal reality of the world and watch that light in his eyes die away.
I HOPE YOU'RE NOT A PROHIBITIONIST, PETER. YOU'RE ABOUT TO ENTER THE HOTTEST SPEAKEASY IN TOWN.
WELCOME TO THE BLACK CAT.
BEN URICH! WHO'S THIS?
DON'T TELL ME YOU'VE TAKEN UP BABYSITTING.
THIS IS PETER PARKER. IGNORE THE BRUISES. HE GOT INTO AN ARGUMENT WITH AN OX.
PETER, MEET FELICIA HARDY, OWNER OF THIS ESTABLISHMENT AND THE ONLY WOMAN I EVER ASKED TO MARRY ME.
SHE TURNED ME DOWN. GOD KNOWS WHY.
SONYA, EVICT WHOEVER IS SQUATTING MISTER URICH'S TABLE AND GET THEM A DRINK ON THE HOUSE.
WHISKEY, IF YOU PLEASE, SONYA.
DOUBLE, ON THE ROCKS. AND A SODA FOR THE KID.
MAKE THAT A WHISKEY.
ARE YOU OLD ENOUGH TO BE DRINKING?
TELL YOU WHAT.
I'LL SHOW YOU MY BIRTH CERTIFICATE AND YOU SHOW ME YOUR LIQUOR LICENSE.
KID'S GOT A MOUTH ON HIM.
HE GETS IT FROM HIS AUNT.

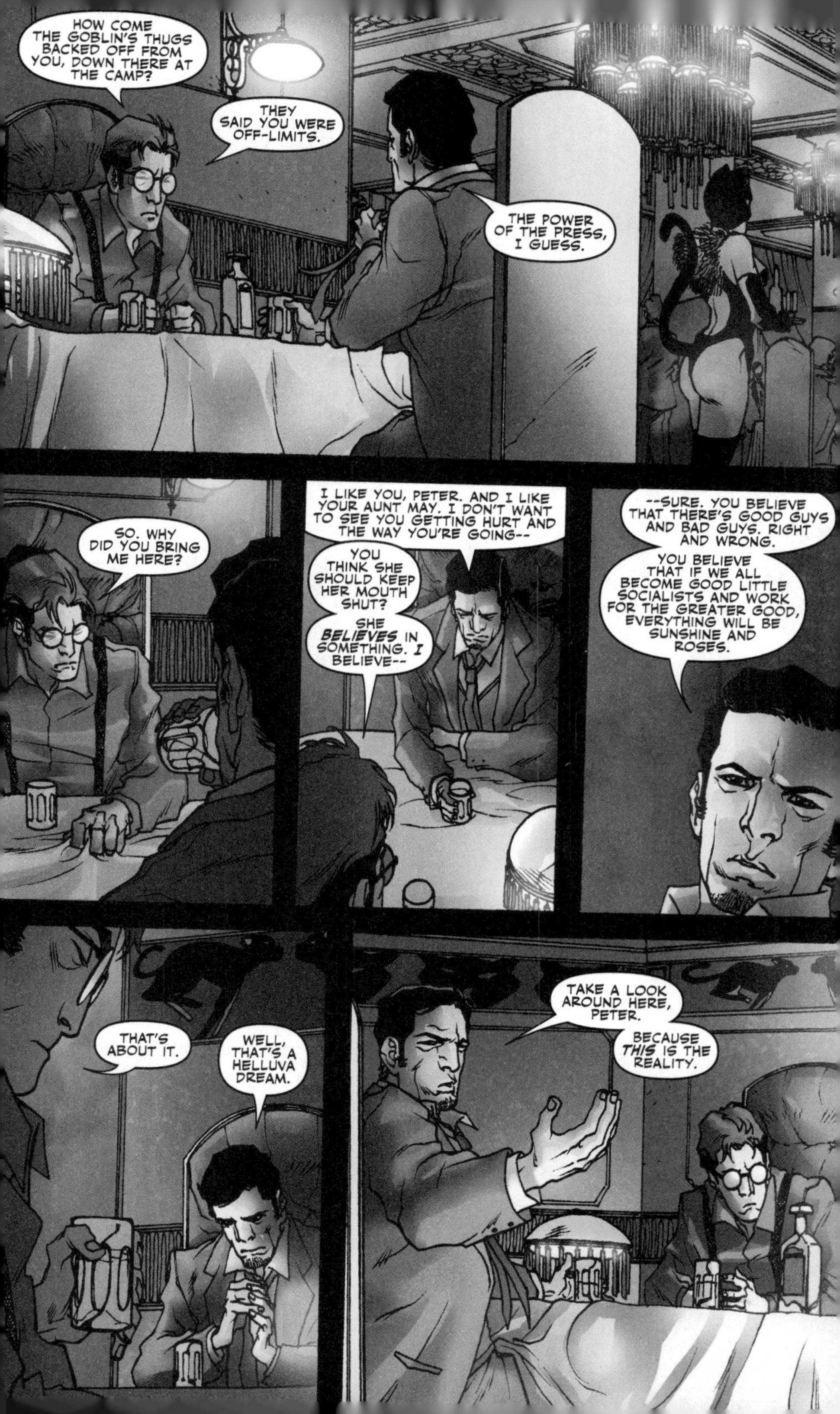
HOW COME THE GOBLIN'S THUGS BACKED OFF FROM YOU, DOWN THERE AT THE CAMP?
THEY SAID YOU WERE OFF-LIMITS.
THE POWER OF THE PRESS, I GUESS.
SO. WHY DID YOU BRING ME HERE?
I LIKE YOU, PETER. AND I LIKE YOUR AUNT MAY. I DON'T WANT TO SEE YOU GETTING HURT AND THE WAY YOU'RE GOING--
YOU THINK SHE SHOULD KEEP HER MOUTH SHUT?
SHE *BELIEVES* IN SOMETHING. *I* BELIEVE--
--SURE. YOU BELIEVE THAT THERE'S GOOD GUYS AND BAD GUYS. RIGHT AND WRONG.
YOU BELIEVE THAT IF WE ALL BECOME GOOD LITTLE SOCIALISTS AND WORK FOR THE GREATER GOOD, EVERYTHING WILL BE SUNSHINE AND ROSES.
THAT'S ABOUT IT.
WELL, THAT'S A HELLUVA DREAM.
TAKE A LOOK AROUND HERE, PETER.
BECAUSE *THIS* IS THE REALITY.

"SEE THE BIG GUY WRESTLING WITH THE BRUNETTE?"

"TO HIS LEFT, CHIEF DETECTIVE RIAN FROM THE VICE SQUAD.

"OH MY GOD! THAT'S JIMMY STRYDER! THE MAYOR OF NEW YORK IS *HERE?!*"

"RIGHT. AND THE DAME WITH HIM IS *NOT* HIS WIFE."

"THE CREEP HE'S SCHMOOZING IS EMILIO ALCUNO. HE RUNS HALF THE BROTHELS IN NEW YORK.

"AND THEN WE HAVE ADOLFUS CRANE, INDUSTRIALIST. YOUR UNCLE BEN HELPED ORGANIZE DEMONSTRATIONS THAT CLOSED DOWN THREE OF HIS SWEATSHOPS LAST YEAR.

"AND MAKING HIS BIG ENTRANCE, NORMAN OSBORN...

"...THE GOBLIN.

"YOU WANTED TO KNOW WHY THE GOBLIN WAS COMING AFTER YOU.

"THE GOBLIN DOESN'T PERSONALLY GIVE A DAMN ABOUT YOU OR YOUR AUNT, OR ANYONE ELSE

"HE'S FREELANCE. HE WORKS FOR THE HIGHEST BIDDER. THEY USE HIM BECAUSE IT WOULDN'T LOOK GOOD TO HAVE THE POLICE SUPPRESSING FREEDOM OF SPEECH."

ARE YOU SAYING *THE MAYOR* HIRED THE GOBLIN TO KILL UNCLE BEN?!

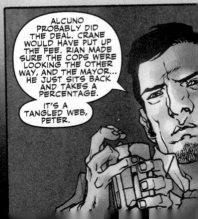

ALCUNO PROBABLY DID THE DEAL. CRANE WOULD HAVE PUT UP THE FEE. RIAN MADE SURE THE COPS WERE LOOKING THE OTHER WAY, AND THE MAYOR... HE JUST SITS BACK AND TAKES A PERCENTAGE.

IT'S A TANGLED WEB, PETER.

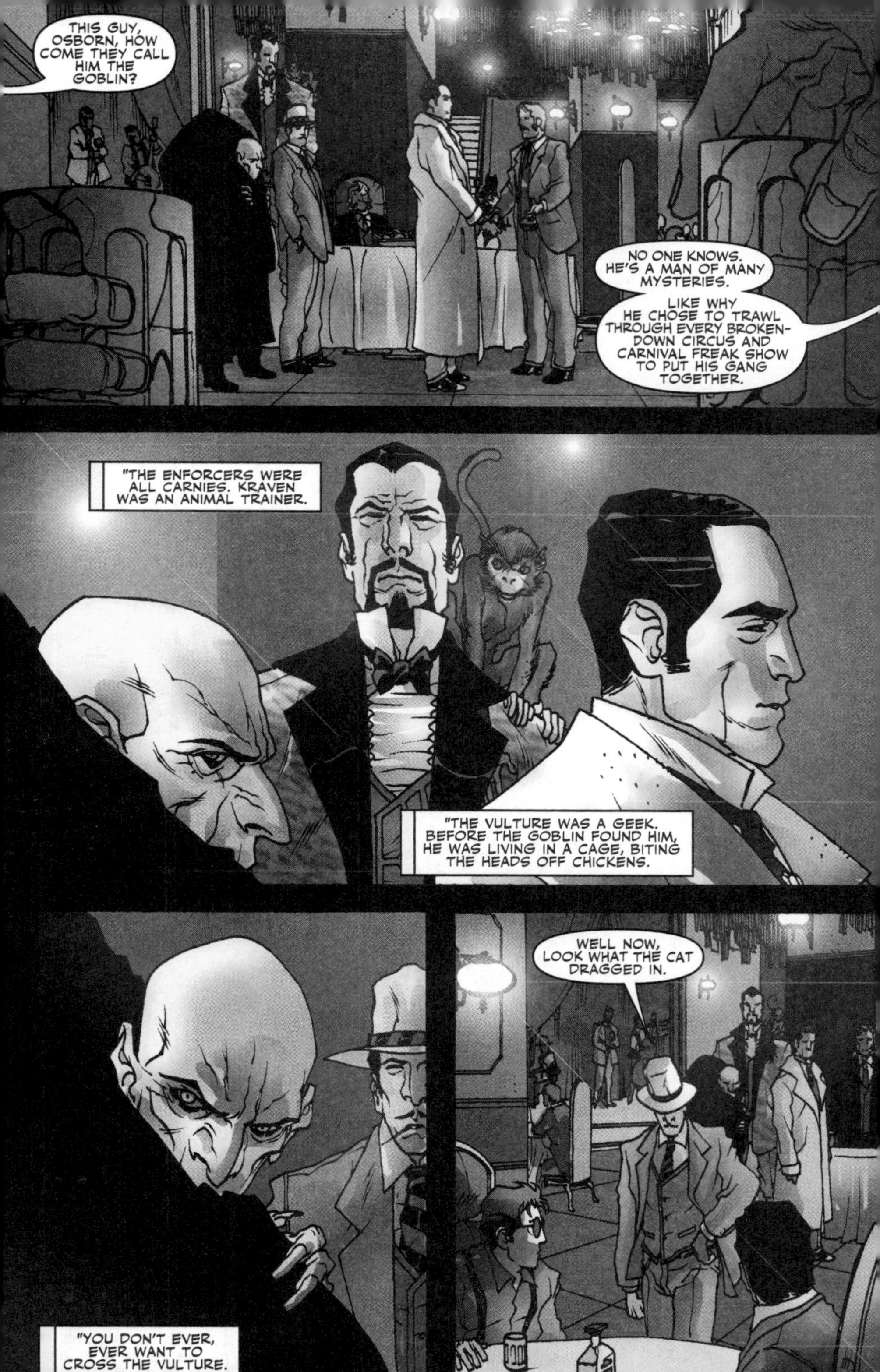
THIS GUY, OSBORN, HOW COME THEY CALL HIM THE GOBLIN?
NO ONE KNOWS. HE'S A MAN OF MANY MYSTERIES.
LIKE WHY HE CHOSE TO TRAWL THROUGH EVERY BROKEN-DOWN CIRCUS AND CARNIVAL FREAK SHOW TO PUT HIS GANG TOGETHER.
"THE ENFORCERS WERE ALL CARNIES. KRAVEN WAS AN ANIMAL TRAINER.
"THE VULTURE WAS A GEEK. BEFORE THE GOBLIN FOUND HIM, HE WAS LIVING IN A CAGE, BITING THE HEADS OFF CHICKENS.
"YOU DON'T EVER, EVER WANT TO CROSS THE VULTURE.
WELL NOW, LOOK WHAT THE CAT DRAGGED IN.

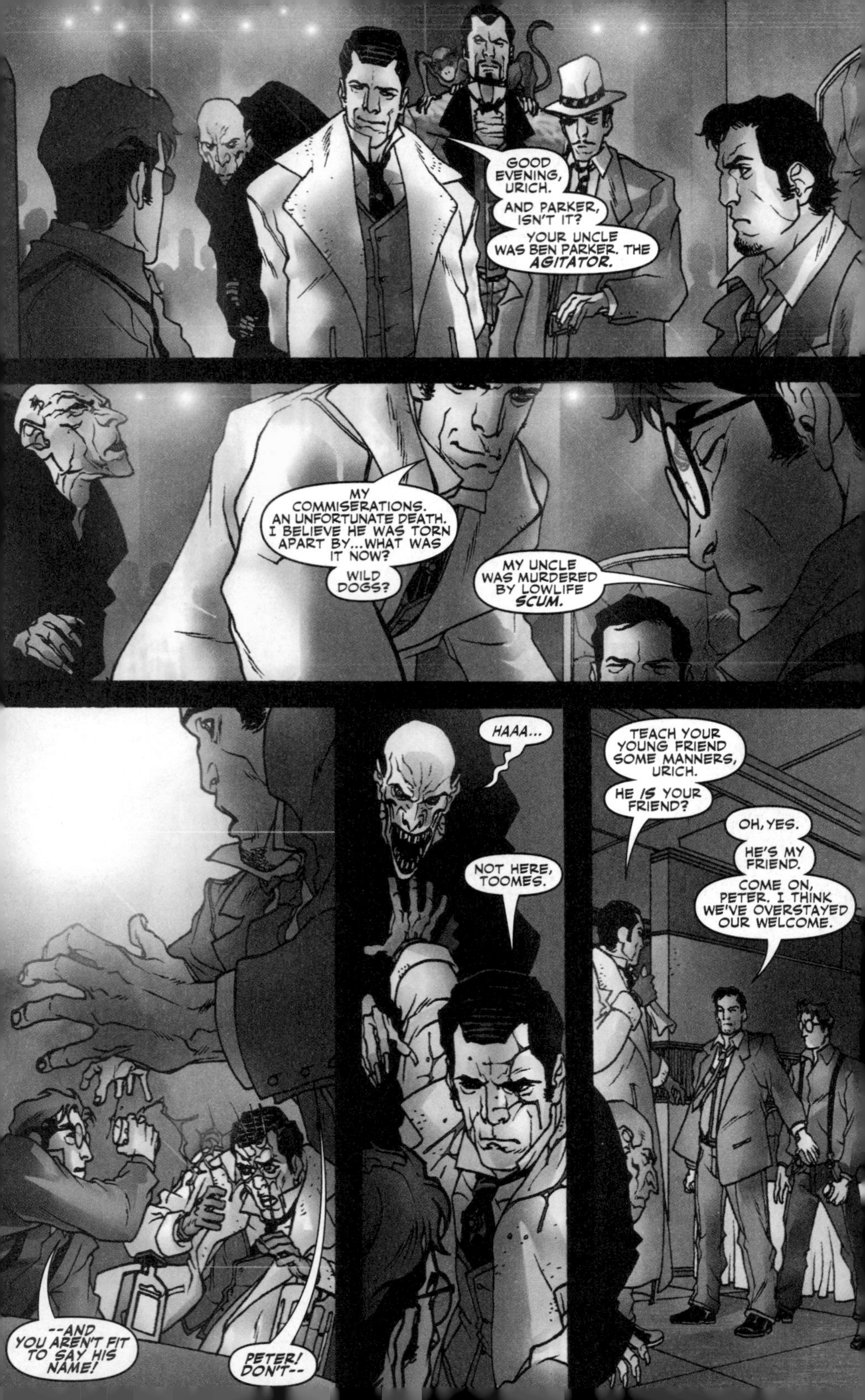
GOOD EVENING, URICH.
AND PARKER, ISN'T IT?
YOUR UNCLE WAS BEN PARKER. THE *AGITATOR*.
MY COMMISERATIONS. AN UNFORTUNATE DEATH. I BELIEVE HE WAS TORN APART BY...WHAT WAS IT NOW?
WILD DOGS?
MY UNCLE WAS MURDERED BY LOWLIFE *SCUM*.
--AND YOU AREN'T FIT TO SAY HIS NAME!
PETER! DON'T--
HAAA...
NOT HERE, TOOMES.
TEACH YOUR YOUNG FRIEND SOME MANNERS, URICH.
HE *IS* YOUR FRIEND?
OH, YES.
HE'S MY FRIEND.
COME ON, PETER. I THINK WE'VE OVERSTAYED OUR WELCOME.

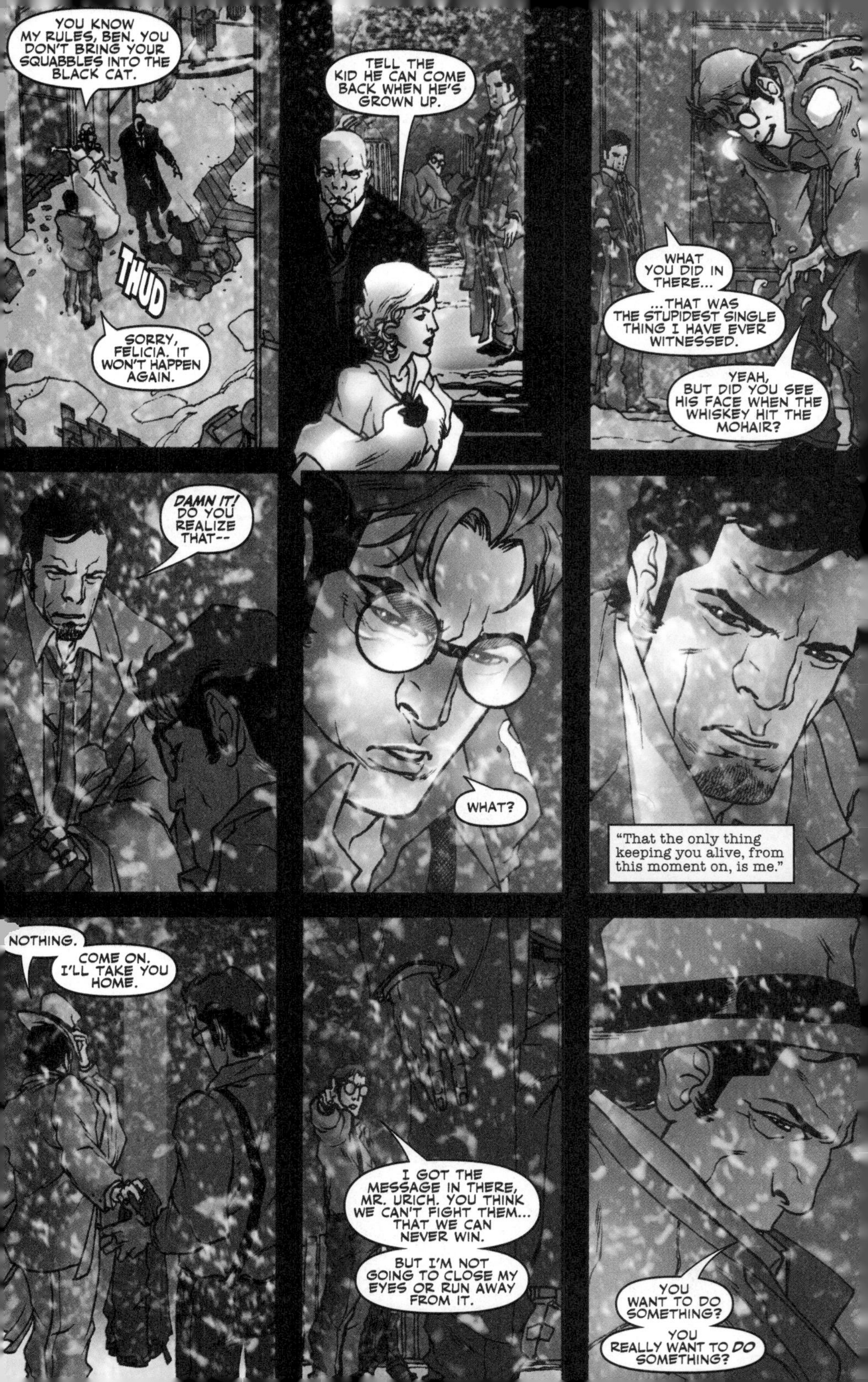
YOU KNOW MY RULES, BEN. YOU DON'T BRING YOUR SQUABBLES INTO THE BLACK CAT.
THUD
SORRY, FELICIA. IT WON'T HAPPEN AGAIN.
TELL THE KID HE CAN COME BACK WHEN HE'S GROWN UP.
WHAT YOU DID IN THERE...
...THAT WAS THE STUPIDEST SINGLE THING I HAVE EVER WITNESSED.
YEAH, BUT DID YOU SEE HIS FACE WHEN THE WHISKEY HIT THE MOHAIR?
DAMN IT! DO YOU REALIZE THAT--
WHAT?
"That the only thing keeping you alive, from this moment on, is me."
NOTHING.
COME ON. I'LL TAKE YOU HOME.
I GOT THE MESSAGE IN THERE, MR. URICH. YOU THINK WE CAN'T FIGHT THEM... THAT WE CAN NEVER WIN.
BUT I'M NOT GOING TO CLOSE MY EYES OR RUN AWAY FROM IT.
YOU WANT TO DO SOMETHING?
YOU REALLY WANT TO DO SOMETHING?

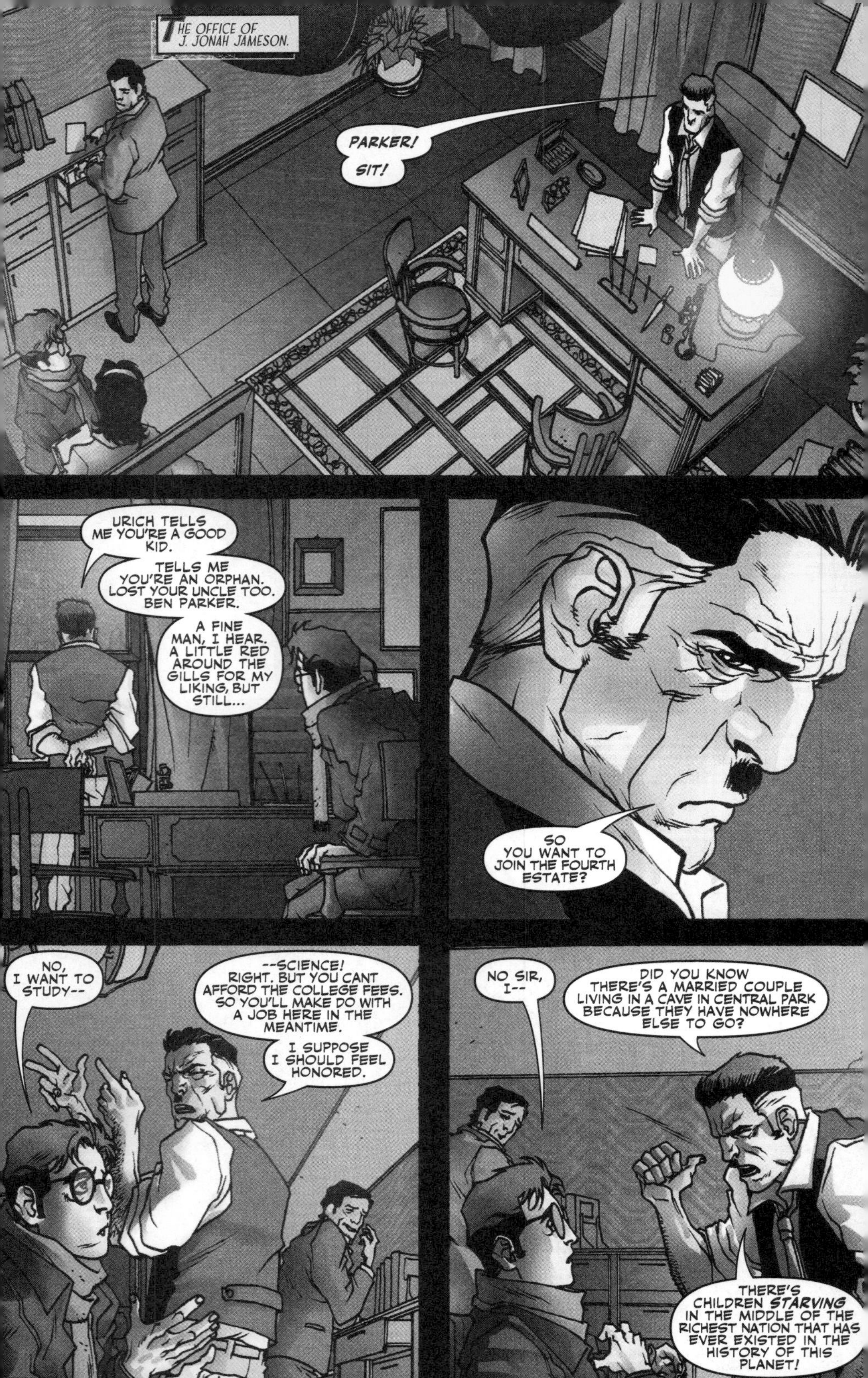
THE OFFICE OF J. JONAH JAMESON.
PARKER!
SIT!
URICH TELLS ME YOU'RE A GOOD KID.
TELLS ME YOU'RE AN ORPHAN. LOST YOUR UNCLE TOO. BEN PARKER.
A FINE MAN, I HEAR. A LITTLE RED AROUND THE GILLS FOR MY LIKING, BUT STILL...
SO YOU WANT TO JOIN THE FOURTH ESTATE?
NO, I WANT TO STUDY--
--SCIENCE! RIGHT. BUT YOU CANT AFFORD THE COLLEGE FEES. SO YOU'LL MAKE DO WITH A JOB HERE IN THE MEANTIME.
I SUPPOSE I SHOULD FEEL HONORED.
NO SIR, I--
DID YOU KNOW THERE'S A MARRIED COUPLE LIVING IN A CAVE IN CENTRAL PARK BECAUSE THEY HAVE NOWHERE ELSE TO GO?
THERE'S CHILDREN STARVING IN THE MIDDLE OF THE RICHEST NATION THAT HAS EVER EXISTED IN THE HISTORY OF THIS PLANET!

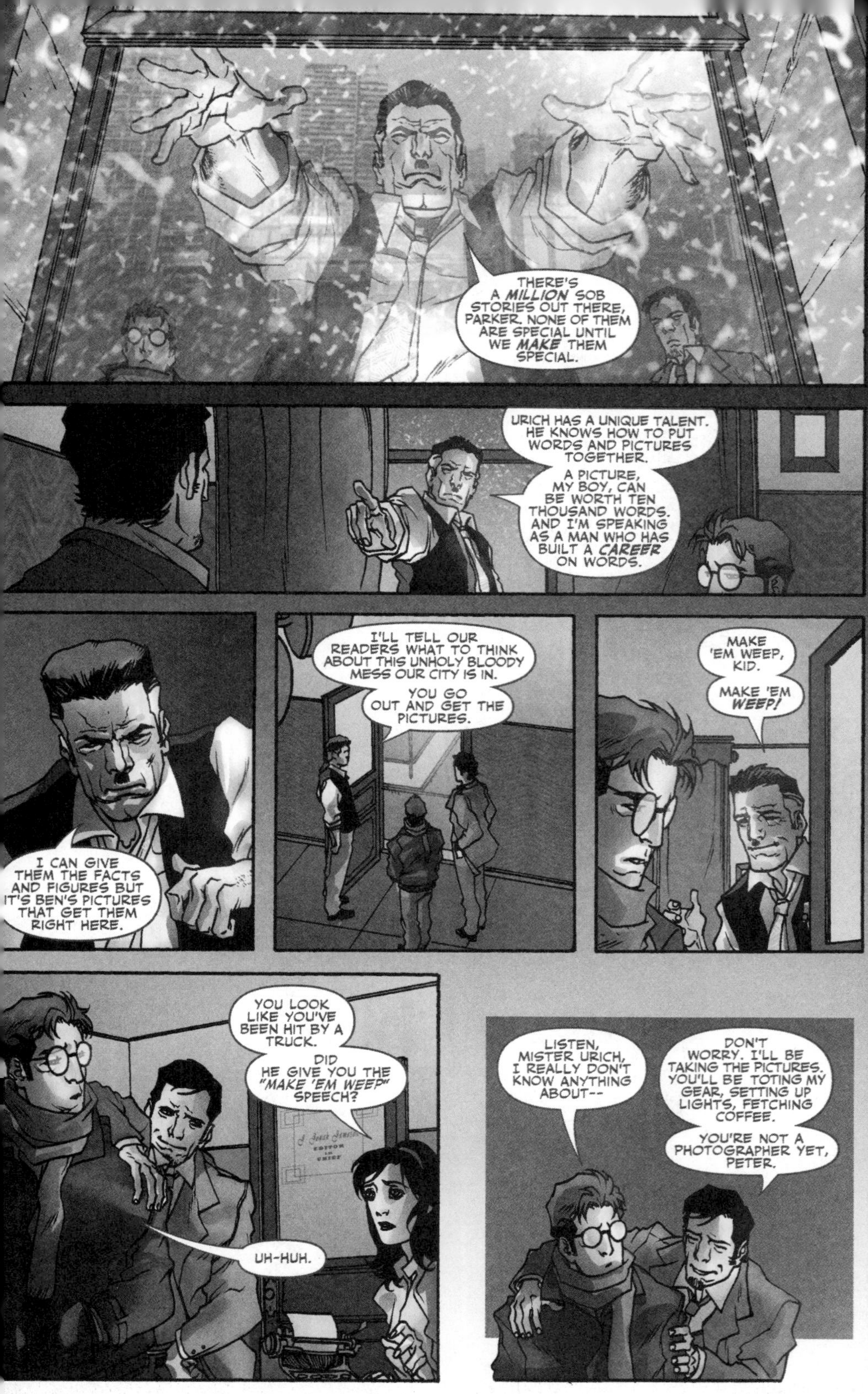
THERE'S A MILLION SOB STORIES OUT THERE, PARKER. NONE OF THEM ARE SPECIAL UNTIL WE MAKE THEM SPECIAL.
URICH HAS A UNIQUE TALENT. HE KNOWS HOW TO PUT WORDS AND PICTURES TOGETHER.
A PICTURE, MY BOY, CAN BE WORTH TEN THOUSAND WORDS. AND I'M SPEAKING AS A MAN WHO HAS BUILT A CAREER ON WORDS.
I CAN GIVE THEM THE FACTS AND FIGURES BUT IT'S BEN'S PICTURES THAT GET THEM RIGHT HERE.
I'LL TELL OUR READERS WHAT TO THINK ABOUT THIS UNHOLY BLOODY MESS OUR CITY IS IN.
YOU GO OUT AND GET THE PICTURES.
MAKE 'EM WEEP, KID.
MAKE 'EM WEEP!
YOU LOOK LIKE YOU'VE BEEN HIT BY A TRUCK.
DID HE GIVE YOU THE "MAKE 'EM WEEP" SPEECH?
UH-HUH.
LISTEN, MISTER URICH, I REALLY DON'T KNOW ANYTHING ABOUT--
DON'T WORRY. I'LL BE TAKING THE PICTURES. YOU'LL BE TOTING MY GEAR, SETTING UP LIGHTS, FETCHING COFFEE.
YOU'RE NOT A PHOTOGRAPHER YET, PETER.

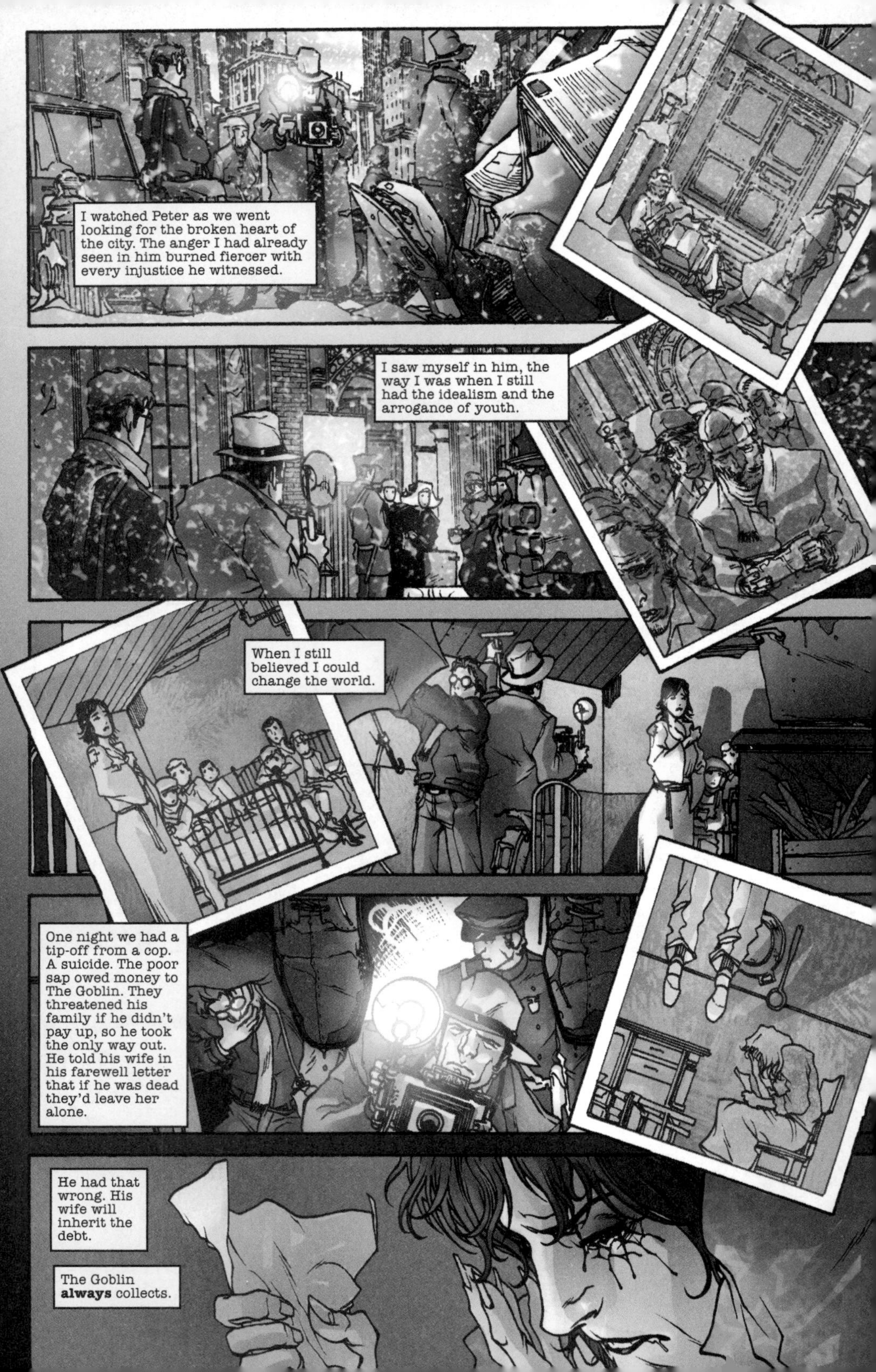
I watched Peter as we went looking for the broken heart of the city. The anger I had already seen in him burned fiercer with every injustice he witnessed.
I saw myself in him, the way I was when I still had the idealism and the arrogance of youth.
When I still believed I could change the world.
One night we had a tip-off from a cop. A suicide. The poor sap owed money to The Goblin. They threatened his family if he didn't pay up, so he took the only way out. He told his wife in his farewell letter that if he was dead they'd leave her alone.
He had that wrong. His wife will inherit the debt.
The Goblin **always** collects.

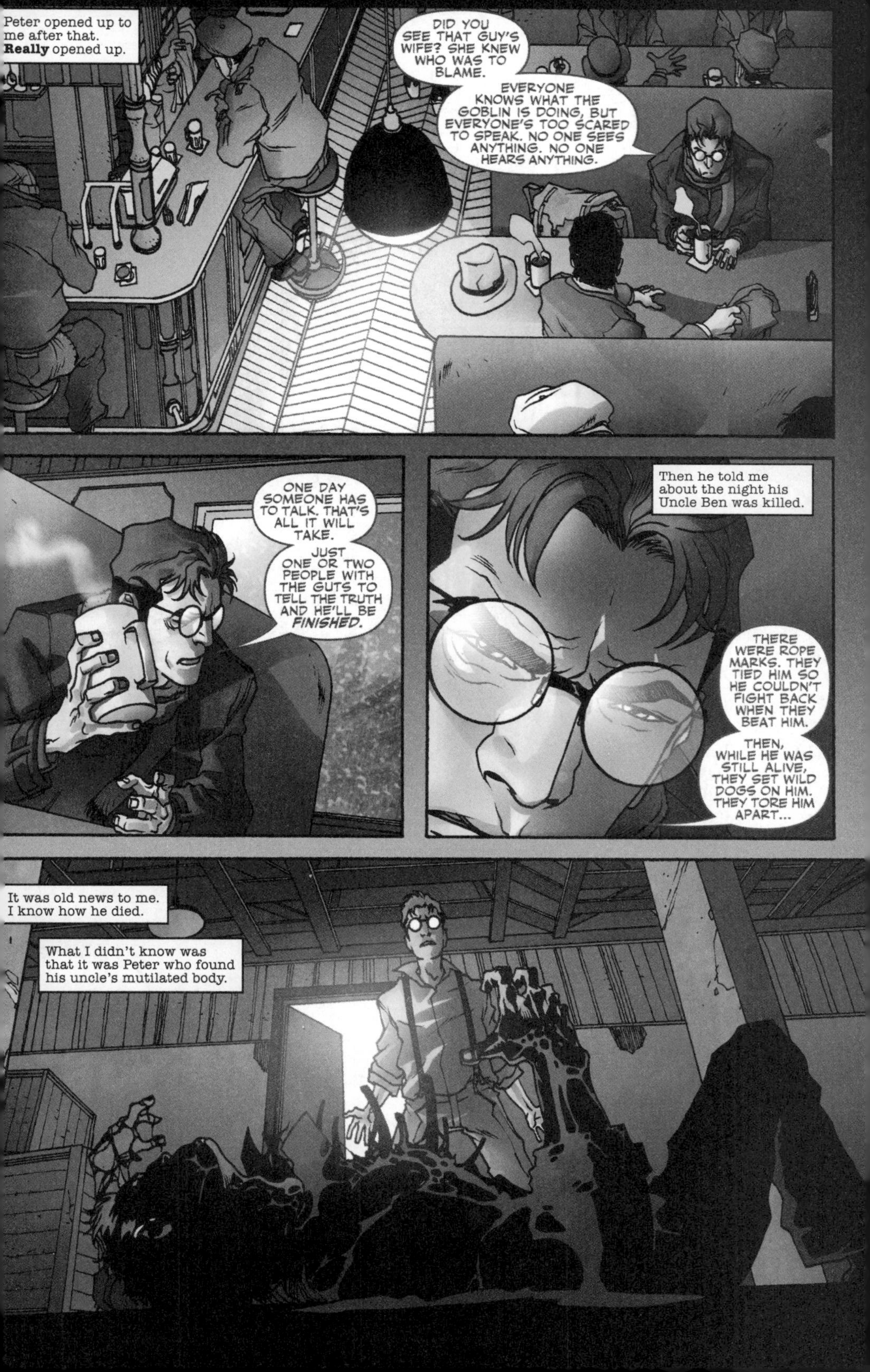

Peter opened up to me after that. **Really** opened up.
DID YOU SEE THAT GUY'S WIFE? SHE KNEW WHO WAS TO BLAME.
EVERYONE KNOWS WHAT THE GOBLIN IS DOING, BUT EVERYONE'S TOO SCARED TO SPEAK. NO ONE SEES ANYTHING. NO ONE HEARS ANYTHING.
ONE DAY SOMEONE HAS TO TALK. THAT'S ALL IT WILL TAKE.
JUST ONE OR TWO PEOPLE WITH THE GUTS TO TELL THE TRUTH AND HE'LL BE *FINISHED*.
Then he told me about the night his Uncle Ben was killed.
THERE WERE ROPE MARKS. THEY TIED HIM SO HE COULDN'T FIGHT BACK WHEN THEY BEAT HIM.
THEN, WHILE HE WAS STILL ALIVE, THEY SET WILD DOGS ON HIM. THEY TORE HIM APART...
It was old news to me. I know how he died.
What I didn't know was that it was Peter who found his uncle's mutilated body.

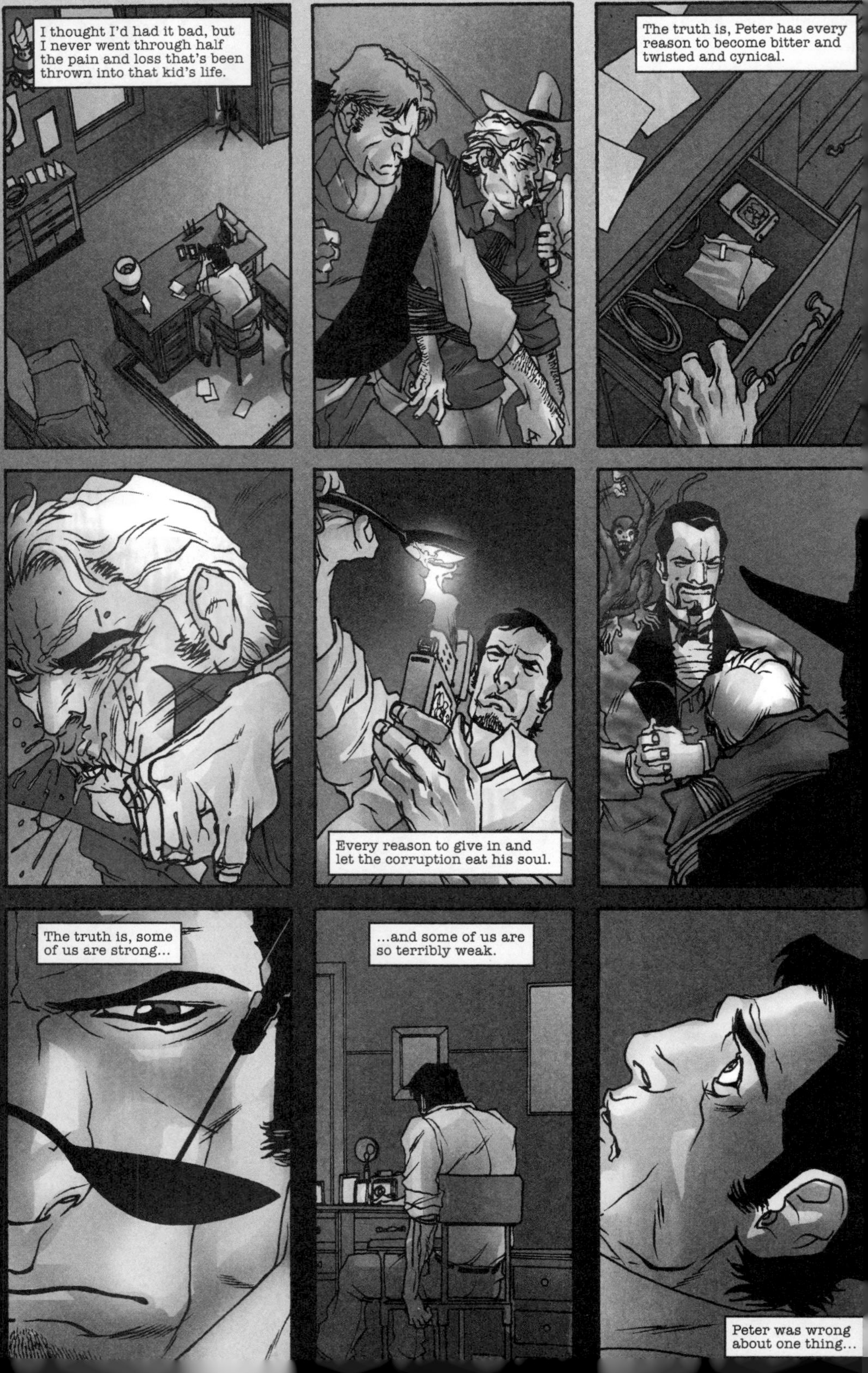
I thought I'd had it bad, but I never went through half the pain and loss that's been thrown into that kid's life.
The truth is, Peter has every reason to become bitter and twisted and cynical.
Every reason to give in and let the corruption eat his soul.
The truth is, some of us are strong...
...and some of us are so terribly weak.
Peter was wrong about one thing...

It wasn't dogs that tore Ben Parker to pieces.

It wasn't dogs.

All those years in the freak show, being treated like an animal, something happened to Adrian Toomes. Somewhere along the line, the last of his humanity finally slipped away.

Sometime, somehow, he developed the taste for human meat...

And how do I know this? How do I know that Ben Parker's living body was cannibalized?

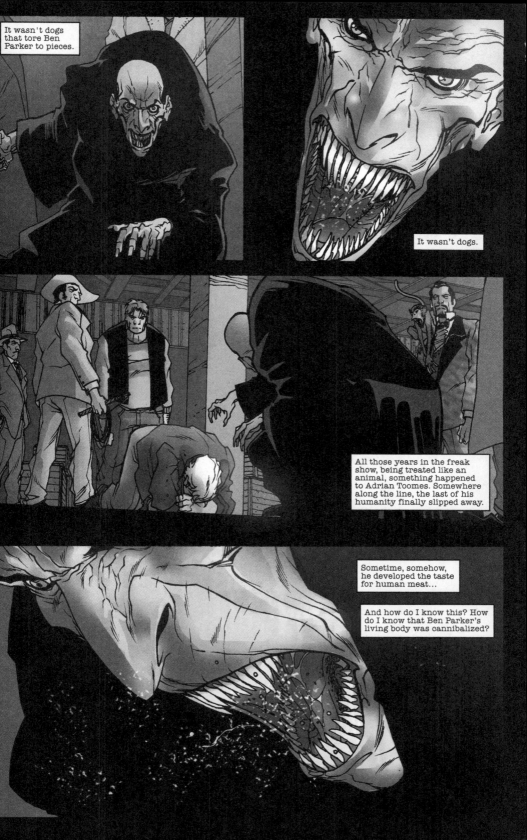

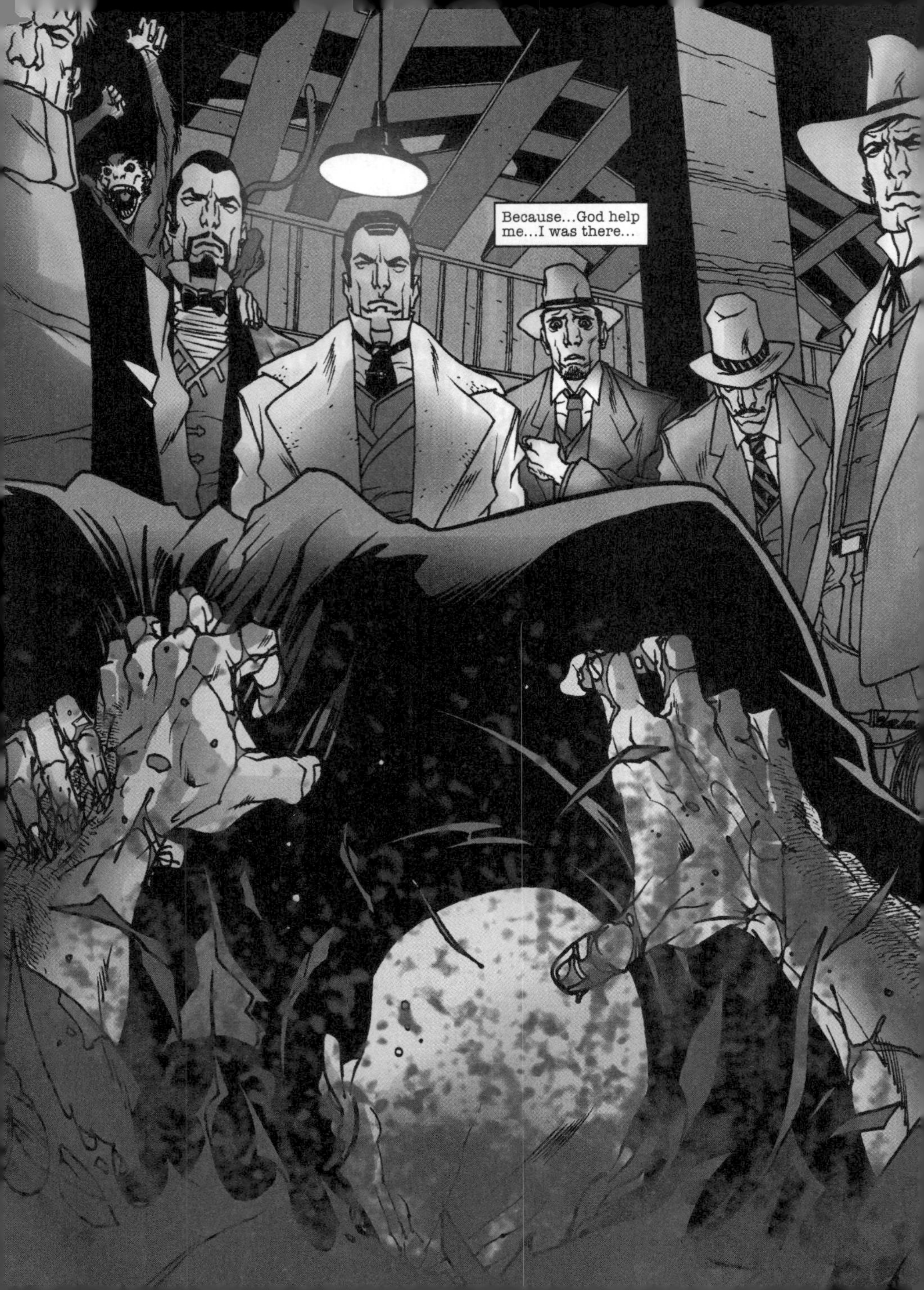
Because...God help me...I was there...

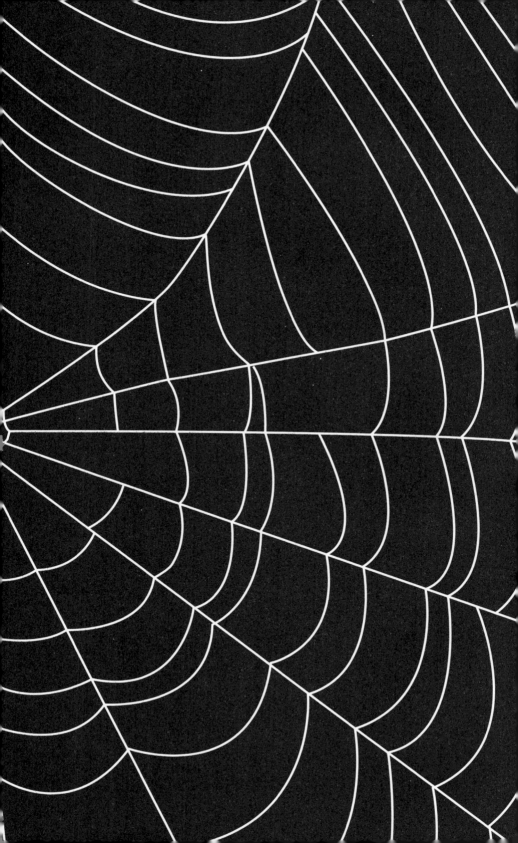

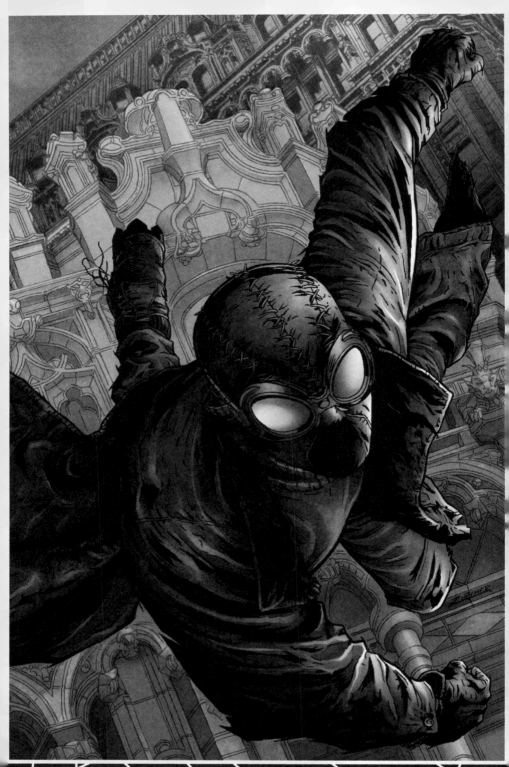

TWO

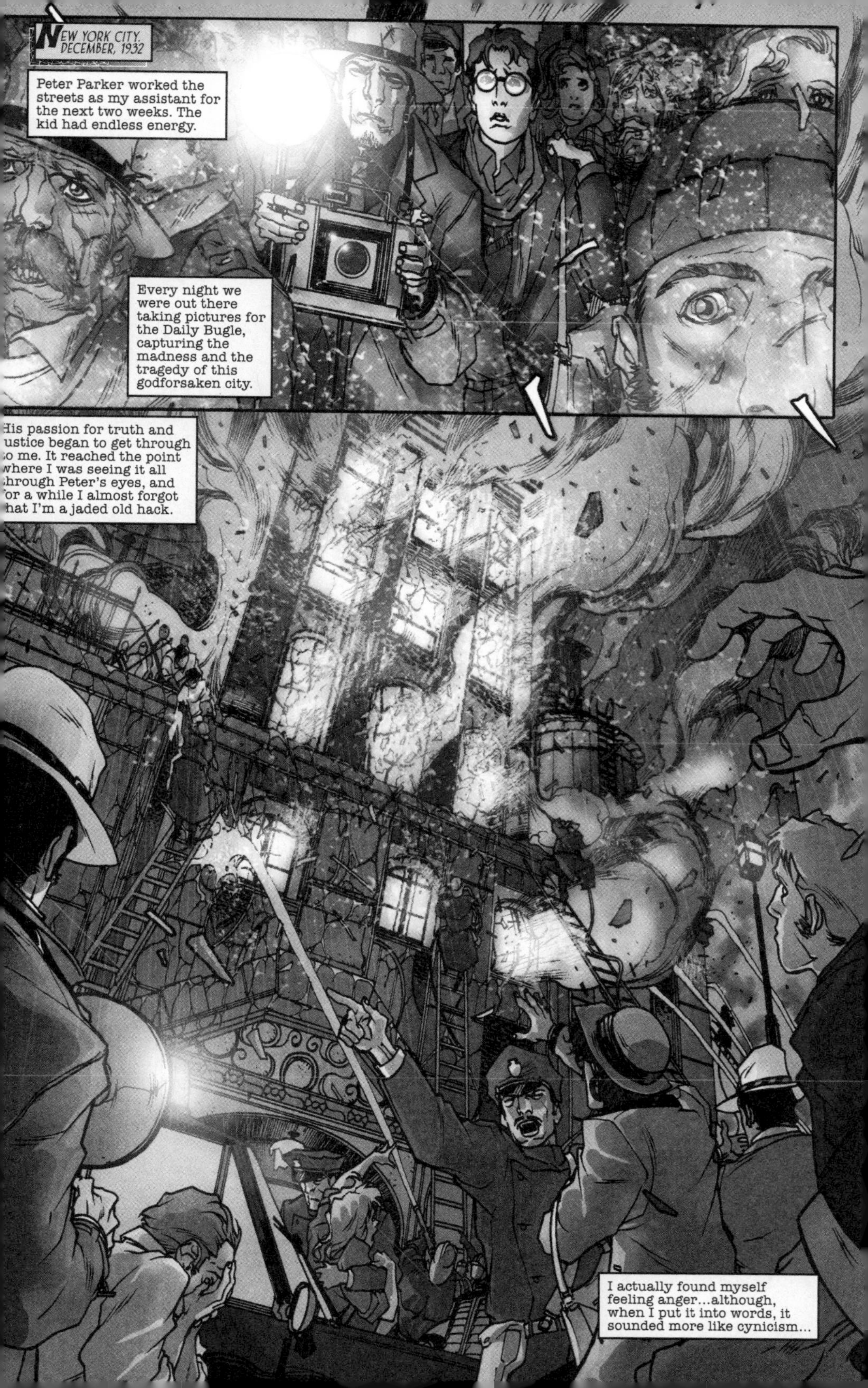
NEW YORK CITY. DECEMBER, 1932
Peter Parker worked the streets as my assistant for the next two weeks. The kid had endless energy.
Every night we were out there taking pictures for the Daily Bugle, capturing the madness and the tragedy of this godforsaken city.
His passion for truth and justice began to get through to me. It reached the point where I was seeing it all through Peter's eyes, and for a while I almost forgot that I'm a jaded old hack.
I actually found myself feeling anger...although, when I put it into words, it sounded more like cynicism...

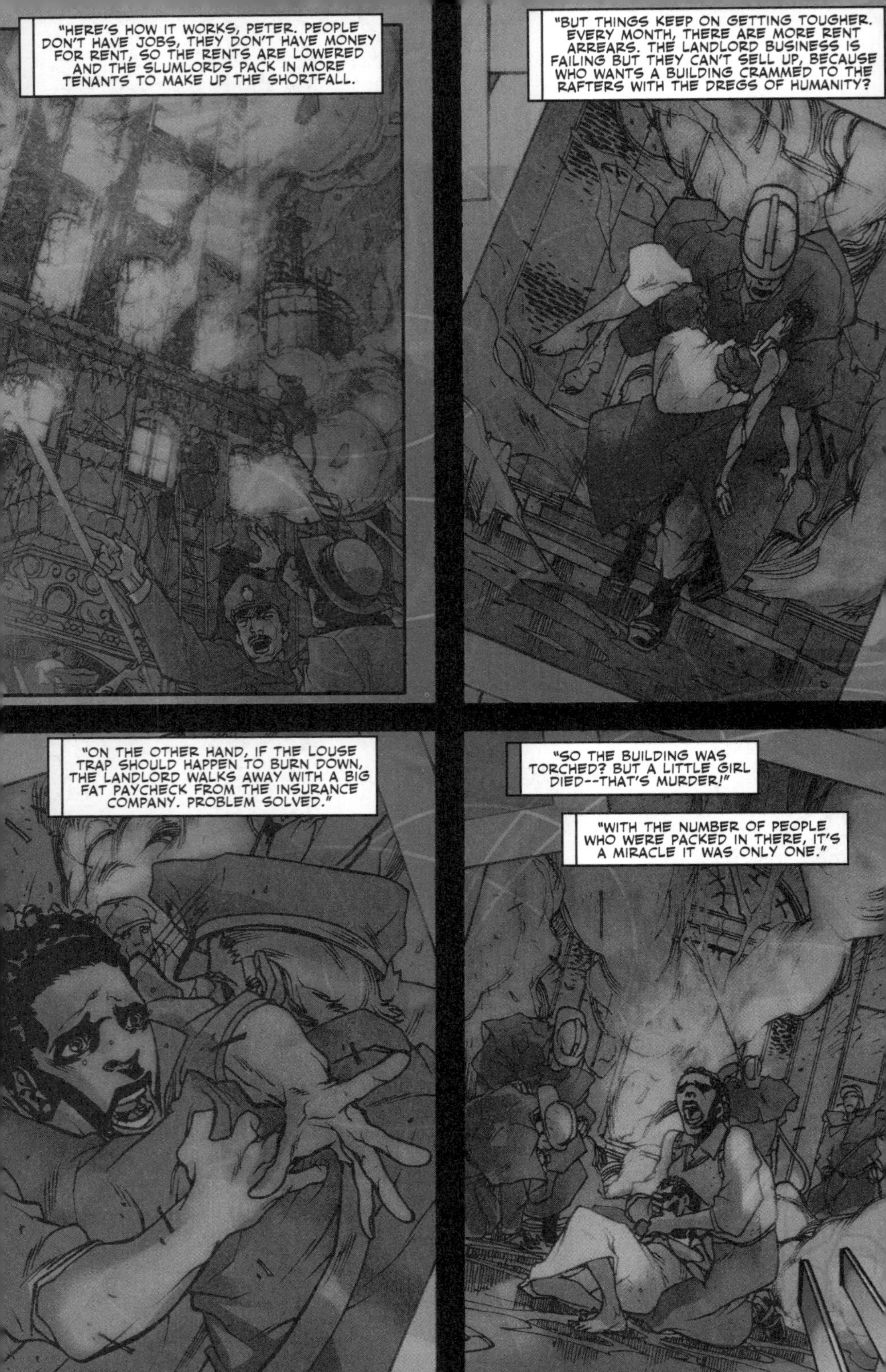
"HERE'S HOW IT WORKS, PETER. PEOPLE DON'T HAVE JOBS, THEY DON'T HAVE MONEY FOR RENT, SO THE RENTS ARE LOWERED AND THE SLUMLORDS PACK IN MORE TENANTS TO MAKE UP THE SHORTFALL.
"BUT THINGS KEEP ON GETTING TOUGHER. EVERY MONTH, THERE ARE MORE RENT ARREARS. THE LANDLORD BUSINESS IS FAILING BUT THEY CAN'T SELL UP, BECAUSE WHO WANTS A BUILDING CRAMMED TO THE RAFTERS WITH THE DREGS OF HUMANITY?
"ON THE OTHER HAND, IF THE LOUSE TRAP SHOULD HAPPEN TO BURN DOWN, THE LANDLORD WALKS AWAY WITH A BIG FAT PAYCHECK FROM THE INSURANCE COMPANY. PROBLEM SOLVED."
"SO THE BUILDING WAS TORCHED? BUT A LITTLE GIRL DIED--THAT'S MURDER!"
"WITH THE NUMBER OF PEOPLE WHO WERE PACKED IN THERE, IT'S A MIRACLE IT WAS ONLY ONE."

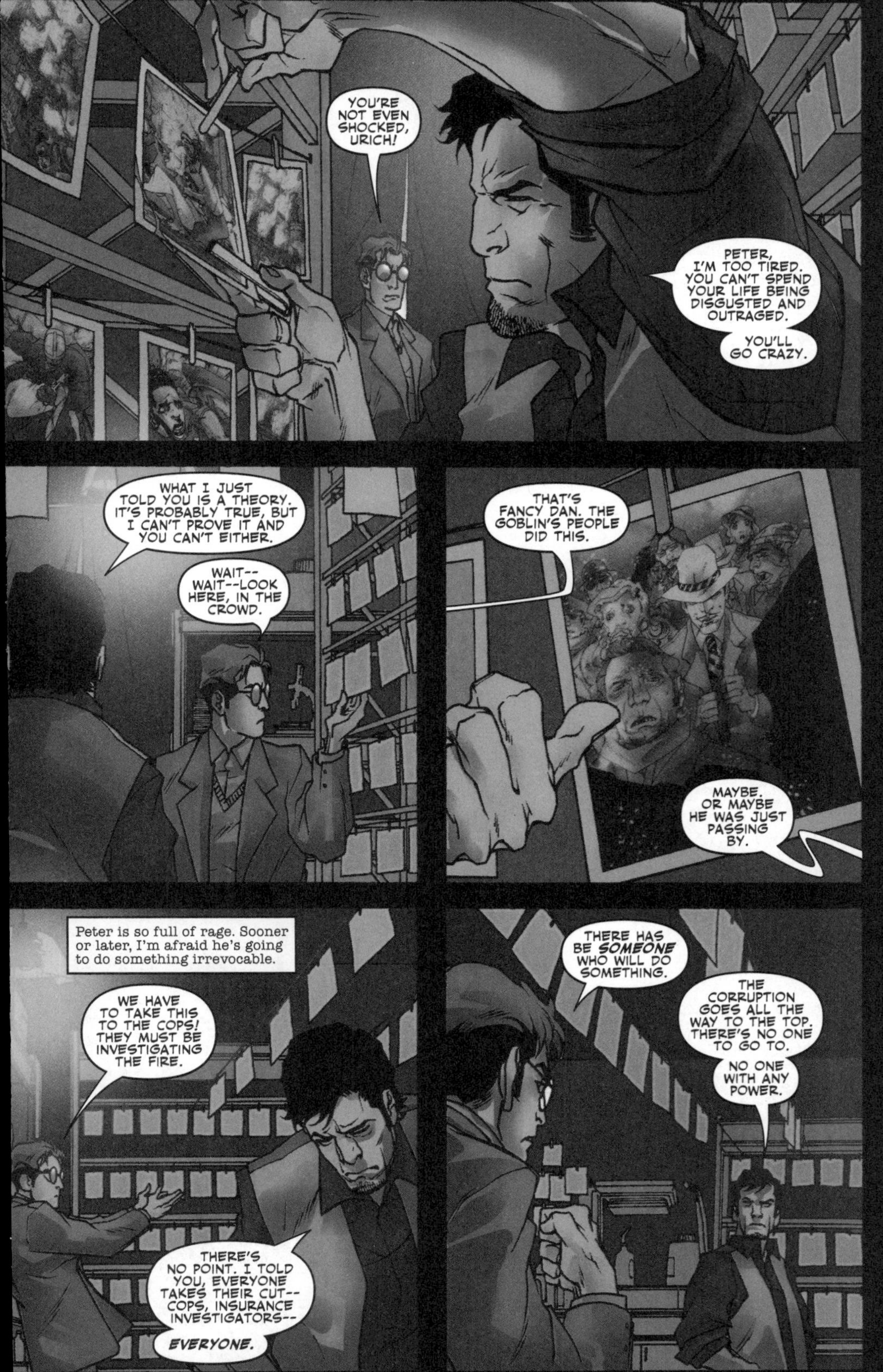
YOU'RE NOT EVEN SHOCKED, URICH!
PETER, I'M TOO TIRED. YOU CAN'T SPEND YOUR LIFE BEING DISGUSTED AND OUTRAGED.
YOU'LL GO CRAZY.
WHAT I JUST TOLD YOU IS A THEORY. IT'S PROBABLY TRUE, BUT I CAN'T PROVE IT AND YOU CAN'T EITHER.
WAIT-- WAIT--LOOK HERE, IN THE CROWD.
THAT'S FANCY DAN. THE GOBLIN'S PEOPLE DID THIS.
MAYBE. OR MAYBE HE WAS JUST PASSING BY.
Peter is so full of rage. Sooner or later, I'm afraid he's going to do something irrevocable.
WE HAVE TO TAKE THIS TO THE COPS! THEY MUST BE INVESTIGATING THE FIRE.
THERE'S NO POINT. I TOLD YOU, EVERYONE TAKES THEIR CUT-- COPS, INSURANCE INVESTIGATORS--
EVERYONE.
THERE HAS BE SOMEONE WHO WILL DO SOMETHING.
THE CORRUPTION GOES ALL THE WAY TO THE TOP. THERE'S NO ONE TO GO TO.
NO ONE WITH ANY POWER.

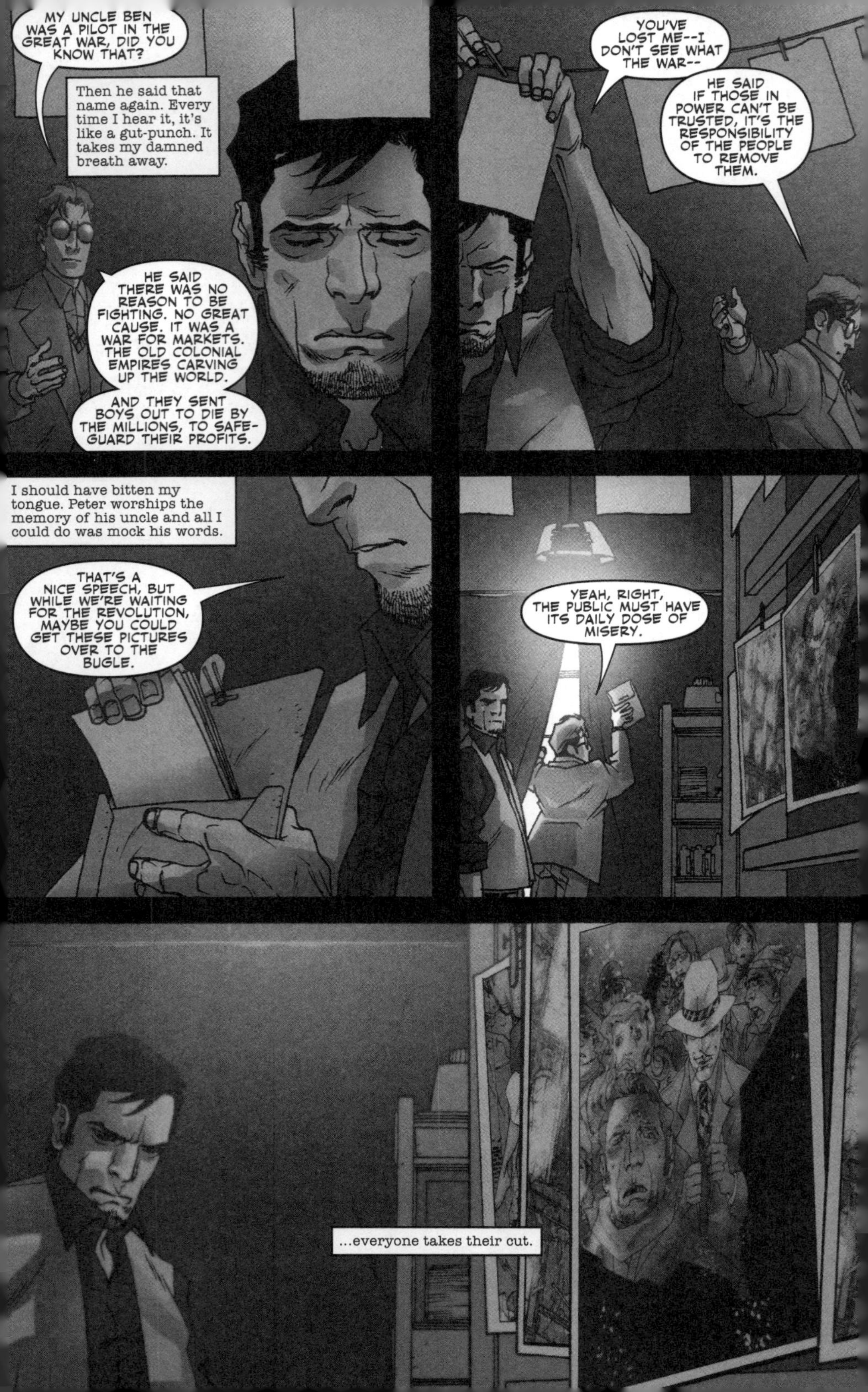
MY UNCLE BEN WAS A PILOT IN THE GREAT WAR, DID YOU KNOW THAT?
Then he said that name again. Every time I hear it, it's like a gut-punch. It takes my damned breath away.
HE SAID THERE WAS NO REASON TO BE FIGHTING. NO GREAT CAUSE. IT WAS A WAR FOR MARKETS. THE OLD COLONIAL EMPIRES CARVING UP THE WORLD.
AND THEY SENT BOYS OUT TO DIE BY THE MILLIONS, TO SAFE-GUARD THEIR PROFITS.
YOU'VE LOST ME--I DON'T SEE WHAT THE WAR--
HE SAID IF THOSE IN POWER CAN'T BE TRUSTED, IT'S THE RESPONSIBILITY OF THE PEOPLE TO REMOVE THEM.
I should have bitten my tongue. Peter worships the memory of his uncle and all I could do was mock his words.
THAT'S A NICE SPEECH, BUT WHILE WE'RE WAITING FOR THE REVOLUTION, MAYBE YOU COULD GET THESE PICTURES OVER TO THE BUGLE.
YEAH, RIGHT, THE PUBLIC MUST HAVE ITS DAILY DOSE OF MISERY.
...everyone takes their cut.

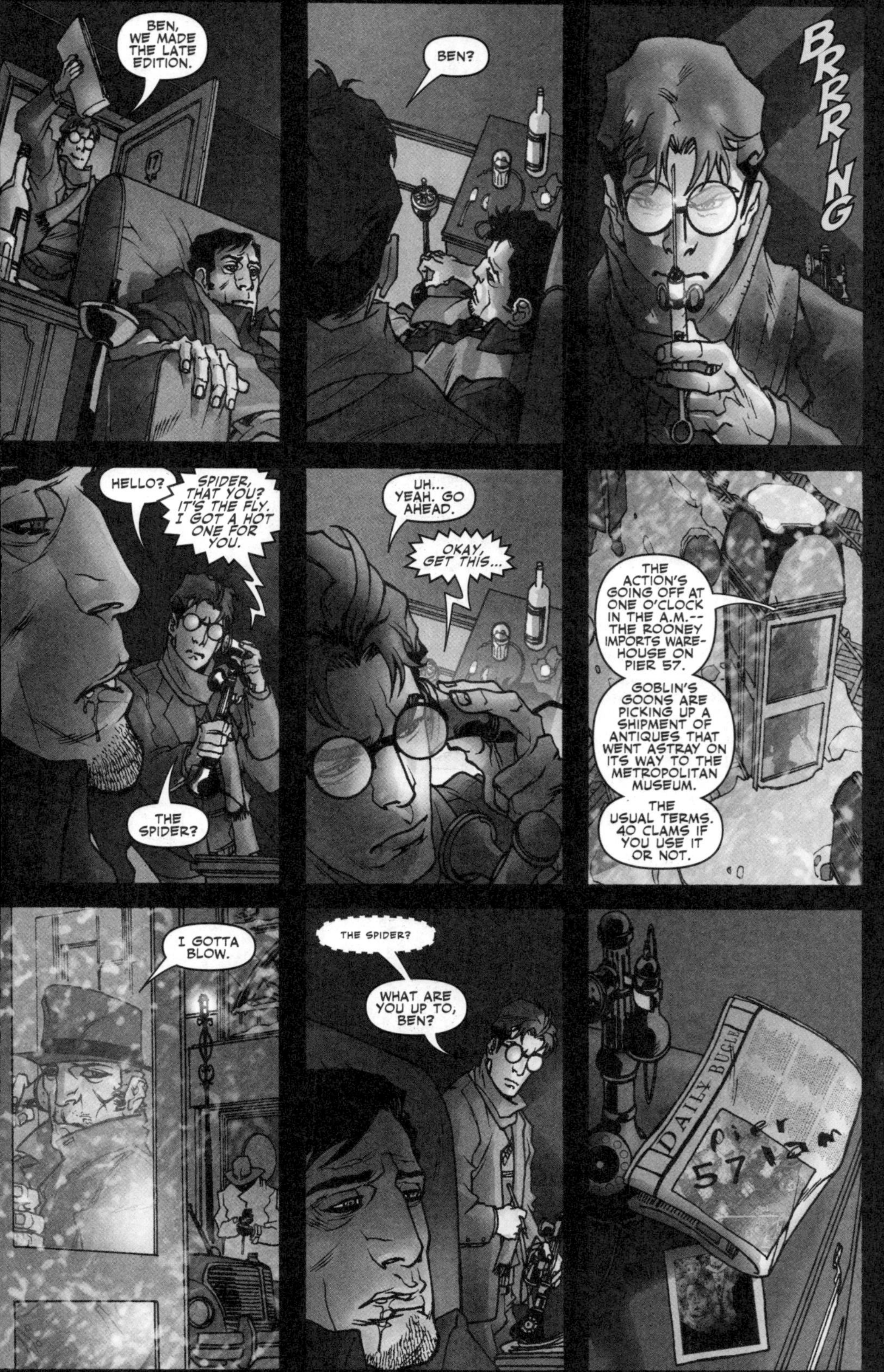
BEN, WE MADE THE LATE EDITION.
BEN?
BRRRING
HELLO?
SPIDER, THAT YOU? IT'S THE FLY. I GOT A HOT ONE FOR YOU.
THE SPIDER?
UH... YEAH. GO AHEAD.
OKAY, GET THIS...
THE ACTION'S GOING OFF AT ONE O'CLOCK IN THE A.M.-- THE ROONEY IMPORTS WARE-HOUSE ON PIER 57.
GOBLIN'S GOONS ARE PICKING UP A SHIPMENT OF ANTIQUES THAT WENT ASTRAY ON ITS WAY TO THE METROPOLITAN MUSEUM.
THE USUAL TERMS. 40 CLAMS IF YOU USE IT OR NOT.
I GOTTA BLOW.
THE SPIDER?
WHAT ARE YOU UP TO, BEN?
DAILY BUGLE
57

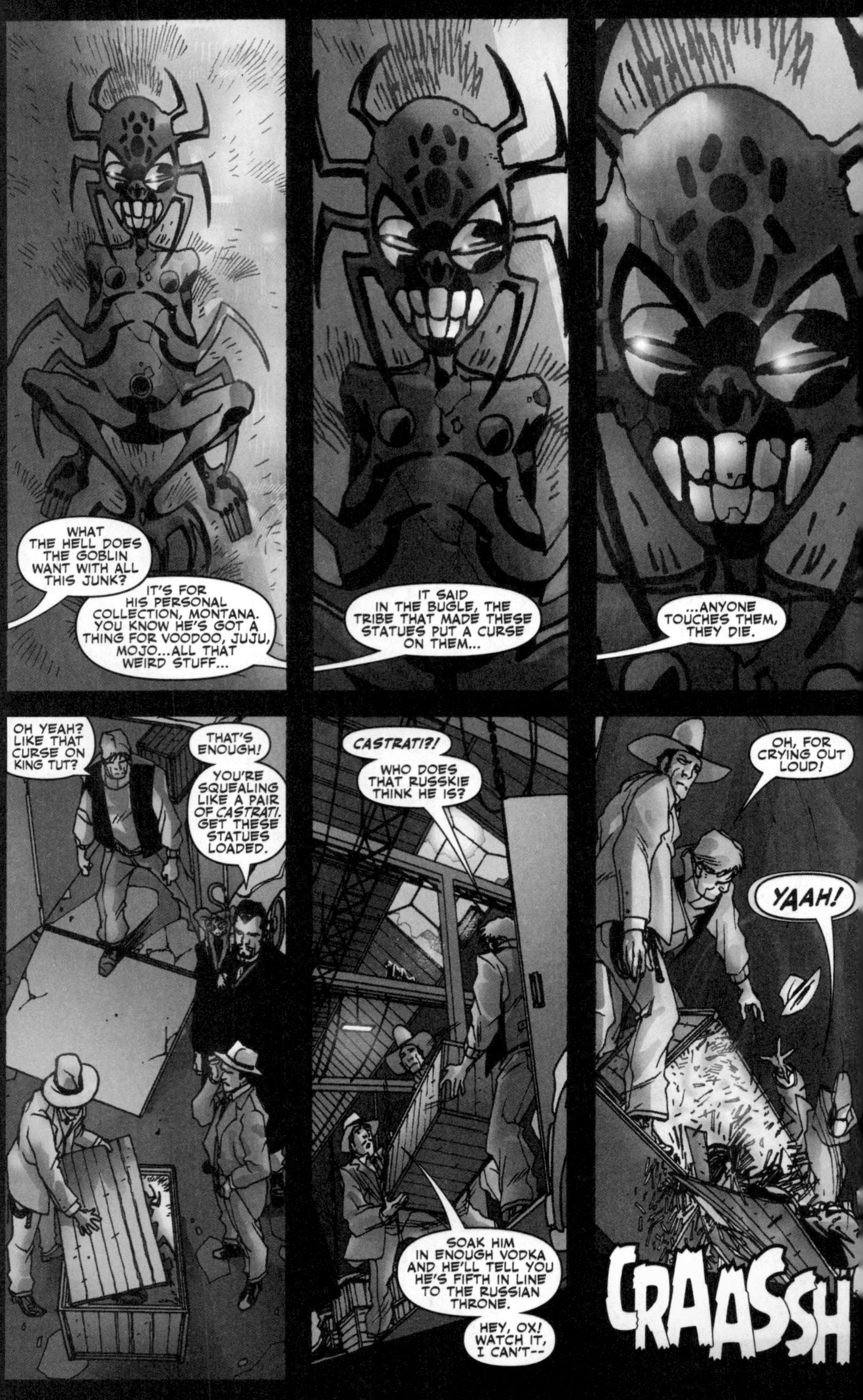

WHAT THE HELL DOES THE GOBLIN WANT WITH ALL THIS JUNK?
IT'S FOR HIS PERSONAL COLLECTION, MONTANA. YOU KNOW HE'S GOT A THING FOR VOODOO, JUJU, MOJO...ALL THAT WEIRD STUFF...
IT SAID IN THE BUGLE, THE TRIBE THAT MADE THESE STATUES PUT A CURSE ON THEM...
...ANYONE TOUCHES THEM, THEY DIE.
OH YEAH? LIKE THAT CURSE ON KING TUT?
THAT'S ENOUGH!
YOU'RE SQUEALING LIKE A PAIR OF CASTRATI. GET THESE STATUES LOADED.
CASTRATI?!
WHO DOES THAT RUSSKIE THINK HE IS?
SOAK HIM IN ENOUGH VODKA AND HE'LL TELL YOU HE'S FIFTH IN LINE TO THE RUSSIAN THRONE.
HEY, OX! WATCH IT, I CAN'T--
OH, FOR CRYING OUT LOUD!
YAAH!
CRAASSH

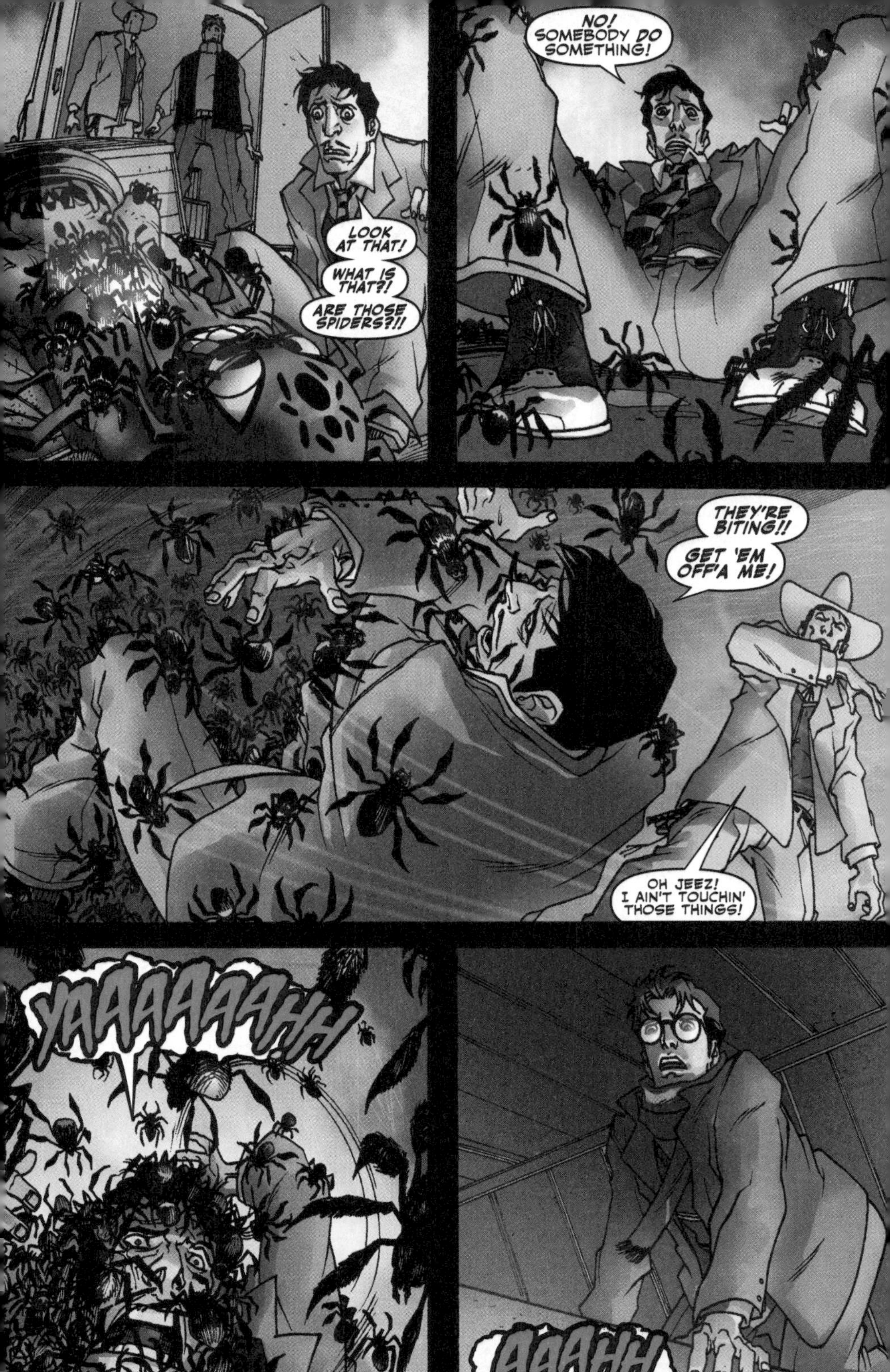
LOOK AT THAT!
WHAT IS THAT?!
ARE THOSE SPIDERS?!!
NO! SOMEBODY DO SOMETHING!
THEY'RE BITING!!
GET 'EM OFF'A ME!
OH JEEZ! I AIN'T TOUCHIN' THOSE THINGS!
YAAAAAAAHH
AAAHH

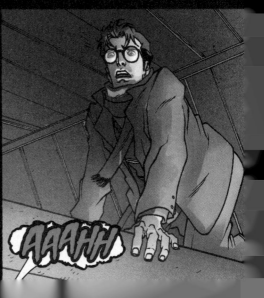

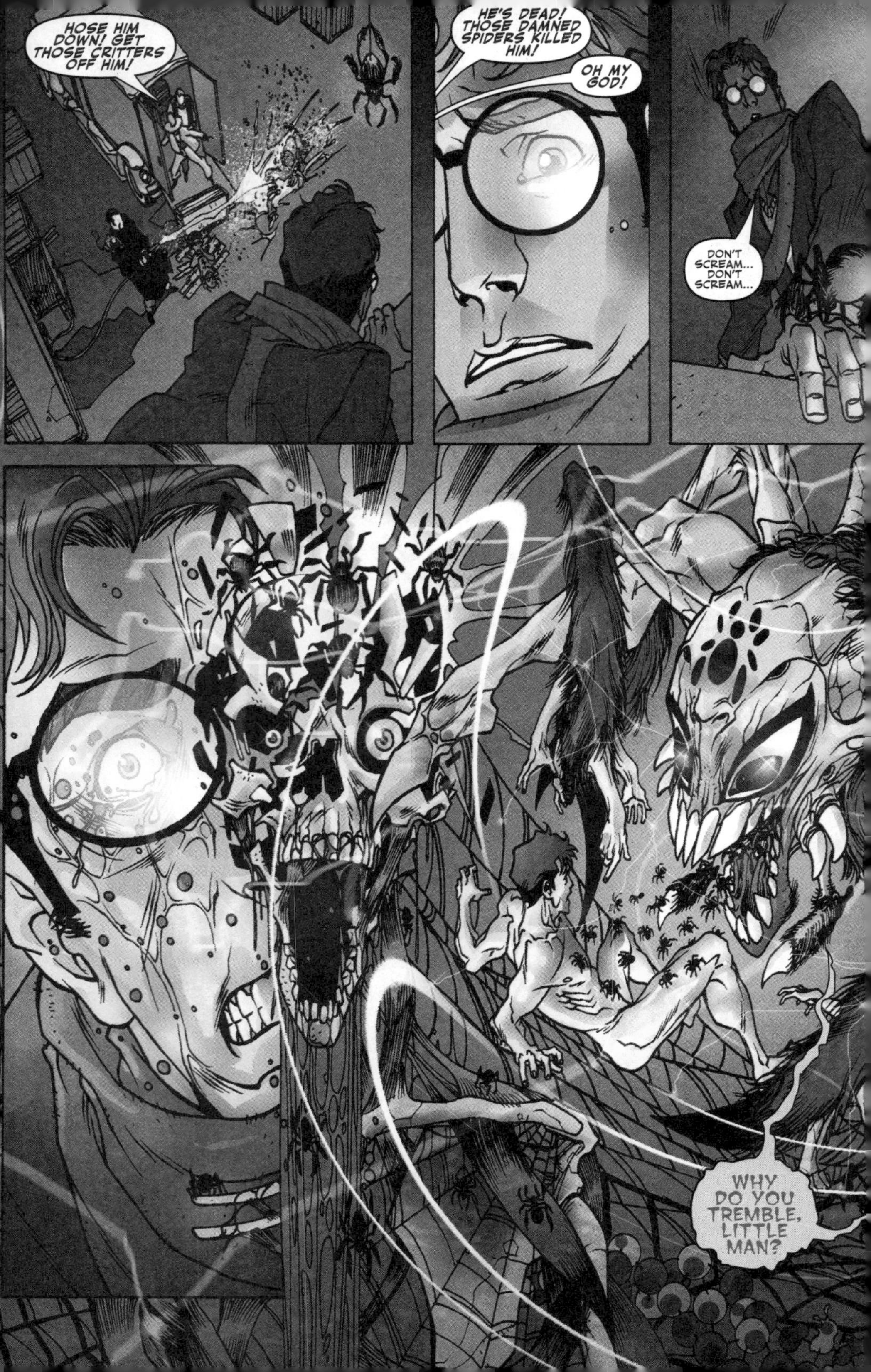
HOSE HIM DOWN! GET THOSE CRITTERS OFF HIM!
HE'S DEAD! THOSE DAMNED SPIDERS KILLED HIM!
OH MY GOD!
DON'T SCREAM... DON'T SCREAM...
WHY DO YOU TREMBLE, LITTLE MAN?

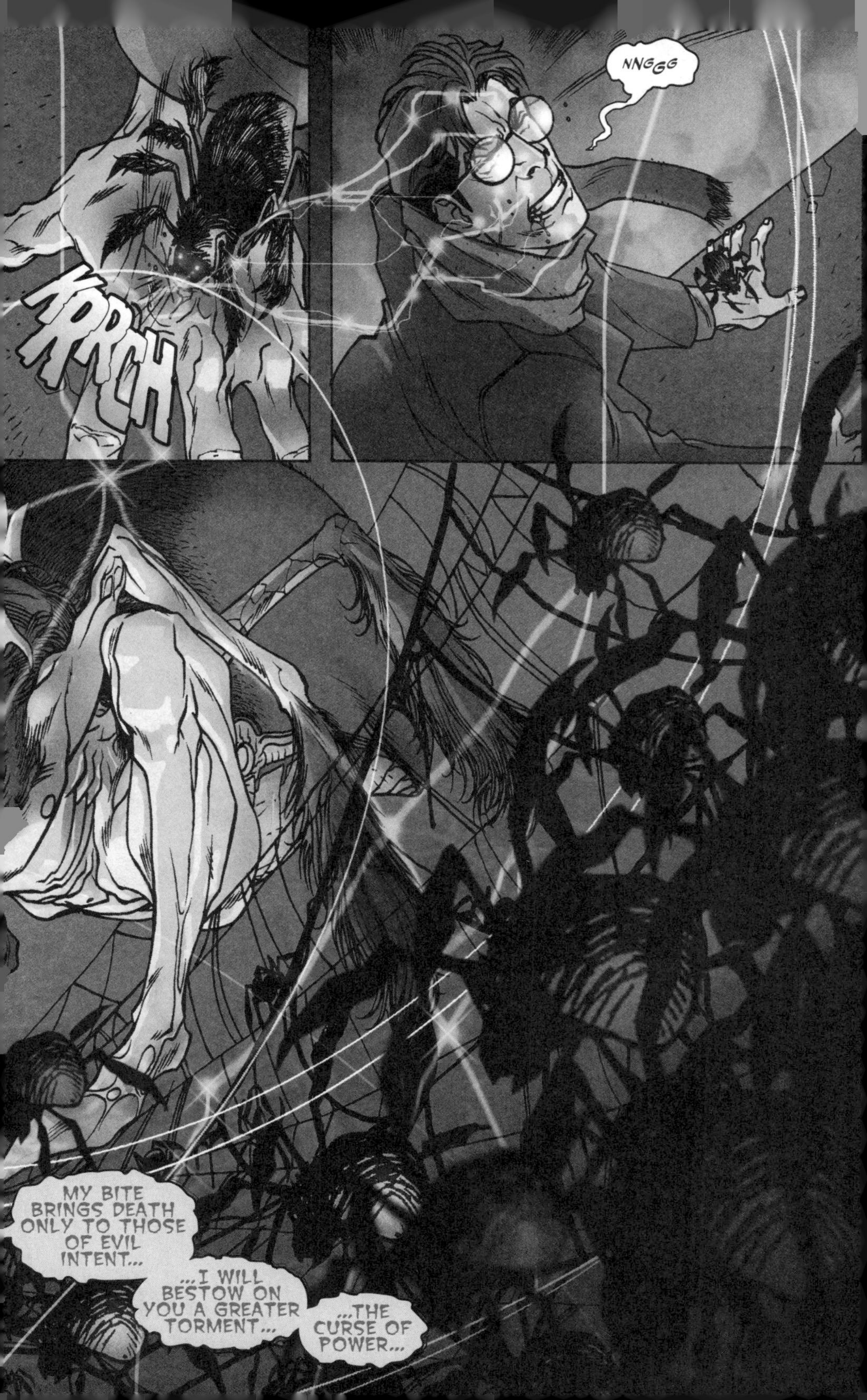
KRRCH
NNGGG
MY BITE BRINGS DEATH ONLY TO THOSE OF EVIL INTENT...
...I WILL BESTOW ON YOU A GREATER TORMENT...
...THE CURSE OF POWER...

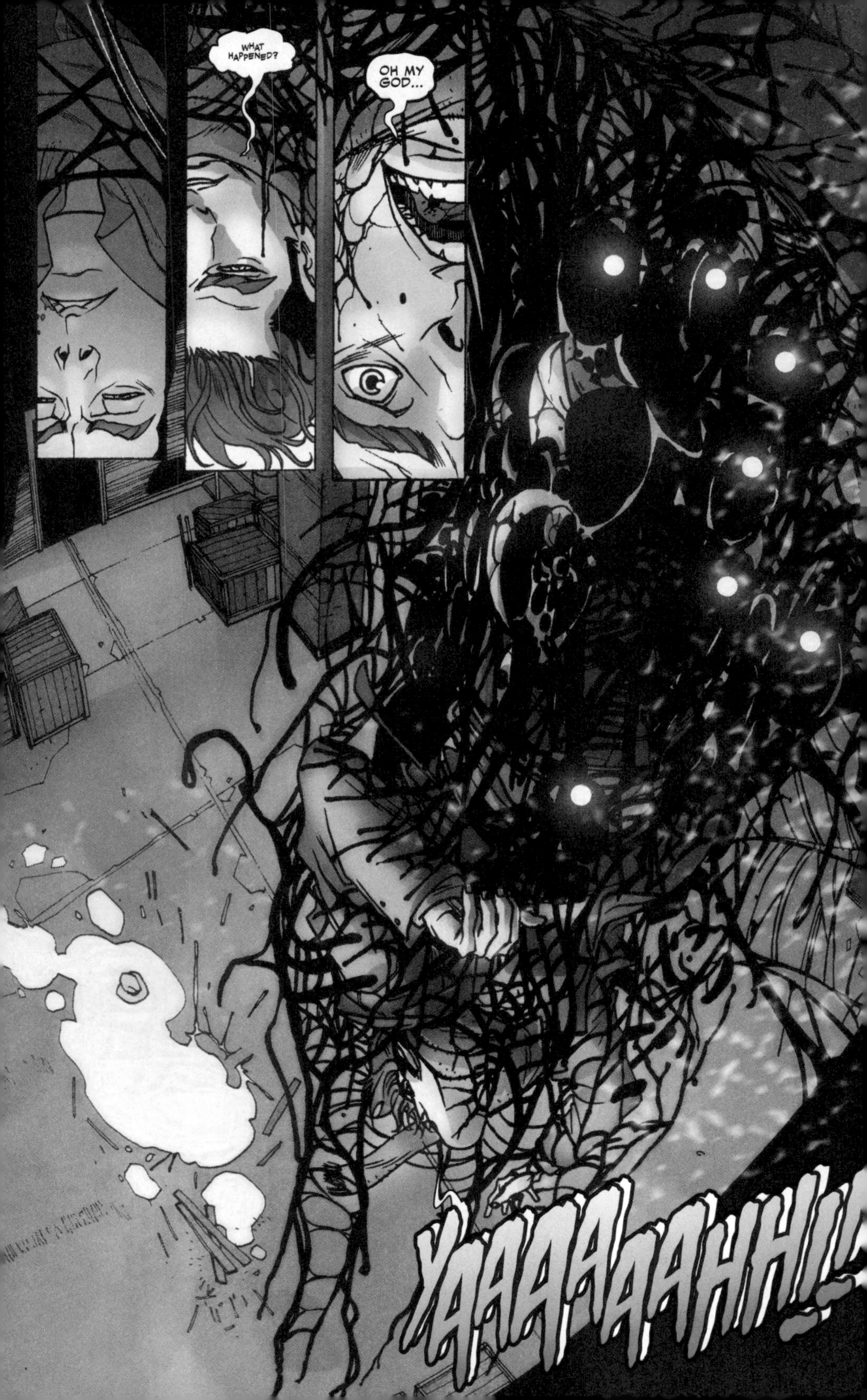
WHAT HAPPENED?
OH MY GOD...
YAAAAAAAHH!!

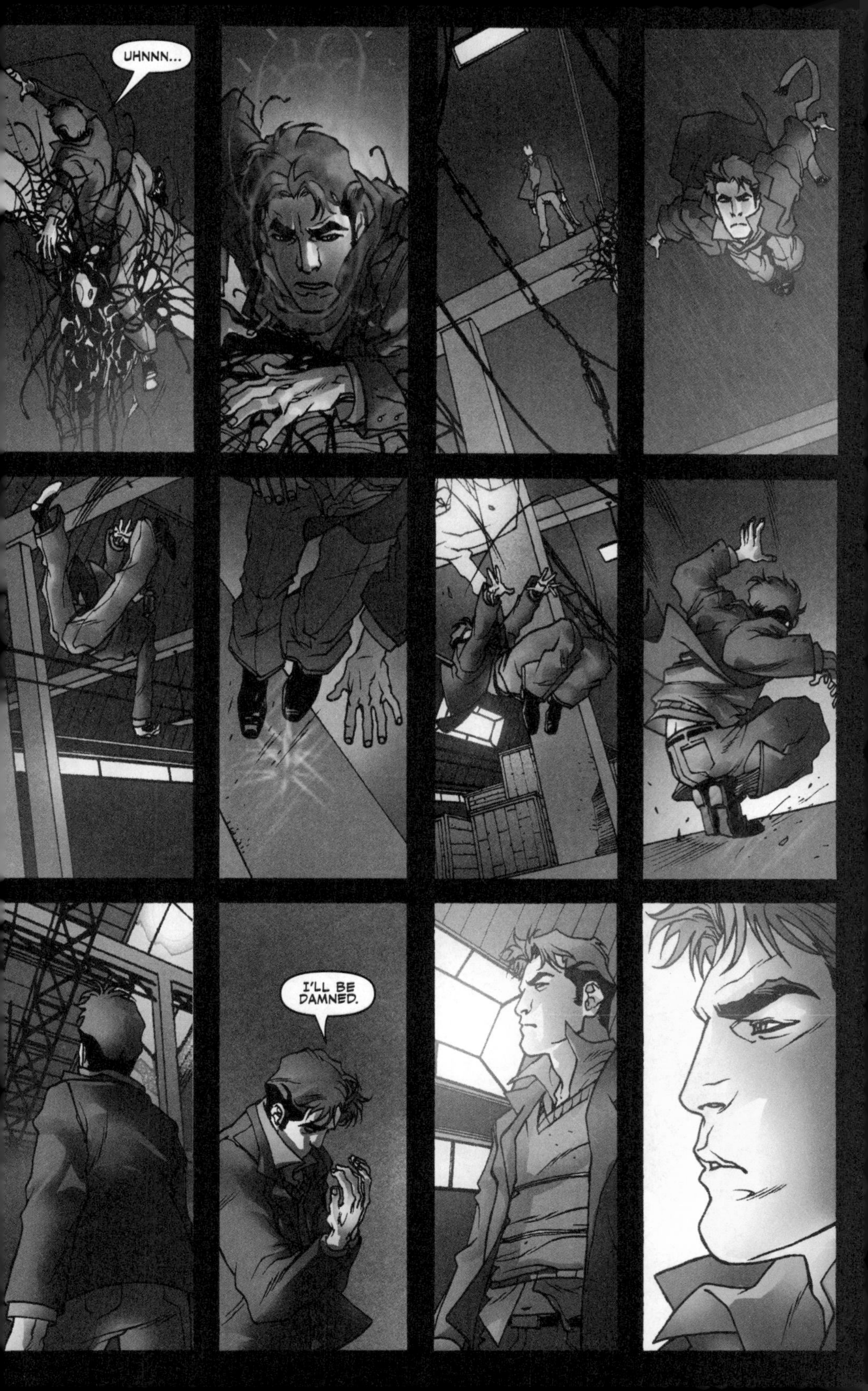
UHNNN...
I'LL BE DAMNED.

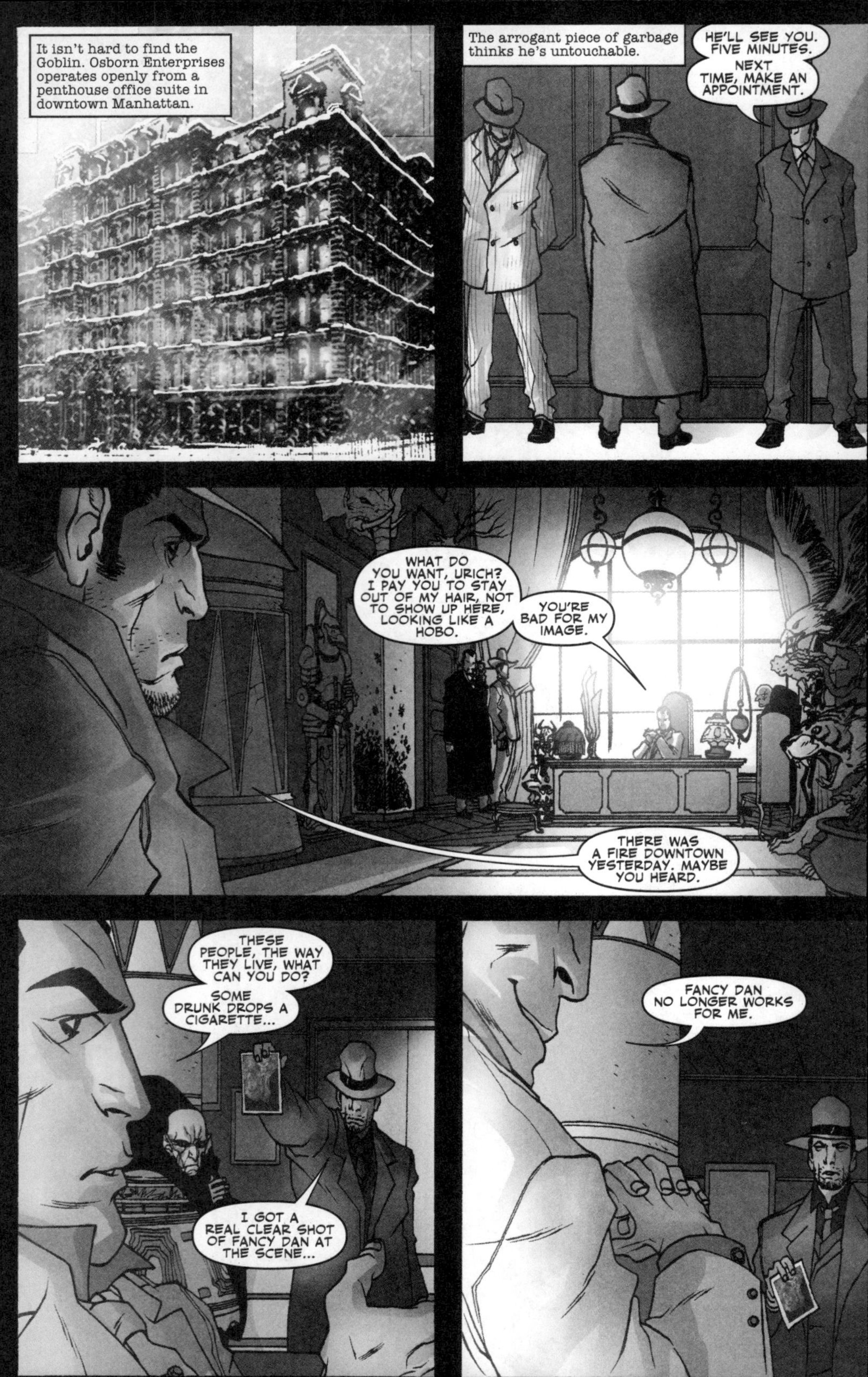

It isn't hard to find the Goblin. Osborn Enterprises operates openly from a penthouse office suite in downtown Manhattan.
The arrogant piece of garbage thinks he's untouchable.
HE'LL SEE YOU. FIVE MINUTES.
NEXT TIME, MAKE AN APPOINTMENT.
WHAT DO YOU WANT, URICH? I PAY YOU TO STAY OUT OF MY HAIR, NOT TO SHOW UP HERE, LOOKING LIKE A HOBO.
YOU'RE BAD FOR MY IMAGE.
THERE WAS A FIRE DOWNTOWN YESTERDAY. MAYBE YOU HEARD.
THESE PEOPLE, THE WAY THEY LIVE, WHAT CAN YOU DO?
SOME DRUNK DROPS A CIGARETTE...
I GOT A REAL CLEAR SHOT OF FANCY DAN AT THE SCENE...
FANCY DAN NO LONGER WORKS FOR ME.

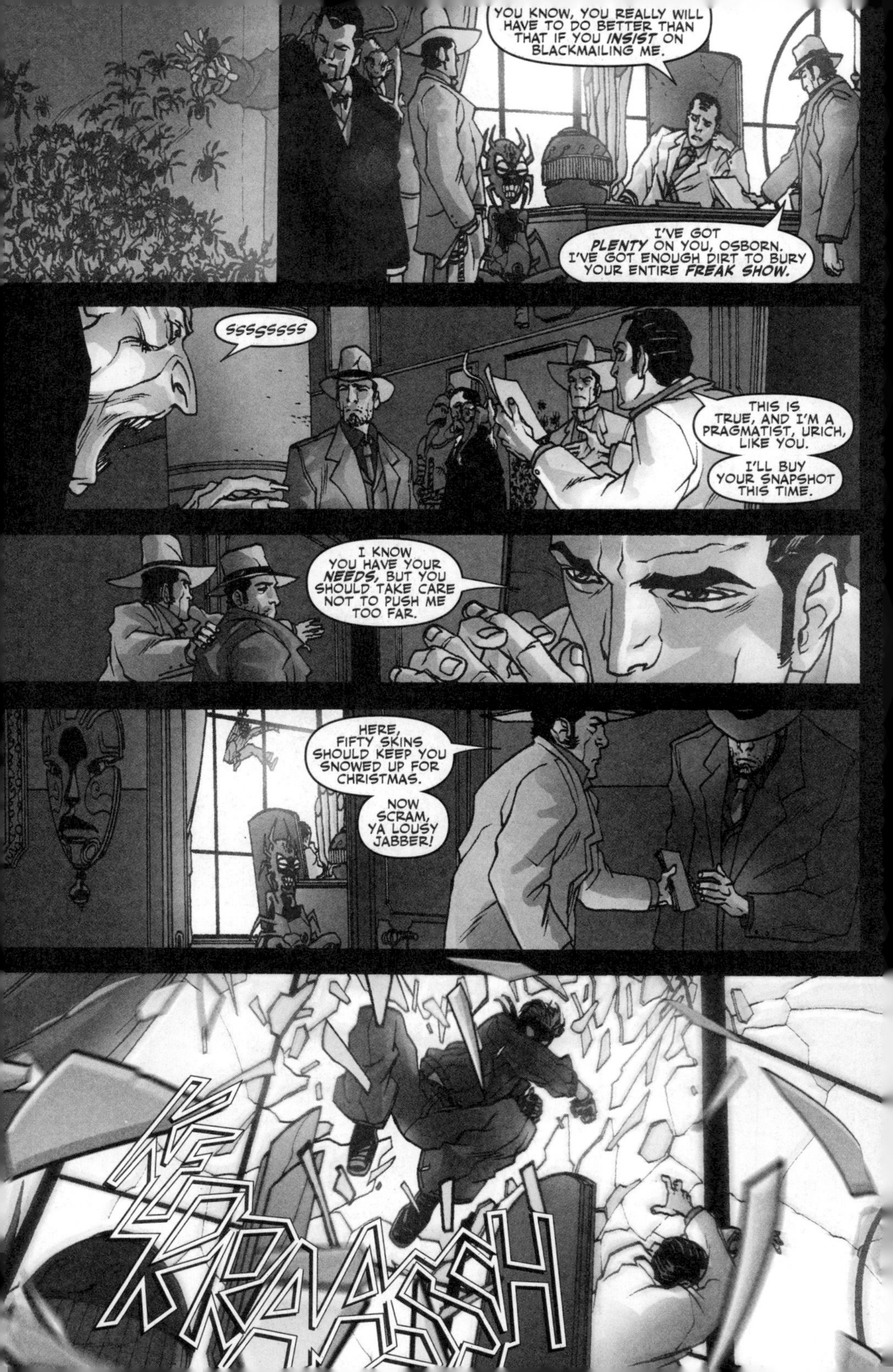
YOU KNOW, YOU REALLY WILL HAVE TO DO BETTER THAN THAT IF YOU INSIST ON BLACKMAILING ME.
I'VE GOT PLENTY ON YOU, OSBORN. I'VE GOT ENOUGH DIRT TO BURY YOUR ENTIRE FREAK SHOW.
SSSSSSSS
THIS IS TRUE, AND I'M A PRAGMATIST, URICH, LIKE YOU.
I'LL BUY YOUR SNAPSHOT THIS TIME.
I KNOW YOU HAVE YOUR NEEDS, BUT YOU SHOULD TAKE CARE NOT TO PUSH ME TOO FAR.
HERE, FIFTY SKINS SHOULD KEEP YOU SNOWED UP FOR CHRISTMAS.
NOW SCRAM, YA LOUSY JABBER!
KRRASSH

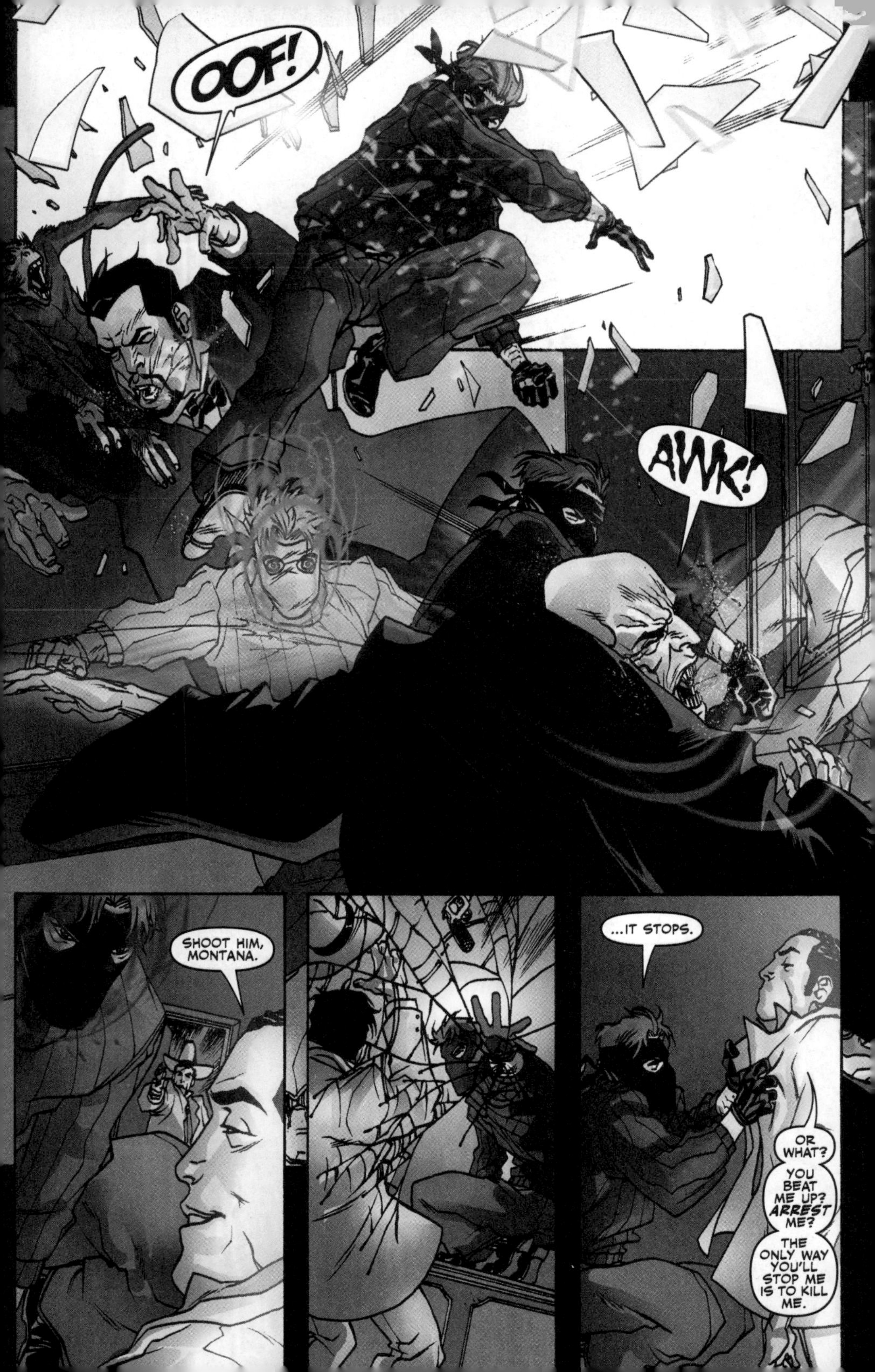
OOF!
AWK!
SHOOT HIM, MONTANA.
...IT STOPS.
OR WHAT?
YOU BEAT ME UP? ARREST ME?
THE ONLY WAY YOU'LL STOP ME IS TO KILL ME.

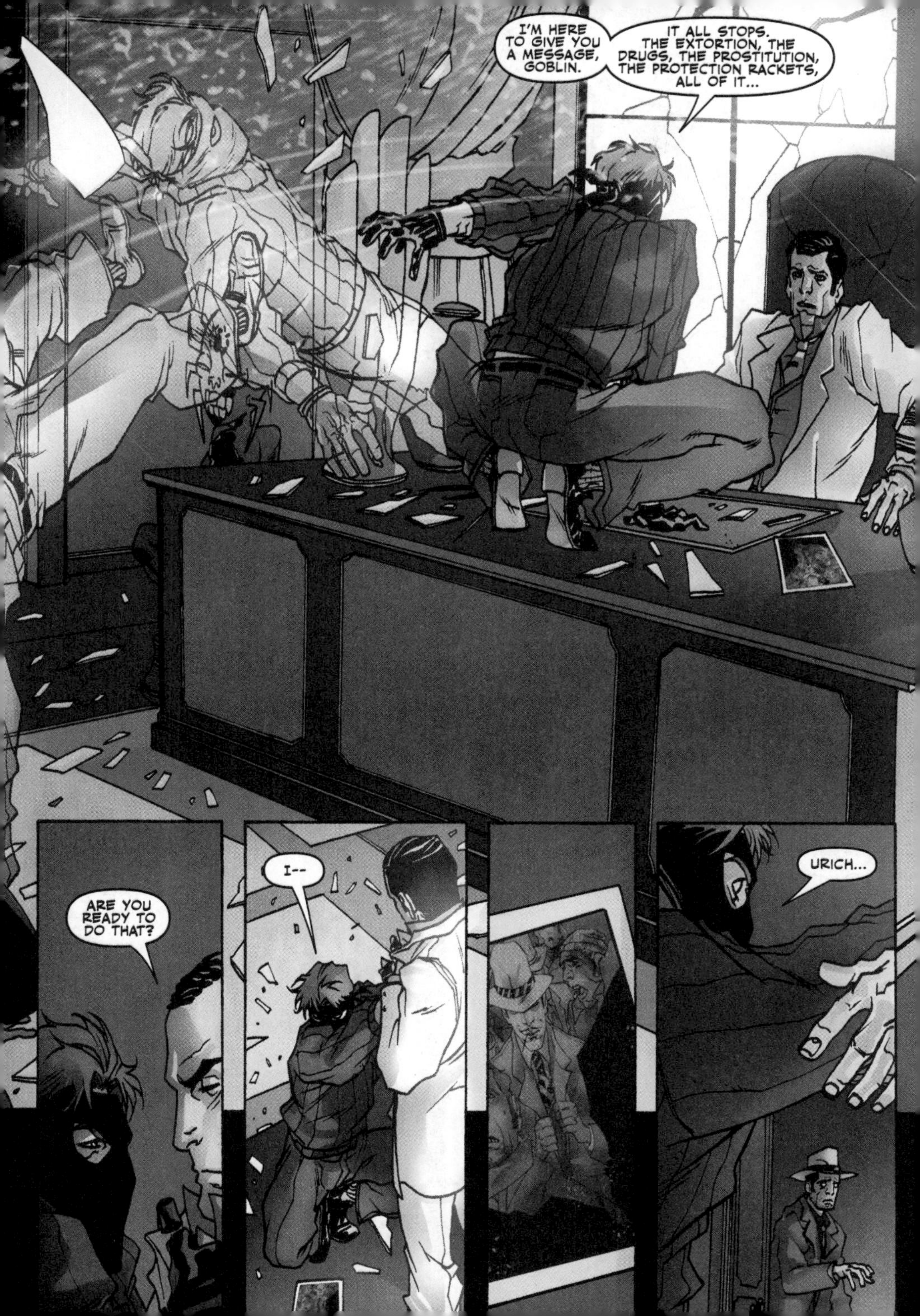
I'M HERE TO GIVE YOU A MESSAGE, GOBLIN.
IT ALL STOPS. THE EXTORTION, THE DRUGS, THE PROSTITUTION, THE PROTECTION RACKETS, ALL OF IT...
ARE YOU READY TO DO THAT?
I--
URICH...

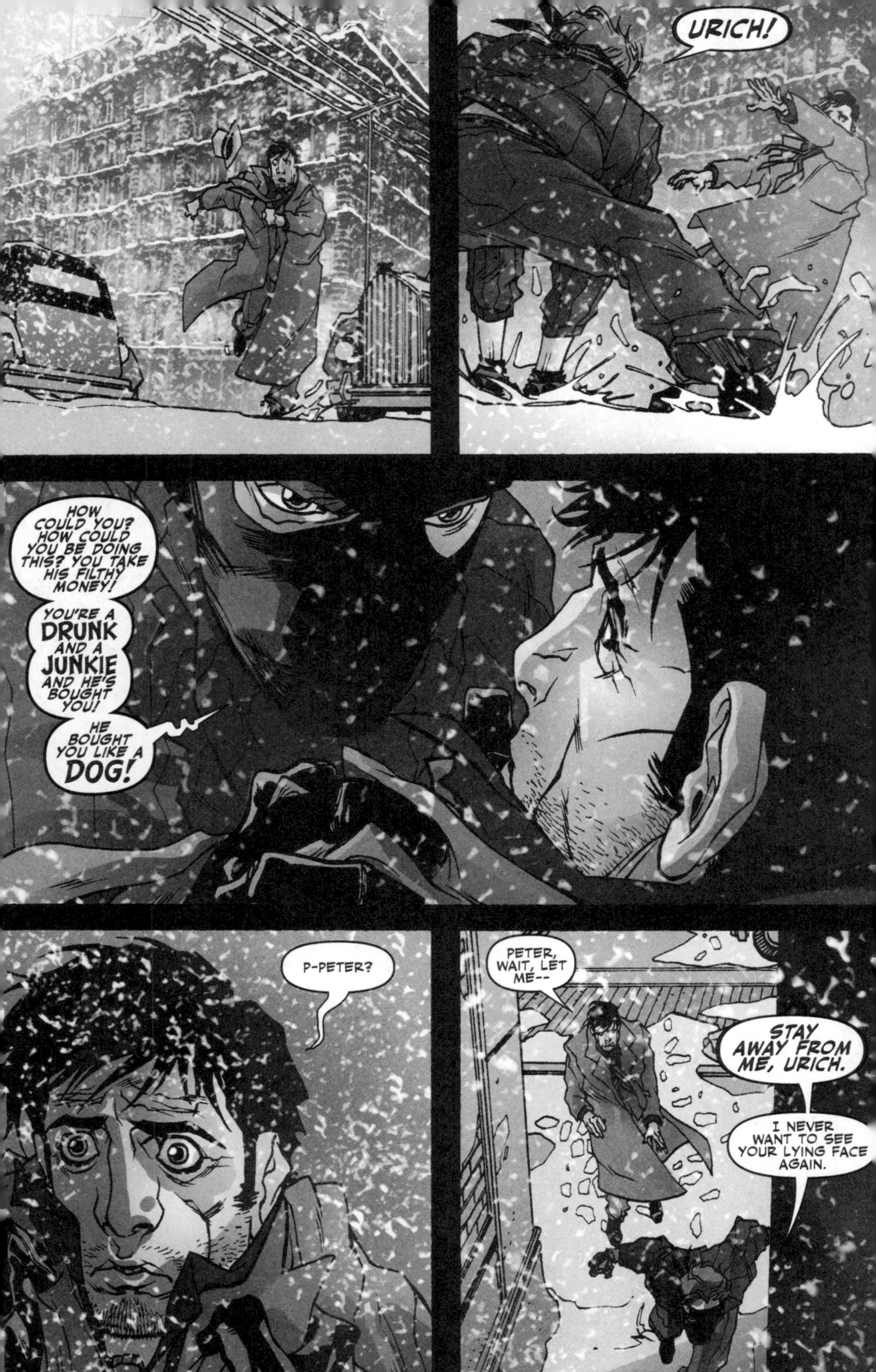
URICH!
HOW COULD YOU? HOW COULD YOU BE DOING THIS? YOU TAKE HIS FILTHY MONEY!
YOU'RE A DRUNK AND A JUNKIE AND HE'S BOUGHT YOU!
HE BOUGHT YOU LIKE A DOG!
P-PETER?
PETER, WAIT, LET ME--
STAY AWAY FROM ME, URICH.
I NEVER WANT TO SEE YOUR LYING FACE AGAIN.

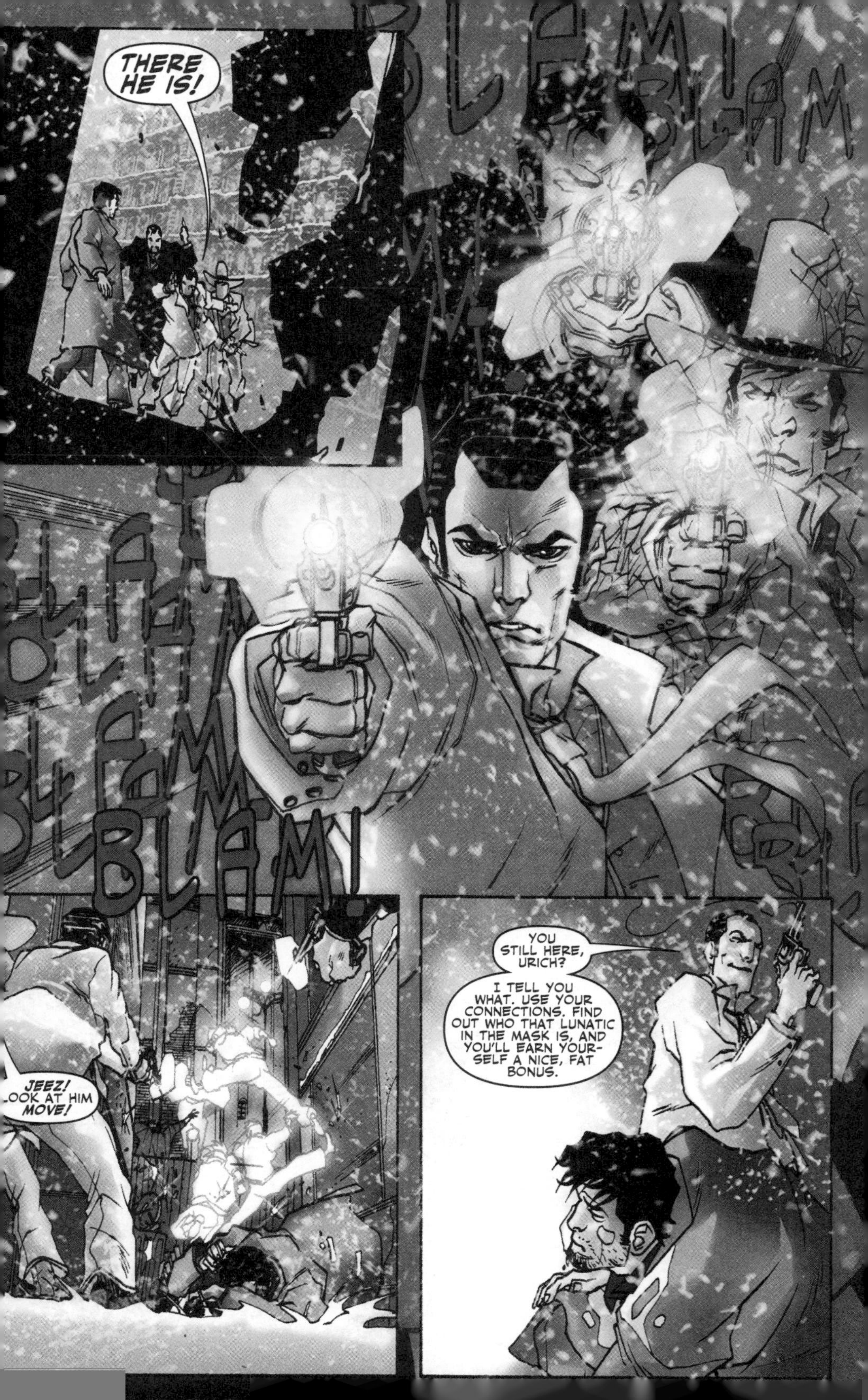
THERE HE IS!
BLAM
BLAM
BLAM
BLAM
BLAM
JEEZ! LOOK AT HIM MOVE!
YOU STILL HERE, URICH?
I TELL YOU WHAT. USE YOUR CONNECTIONS. FIND OUT WHO THAT LUNATIC IN THE MASK IS, AND YOU'LL EARN YOURSELF A NICE, FAT BONUS.

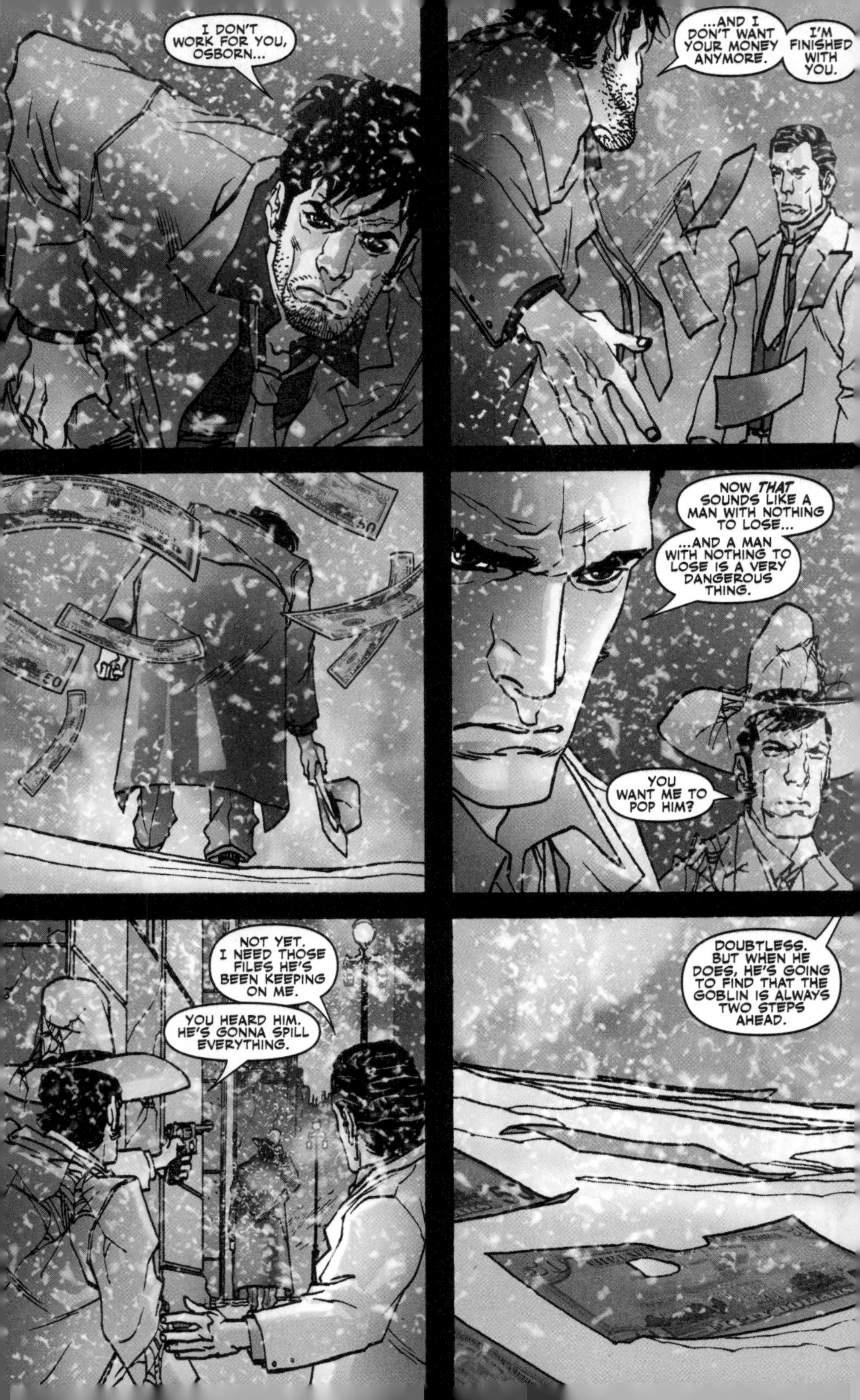
I DON'T WORK FOR YOU, OSBORN...
...AND I DON'T WANT YOUR MONEY ANYMORE.
I'M FINISHED WITH YOU.
NOW THAT SOUNDS LIKE A MAN WITH NOTHING TO LOSE...
...AND A MAN WITH NOTHING TO LOSE IS A VERY DANGEROUS THING.
YOU WANT ME TO POP HIM?
NOT YET. I NEED THOSE FILES HE'S BEEN KEEPING ON ME.
YOU HEARD HIM. HE'S GONNA SPILL EVERYTHING.
DOUBTLESS. BUT WHEN HE DOES, HE'S GOING TO FIND THAT THE GOBLIN IS ALWAYS TWO STEPS AHEAD.

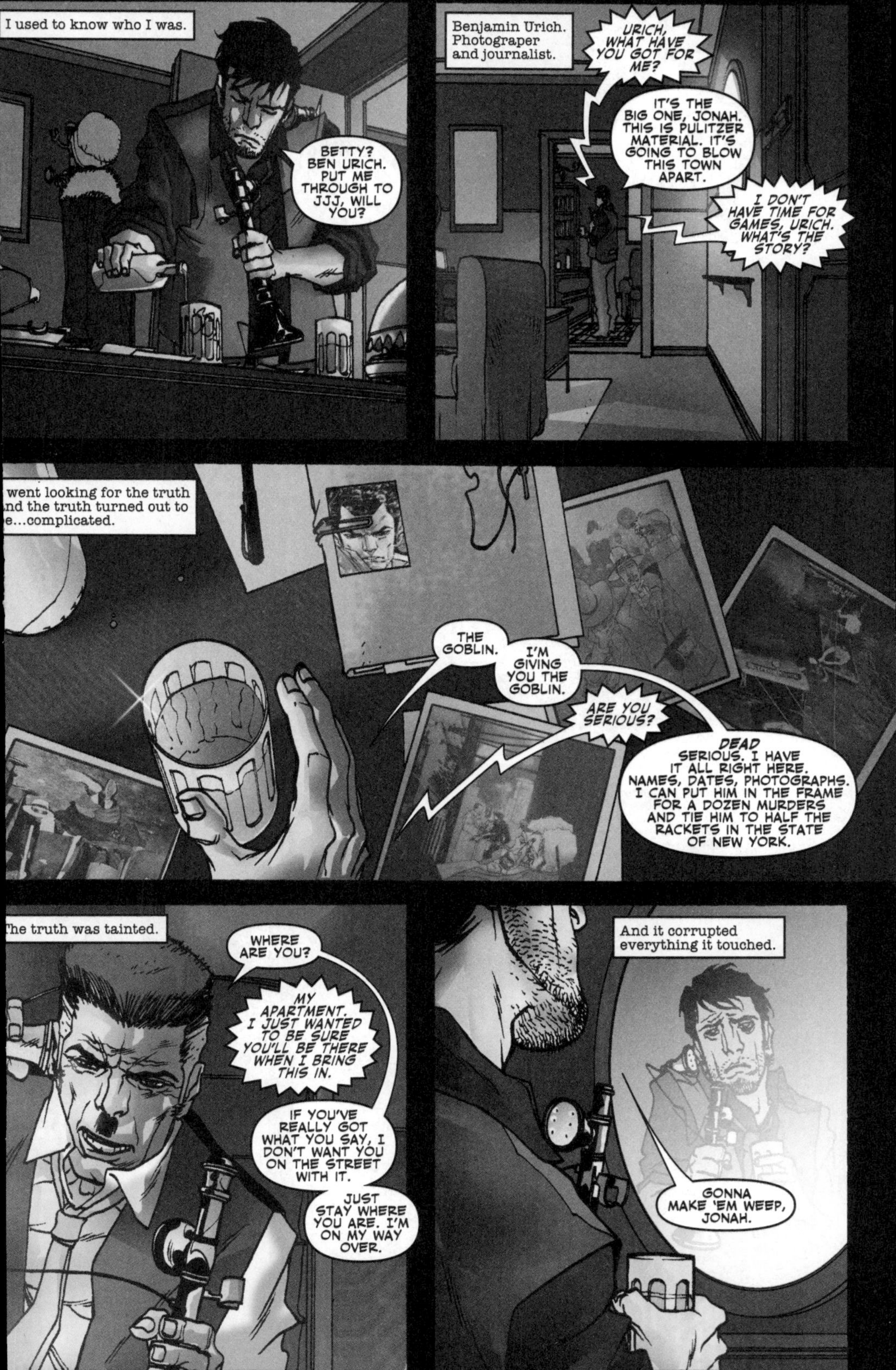
I used to know who I was.
BETTY? BEN URICH. PUT ME THROUGH TO JJJ, WILL YOU?
Benjamin Urich. Photograper and journalist.
URICH, WHAT HAVE YOU GOT FOR ME?
IT'S THE BIG ONE, JONAH. THIS IS PULITZER MATERIAL. IT'S GOING TO BLOW THIS TOWN APART.
I DON'T HAVE TIME FOR GAMES, URICH. WHAT'S THE STORY?
went looking for the truth nd the truth turned out to e...complicated.
THE GOBLIN.
I'M GIVING YOU THE GOBLIN.
ARE YOU SERIOUS?
DEAD SERIOUS. I HAVE IT ALL RIGHT HERE. NAMES, DATES, PHOTOGRAPHS. I CAN PUT HIM IN THE FRAME FOR A DOZEN MURDERS AND TIE HIM TO HALF THE RACKETS IN THE STATE OF NEW YORK.
The truth was tainted.
WHERE ARE YOU?
MY APARTMENT. I JUST WANTED TO BE SURE YOU'LL BE THERE WHEN I BRING THIS IN.
IF YOU'VE REALLY GOT WHAT YOU SAY, I DON'T WANT YOU ON THE STREET WITH IT.
JUST STAY WHERE YOU ARE. I'M ON MY WAY OVER.
And it corrupted everything it touched.
GONNA MAKE 'EM WEEP, JONAH.

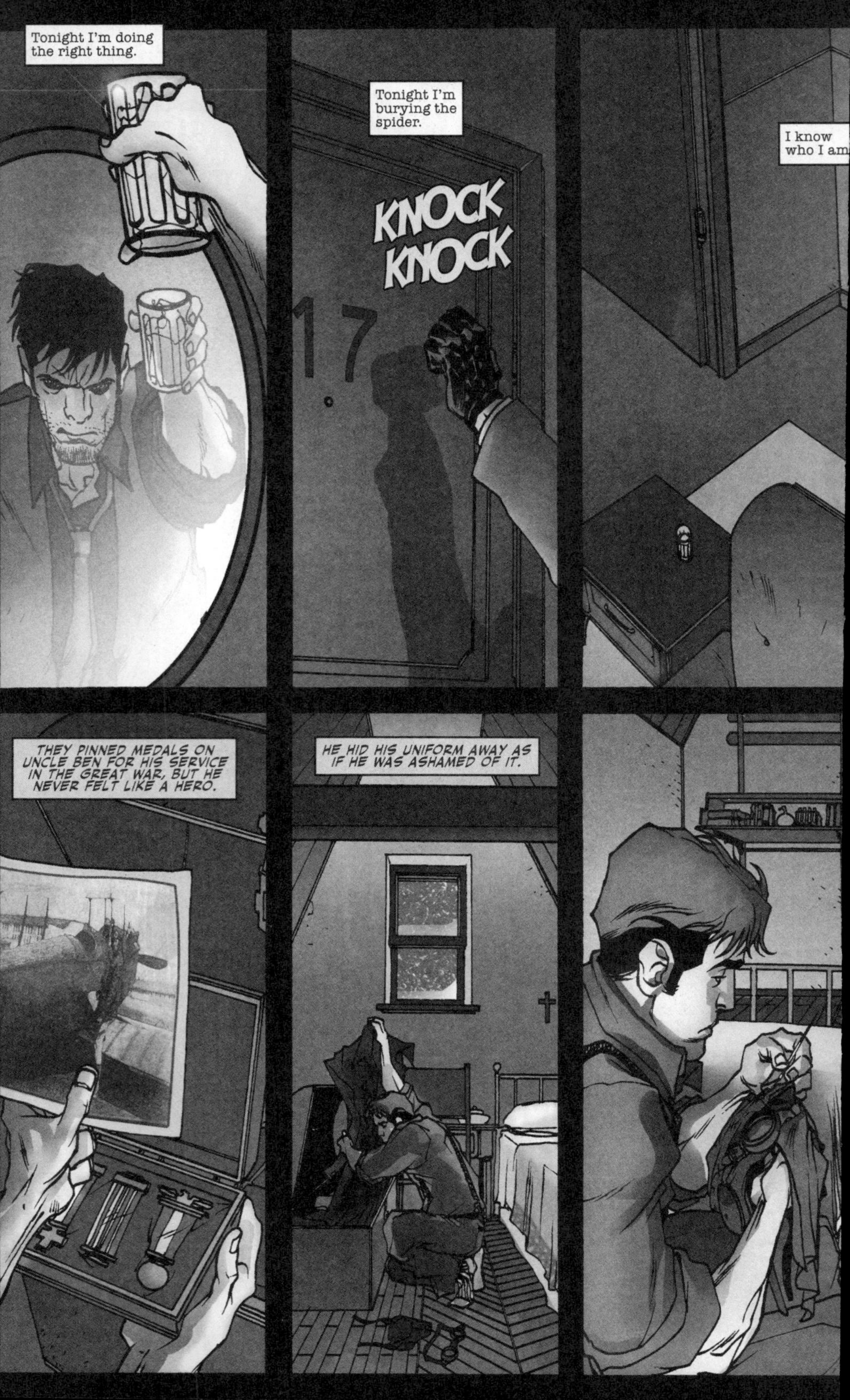
Tonight I'm doing the right thing.
Tonight I'm burying the spider.
KNOCK KNOCK
17
I know who I am
THEY PINNED MEDALS ON UNCLE BEN FOR HIS SERVICE IN THE GREAT WAR, BUT HE NEVER FELT LIKE A HERO.
HE HID HIS UNIFORM AWAY AS IF HE WAS ASHAMED OF IT.

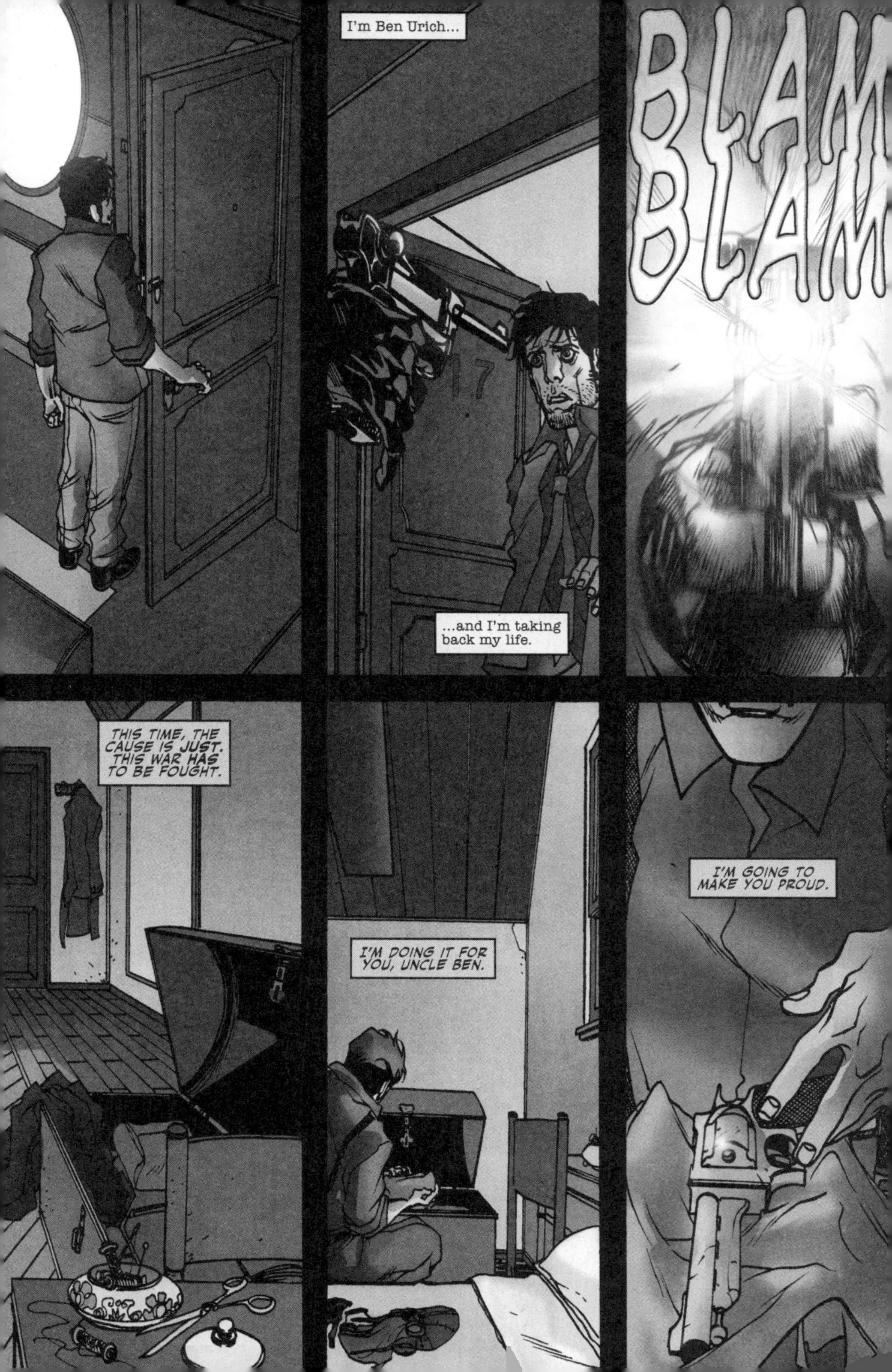
I'm Ben Urich...
...and I'm taking back my life.
BLAM BLAM
THIS TIME, THE CAUSE IS JUST. THIS WAR HAS TO BE FOUGHT.
I'M DOING IT FOR YOU, UNCLE BEN.
I'M GOING TO MAKE YOU PROUD.

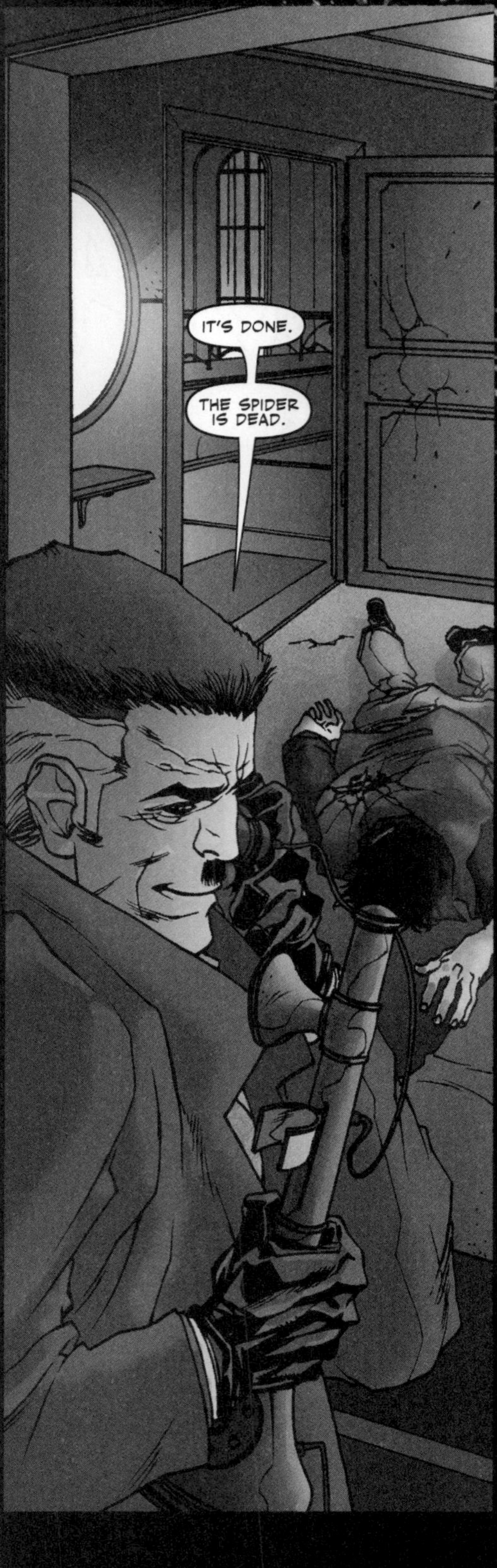
IT'S DONE.
THE SPIDER IS DEAD.

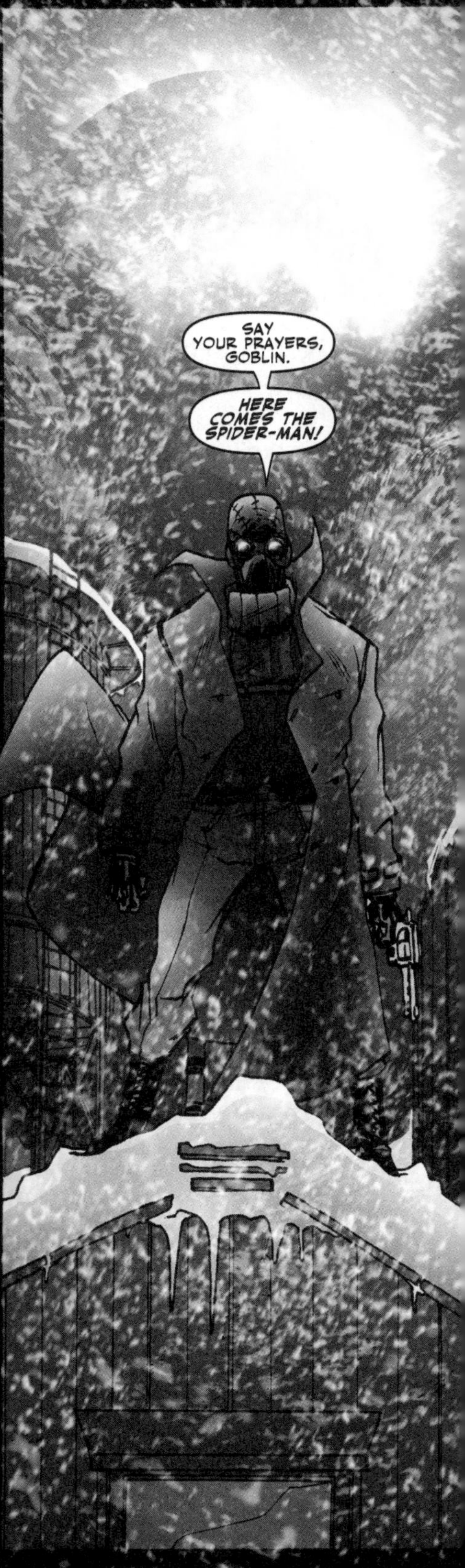
SAY YOUR PRAYERS, GOBLIN.
HERE COMES THE SPIDER-MAN!

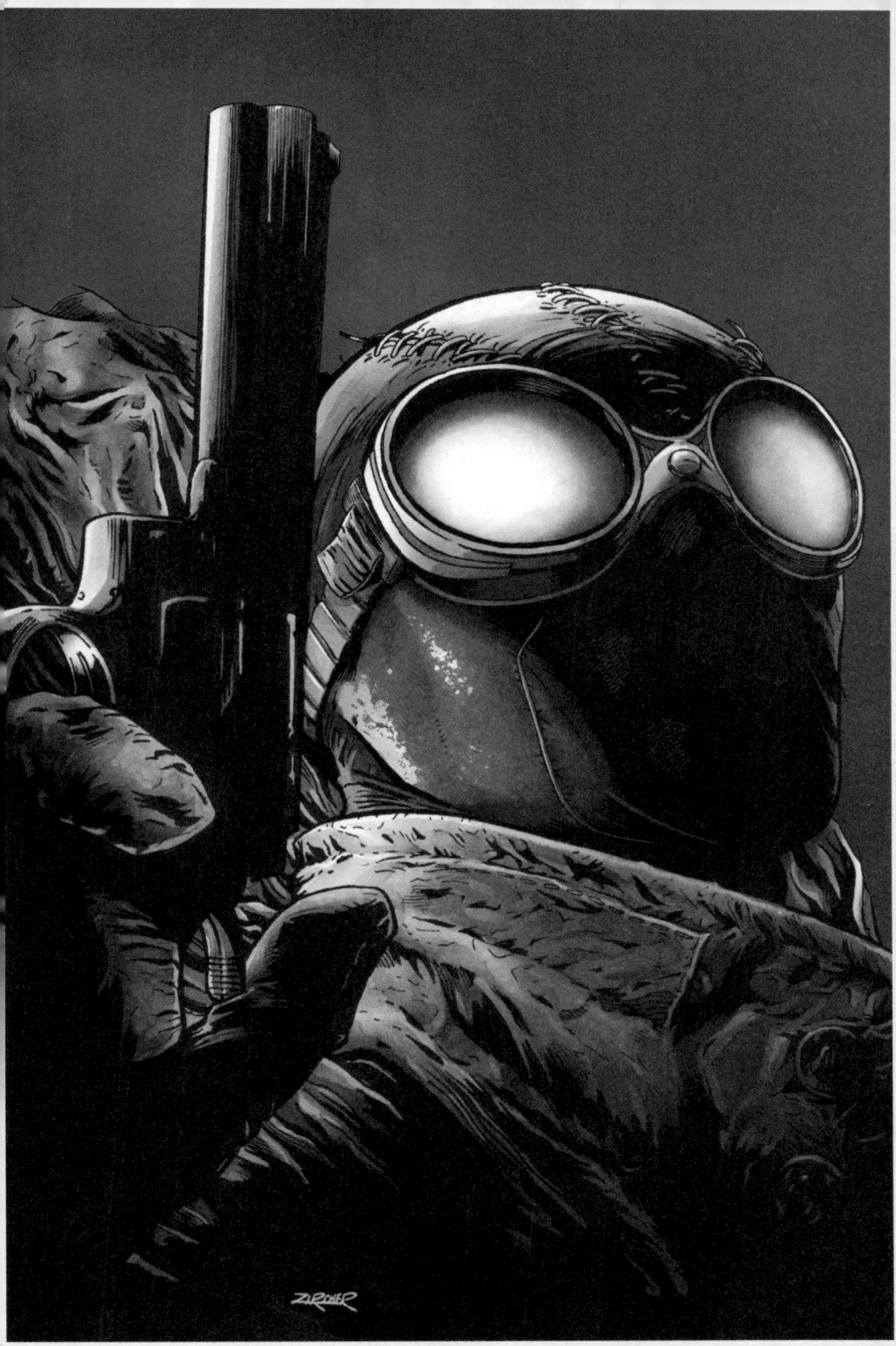

THREE

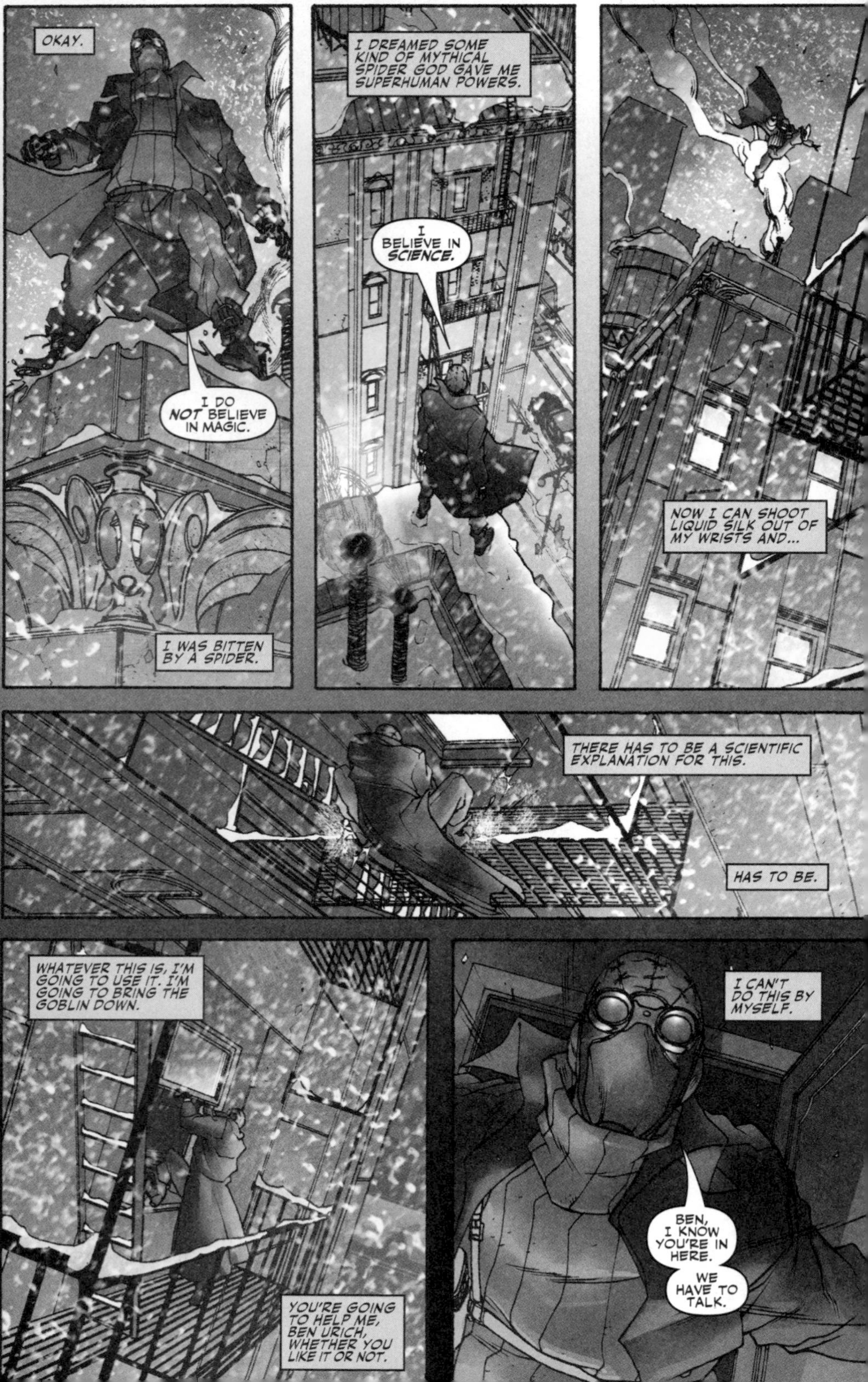
OKAY.
I DO NOT BELIEVE IN MAGIC.
I WAS BITTEN BY A SPIDER.
I DREAMED SOME KIND OF MYTHICAL SPIDER GOD GAVE ME SUPERHUMAN POWERS.
I BELIEVE IN SCIENCE.
NOW I CAN SHOOT LIQUID SILK OUT OF MY WRISTS AND...
THERE HAS TO BE A SCIENTIFIC EXPLANATION FOR THIS.
HAS TO BE.
WHATEVER THIS IS, I'M GOING TO USE IT. I'M GOING TO BRING THE GOBLIN DOWN.
YOU'RE GOING TO HELP ME, BEN URICH, WHETHER YOU LIKE IT OR NOT.
I CAN'T DO THIS BY MYSELF.
BEN, I KNOW YOU'RE IN HERE.
WE HAVE TO TALK.

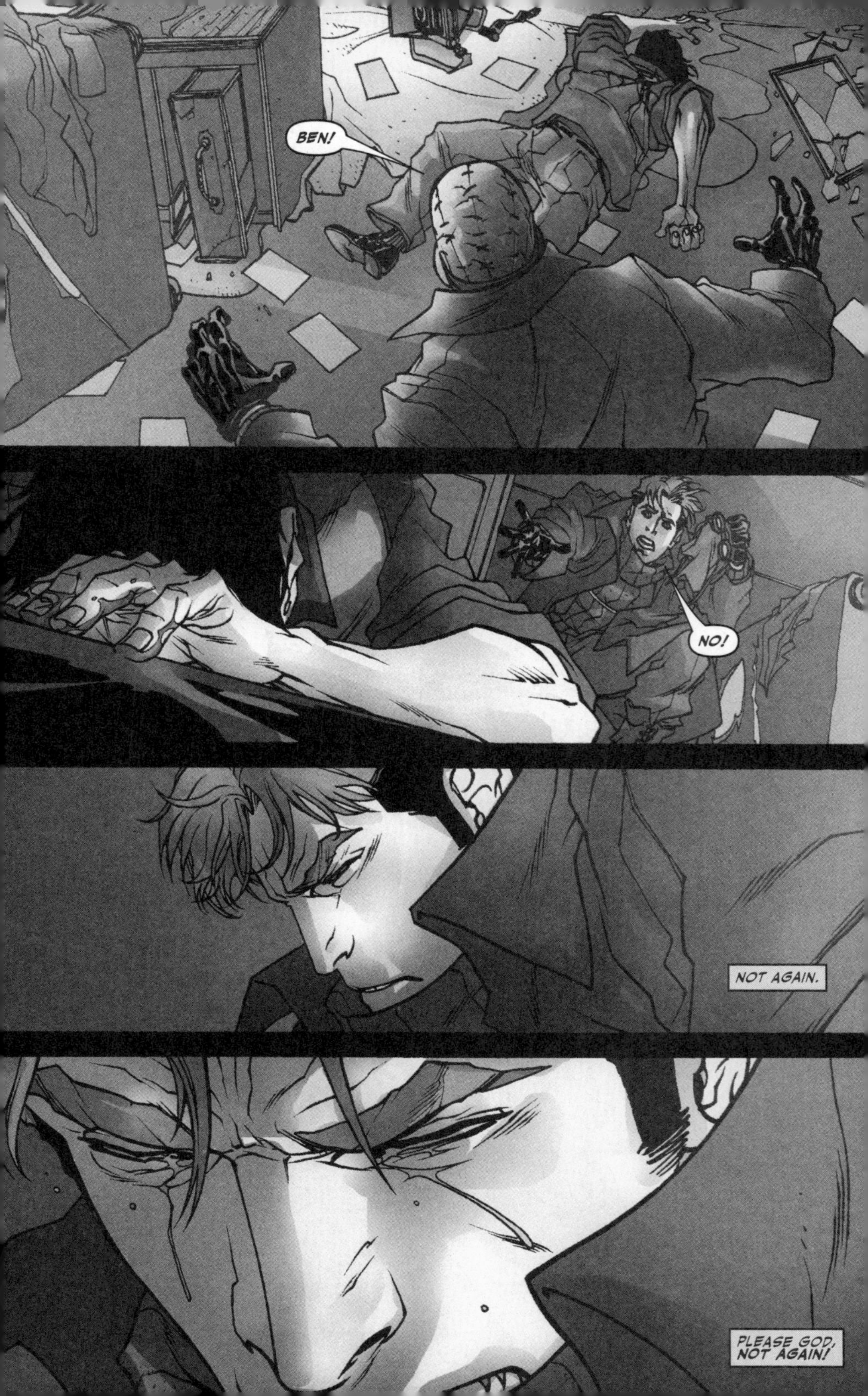
BEN!
NO!
NOT AGAIN.
PLEASE GOD, NOT AGAIN!

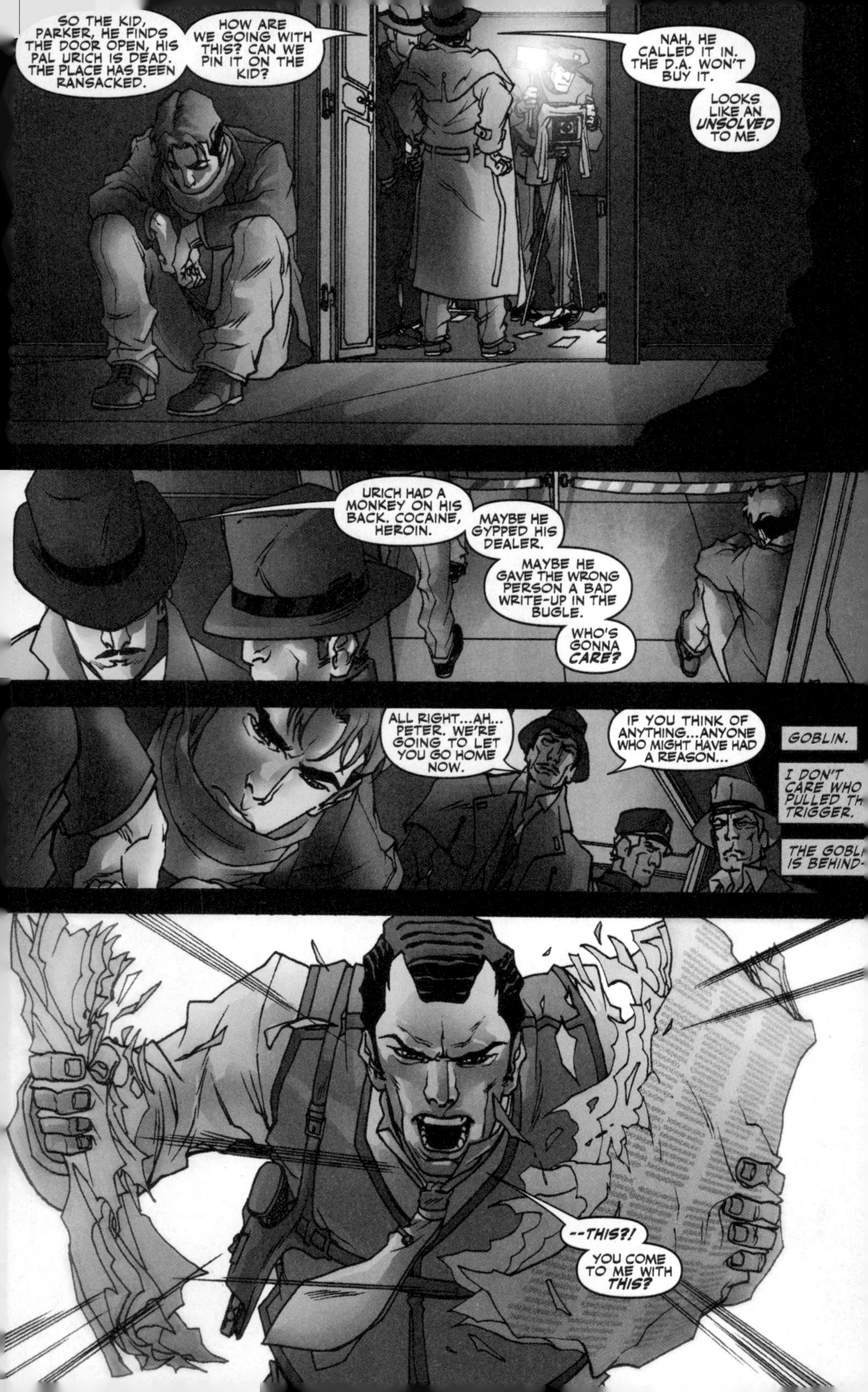
SO THE KID, PARKER, HE FINDS THE DOOR OPEN, HIS PAL URICH IS DEAD. THE PLACE HAS BEEN RANSACKED.
HOW ARE WE GOING WITH THIS? CAN WE PIN IT ON THE KID?
NAH, HE CALLED IT IN. THE D.A. WON'T BUY IT.
LOOKS LIKE AN *UNSOLVED* TO ME.
URICH HAD A MONKEY ON HIS BACK. COCAINE, HEROIN.
MAYBE HE GYPPED HIS DEALER.
MAYBE HE GAVE THE WRONG PERSON A BAD WRITE-UP IN THE BUGLE.
WHO'S GONNA *CARE?*
ALL RIGHT...AH... PETER. WE'RE GOING TO LET YOU GO HOME NOW.
IF YOU THINK OF ANYTHING...ANYONE WHO MIGHT HAVE HAD A REASON...
GOBLIN.
I DON'T CARE WHO PULLED TH TRIGGER.
THE GOBL IS BEHIND-
--THIS?!
YOU COME TO ME WITH *THIS?*

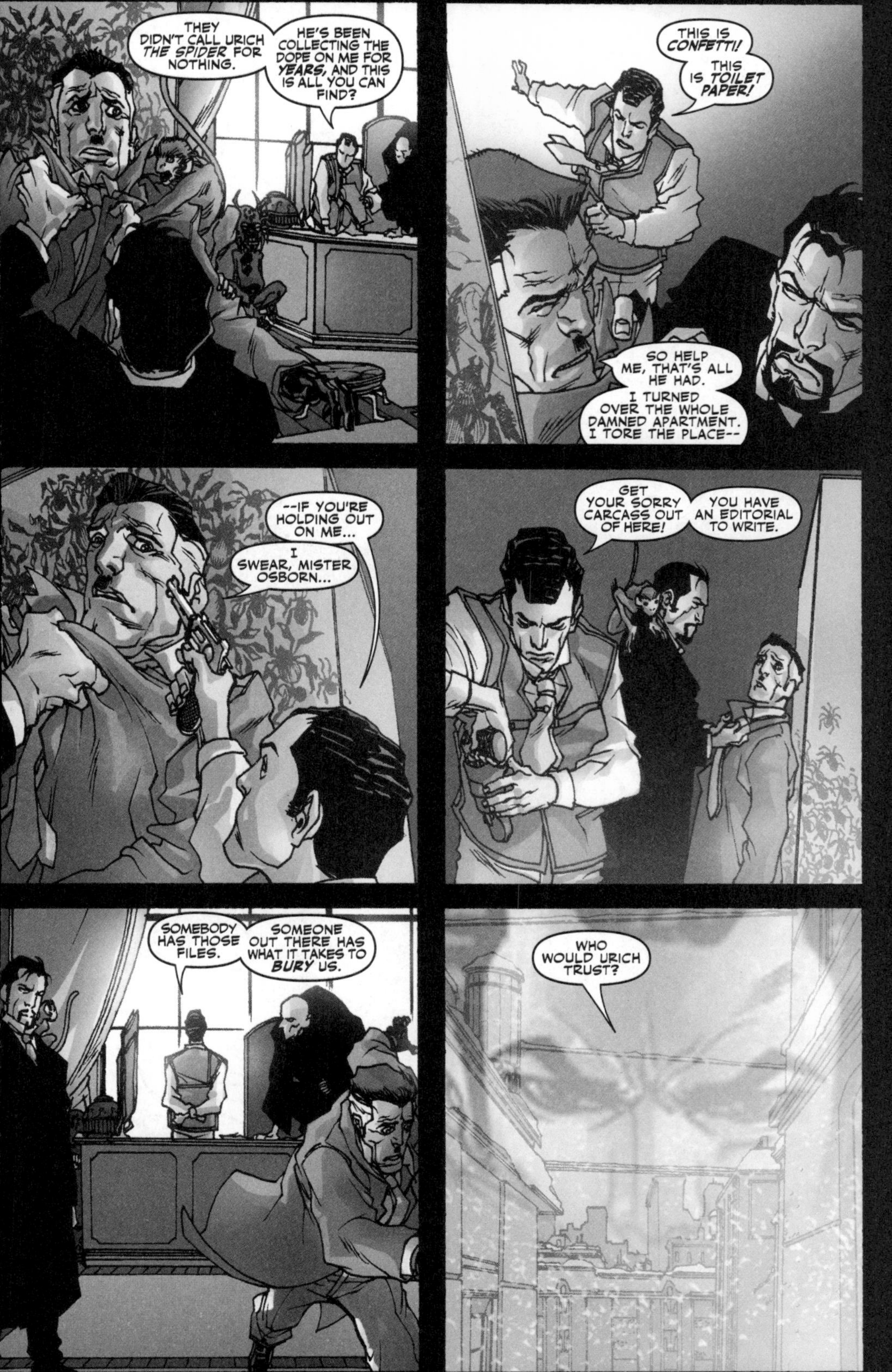
THEY DIDN'T CALL URICH THE SPIDER FOR NOTHING.
HE'S BEEN COLLECTING THE DOPE ON ME FOR YEARS, AND THIS IS ALL YOU CAN FIND?
THIS IS CONFETTI!
THIS IS TOILET PAPER!
SO HELP ME, THAT'S ALL HE HAD.
I TURNED OVER THE WHOLE DAMNED APARTMENT. I TORE THE PLACE--
--IF YOU'RE HOLDING OUT ON ME...
I SWEAR, MISTER OSBORN...
GET YOUR SORRY CARCASS OUT OF HERE!
YOU HAVE AN EDITORIAL TO WRITE.
SOMEBODY HAS THOSE FILES.
SOMEONE OUT THERE HAS WHAT IT TAKES TO BURY US.
WHO WOULD URICH TRUST?

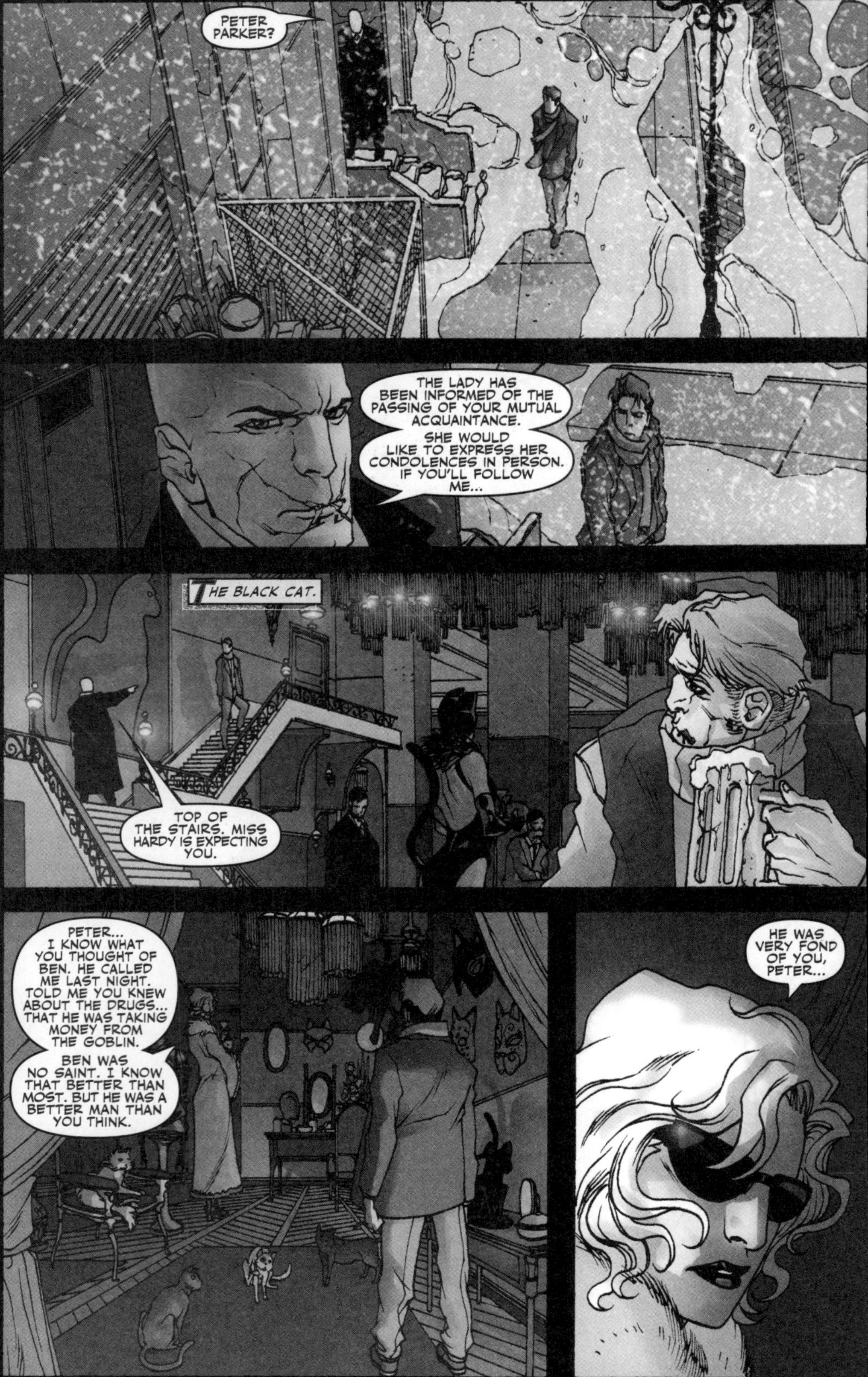
PETER PARKER?
THE LADY HAS BEEN INFORMED OF THE PASSING OF YOUR MUTUAL ACQUAINTANCE.
SHE WOULD LIKE TO EXPRESS HER CONDOLENCES IN PERSON. IF YOU'LL FOLLOW ME...
THE BLACK CAT.
TOP OF THE STAIRS. MISS HARDY IS EXPECTING YOU.
PETER... I KNOW WHAT YOU THOUGHT OF BEN. HE CALLED ME LAST NIGHT. TOLD ME YOU KNEW ABOUT THE DRUGS... THAT HE WAS TAKING MONEY FROM THE GOBLIN.
BEN WAS NO SAINT. I KNOW THAT BETTER THAN MOST. BUT HE WAS A BETTER MAN THAN YOU THINK.
HE WAS VERY FOND OF YOU, PETER...

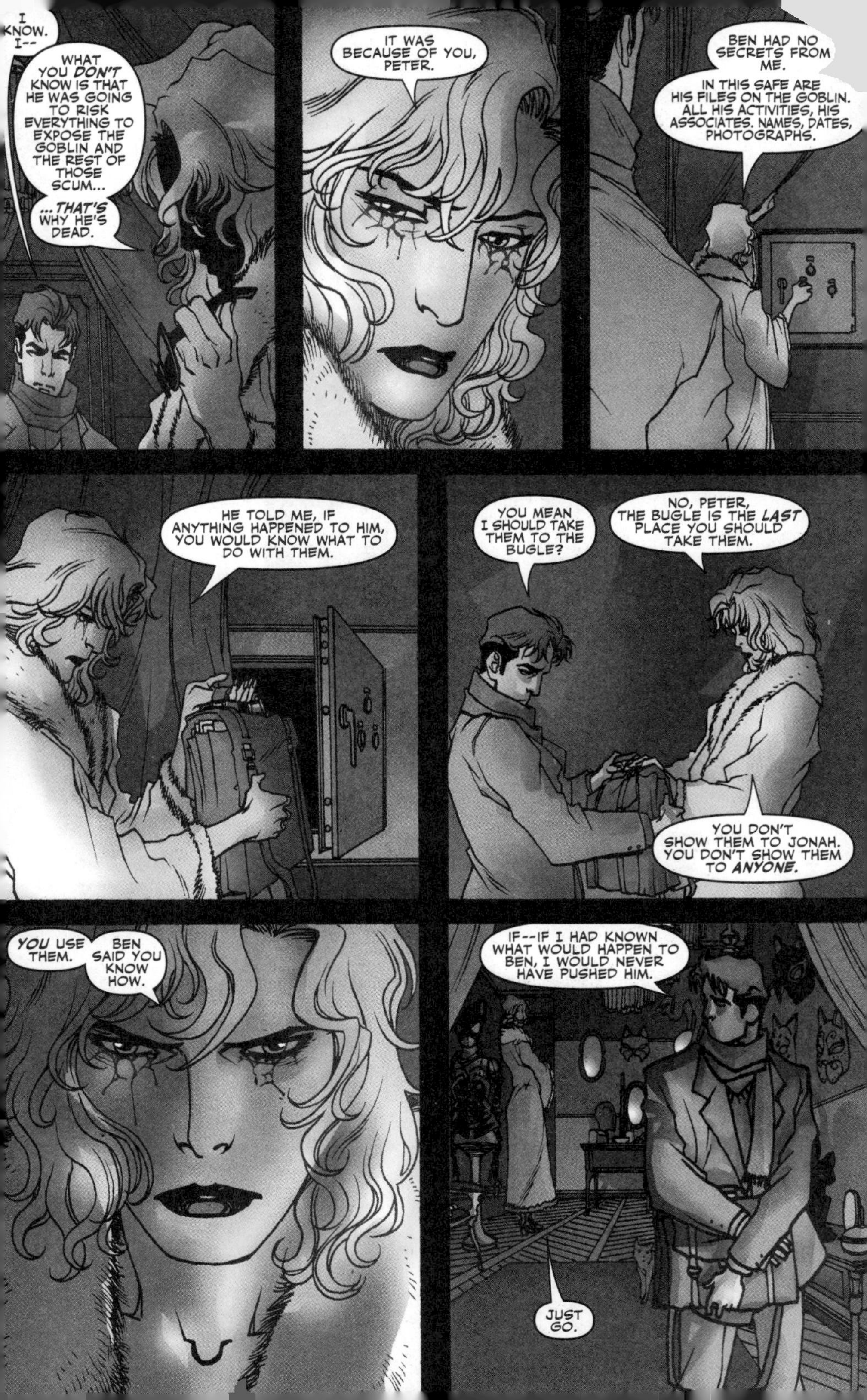
I KNOW. I--
WHAT YOU DON'T KNOW IS THAT HE WAS GOING TO RISK EVERYTHING TO EXPOSE THE GOBLIN AND THE REST OF THOSE SCUM...
...THAT'S WHY HE'S DEAD.
IT WAS BECAUSE OF YOU, PETER.
BEN HAD NO SECRETS FROM ME.
IN THIS SAFE ARE HIS FILES ON THE GOBLIN. ALL HIS ACTIVITIES, HIS ASSOCIATES. NAMES, DATES, PHOTOGRAPHS.
HE TOLD ME, IF ANYTHING HAPPENED TO HIM, YOU WOULD KNOW WHAT TO DO WITH THEM.
YOU MEAN I SHOULD TAKE THEM TO THE BUGLE?
NO, PETER, THE BUGLE IS THE LAST PLACE YOU SHOULD TAKE THEM.
YOU DON'T SHOW THEM TO JONAH. YOU DON'T SHOW THEM TO ANYONE.
YOU USE THEM.
BEN SAID YOU KNOW HOW.
IF--IF I HAD KNOWN WHAT WOULD HAPPEN TO BEN, I WOULD NEVER HAVE PUSHED HIM.
JUST GO.

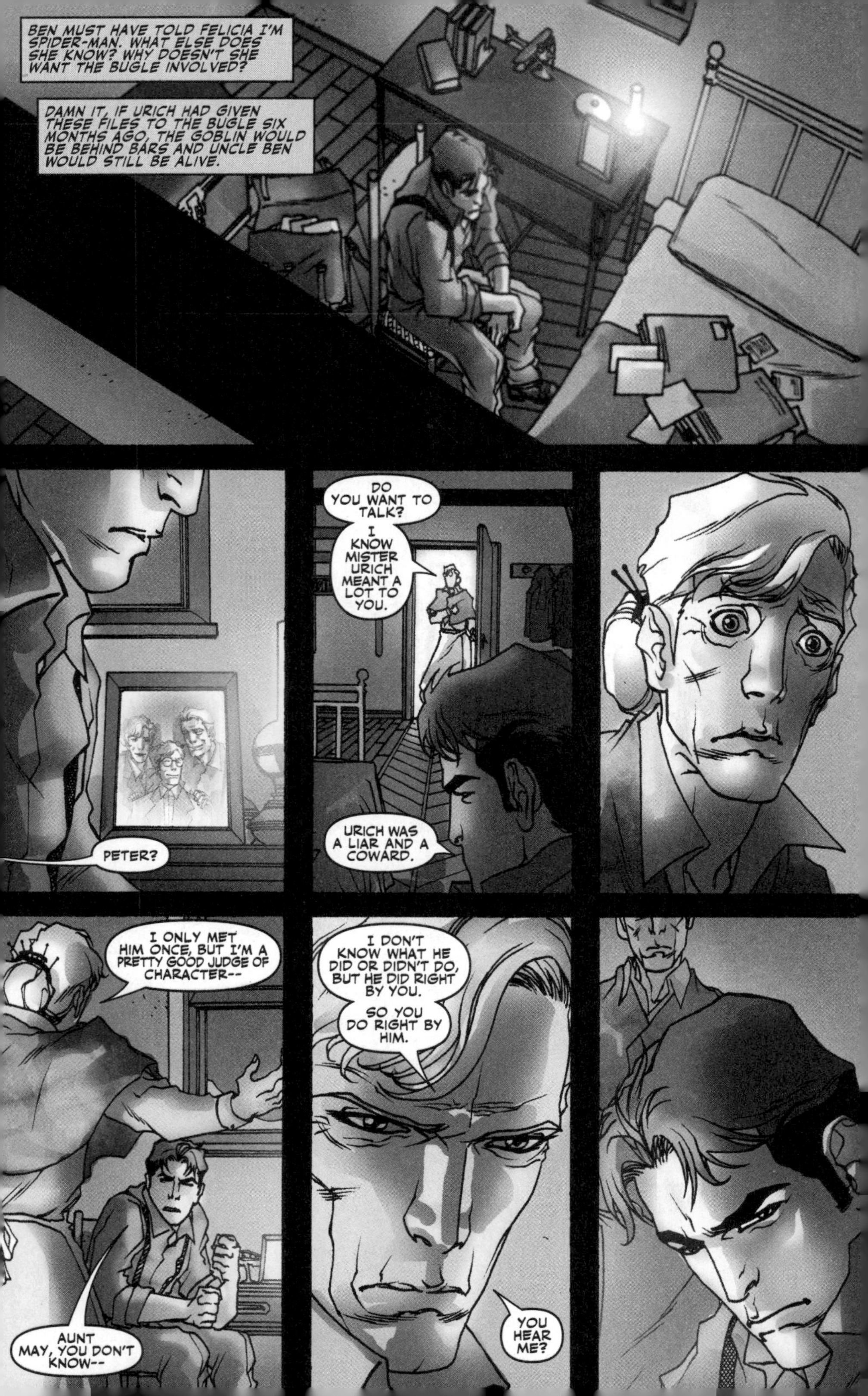
BEN MUST HAVE TOLD FELICIA I'M SPIDER-MAN. WHAT ELSE DOES SHE KNOW? WHY DOESN'T SHE WANT THE BUGLE INVOLVED?
DAMN IT, IF URICH HAD GIVEN THESE FILES TO THE BUGLE SIX MONTHS AGO, THE GOBLIN WOULD BE BEHIND BARS AND UNCLE BEN WOULD STILL BE ALIVE.
PETER?
DO YOU WANT TO TALK?
I KNOW MISTER URICH MEANT A LOT TO YOU.
URICH WAS A LIAR AND A COWARD.
I ONLY MET HIM ONCE, BUT I'M A PRETTY GOOD JUDGE OF CHARACTER--
AUNT MAY, YOU DON'T KNOW--
I DON'T KNOW WHAT HE DID OR DIDN'T DO, BUT HE DID RIGHT BY YOU.
SO YOU DO RIGHT BY HIM.
YOU HEAR ME?

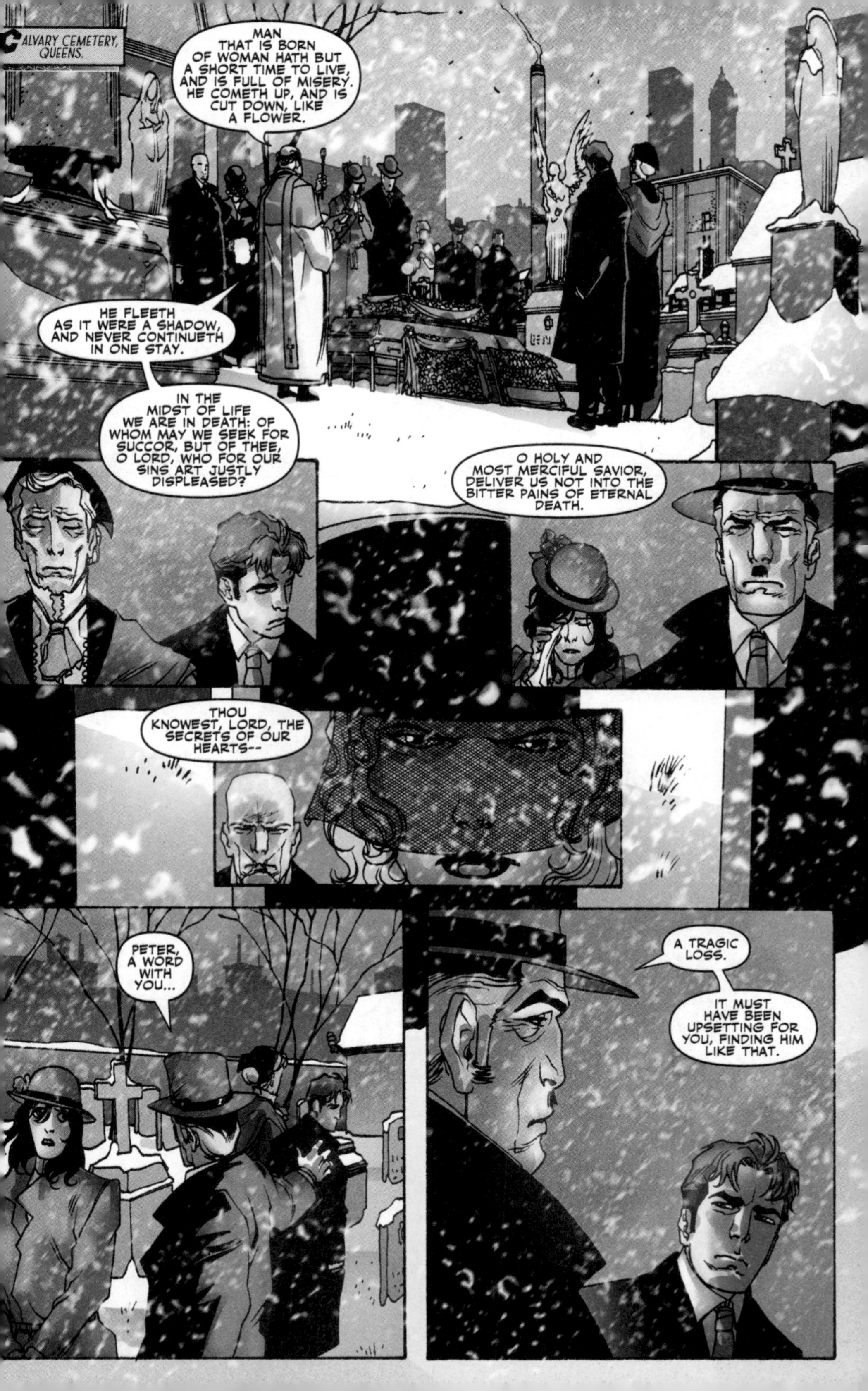
CALVARY CEMETERY, QUEENS.
MAN THAT IS BORN OF WOMAN HATH BUT A SHORT TIME TO LIVE, AND IS FULL OF MISERY. HE COMETH UP, AND IS CUT DOWN, LIKE A FLOWER.
HE FLEETH AS IT WERE A SHADOW, AND NEVER CONTINUETH IN ONE STAY.
IN THE MIDST OF LIFE WE ARE IN DEATH: OF WHOM MAY WE SEEK FOR SUCCOR, BUT OF THEE, O LORD, WHO FOR OUR SINS ART JUSTLY DISPLEASED?
O HOLY AND MOST MERCIFUL SAVIOR, DELIVER US NOT INTO THE BITTER PAINS OF ETERNAL DEATH.
THOU KNOWEST, LORD, THE SECRETS OF OUR HEARTS--
PETER, A WORD WITH YOU...
A TRAGIC LOSS.
IT MUST HAVE BEEN UPSETTING FOR YOU, FINDING HIM LIKE THAT.

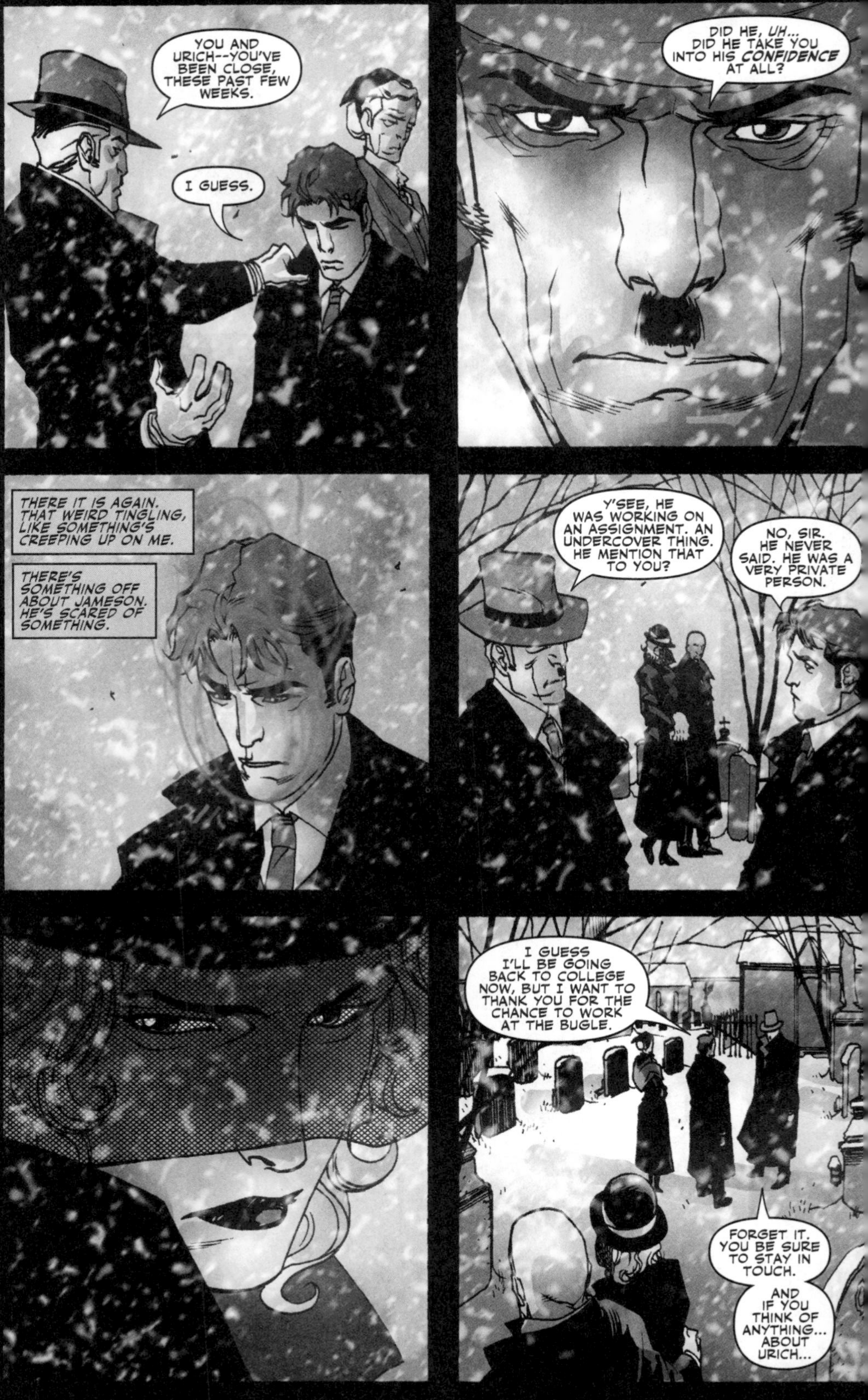
YOU AND URICH--YOU'VE BEEN CLOSE, THESE PAST FEW WEEKS.
I GUESS.
DID HE, UH... DID HE TAKE YOU INTO HIS CONFIDENCE AT ALL?
THERE IT IS AGAIN. THAT WEIRD TINGLING, LIKE SOMETHING'S CREEPING UP ON ME.
THERE'S SOMETHING OFF ABOUT JAMESON. HE'S SCARED OF SOMETHING.
Y'SEE, HE WAS WORKING ON AN ASSIGNMENT. AN UNDERCOVER THING. HE MENTION THAT TO YOU?
NO, SIR. HE NEVER SAID. HE WAS A VERY PRIVATE PERSON.
I GUESS I'LL BE GOING BACK TO COLLEGE NOW, BUT I WANT TO THANK YOU FOR THE CHANCE TO WORK AT THE BUGLE.
FORGET IT. YOU BE SURE TO STAY IN TOUCH.
AND IF YOU THINK OF ANYTHING... ABOUT URICH...

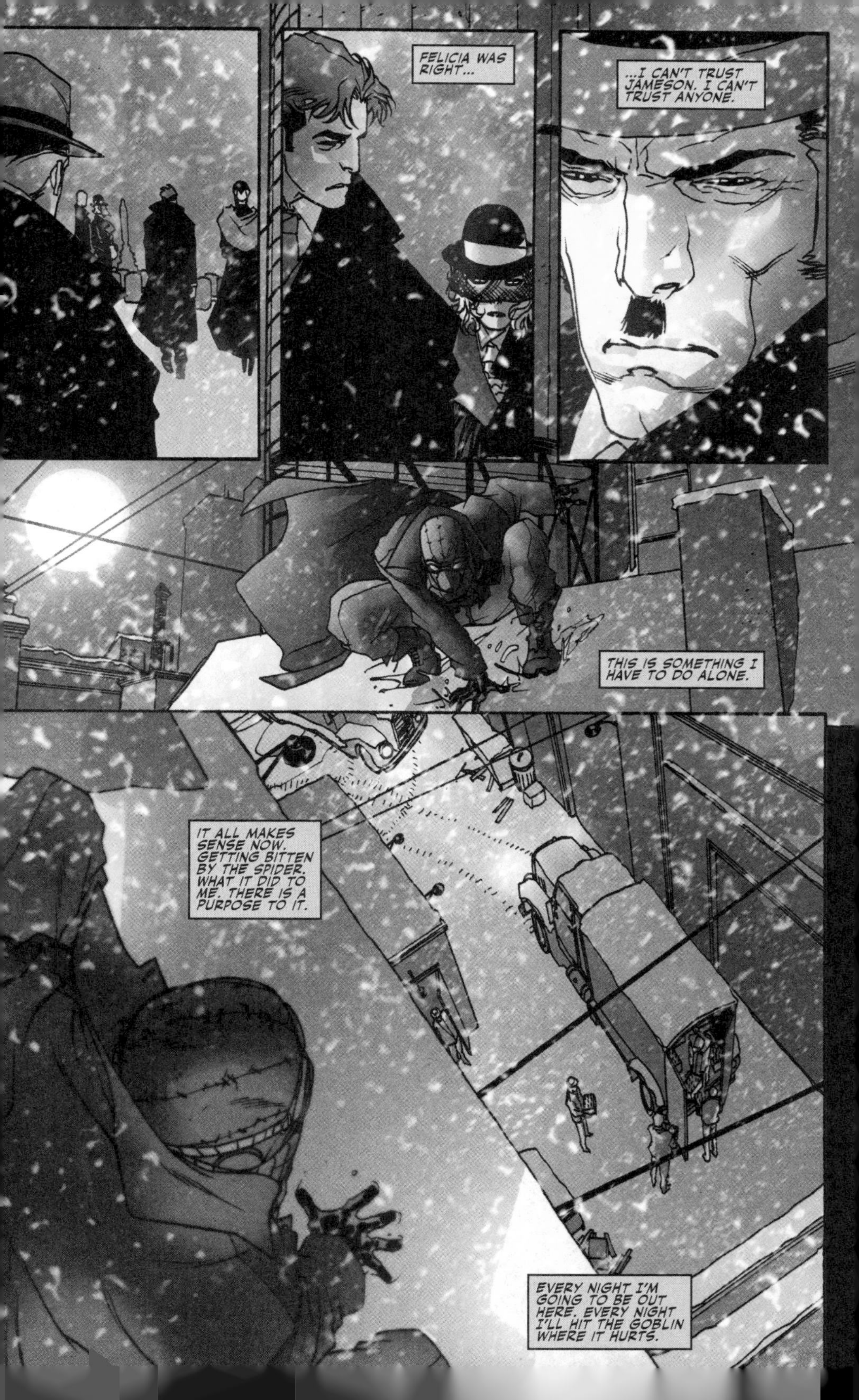
FELICIA WAS RIGHT...
...I CAN'T TRUST JAMESON. I CAN'T TRUST ANYONE.
THIS IS SOMETHING I HAVE TO DO ALONE.
IT ALL MAKES SENSE NOW. GETTING BITTEN BY THE SPIDER. WHAT IT DID TO ME. THERE IS A PURPOSE TO IT.
EVERY NIGHT I'M GOING TO BE OUT HERE. EVERY NIGHT I'LL HIT THE GOBLIN WHERE IT HURTS.

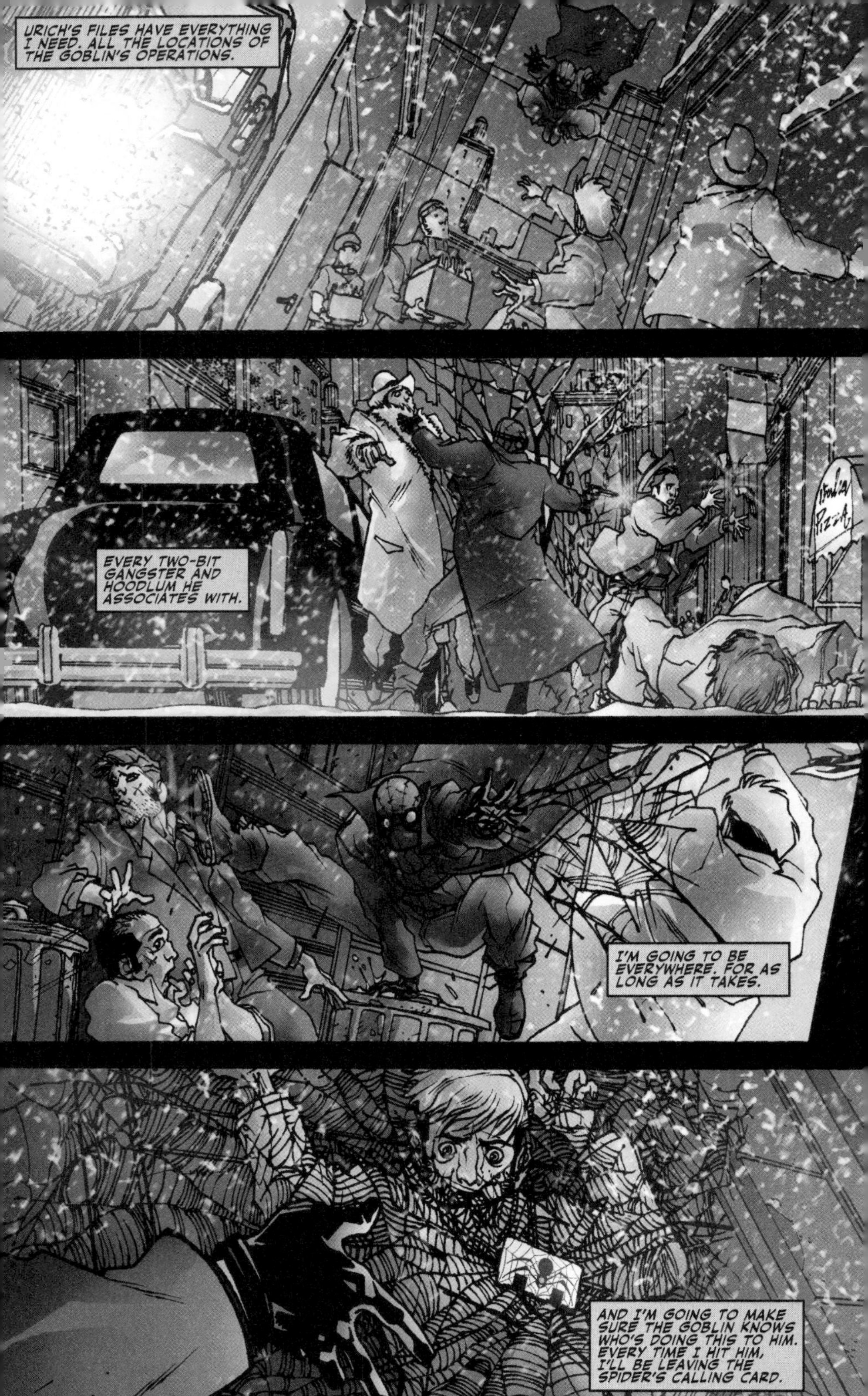
URICH'S FILES HAVE EVERYTHING I NEED. ALL THE LOCATIONS OF THE GOBLIN'S OPERATIONS.
EVERY TWO-BIT GANGSTER AND HOODLUM HE ASSOCIATES WITH.
I'M GOING TO BE EVERYWHERE. FOR AS LONG AS IT TAKES.
AND I'M GOING TO MAKE SURE THE GOBLIN KNOWS WHO'S DOING THIS TO HIM. EVERY TIME I HIT HIM, I'LL BE LEAVING THE SPIDER'S CALLING CARD.

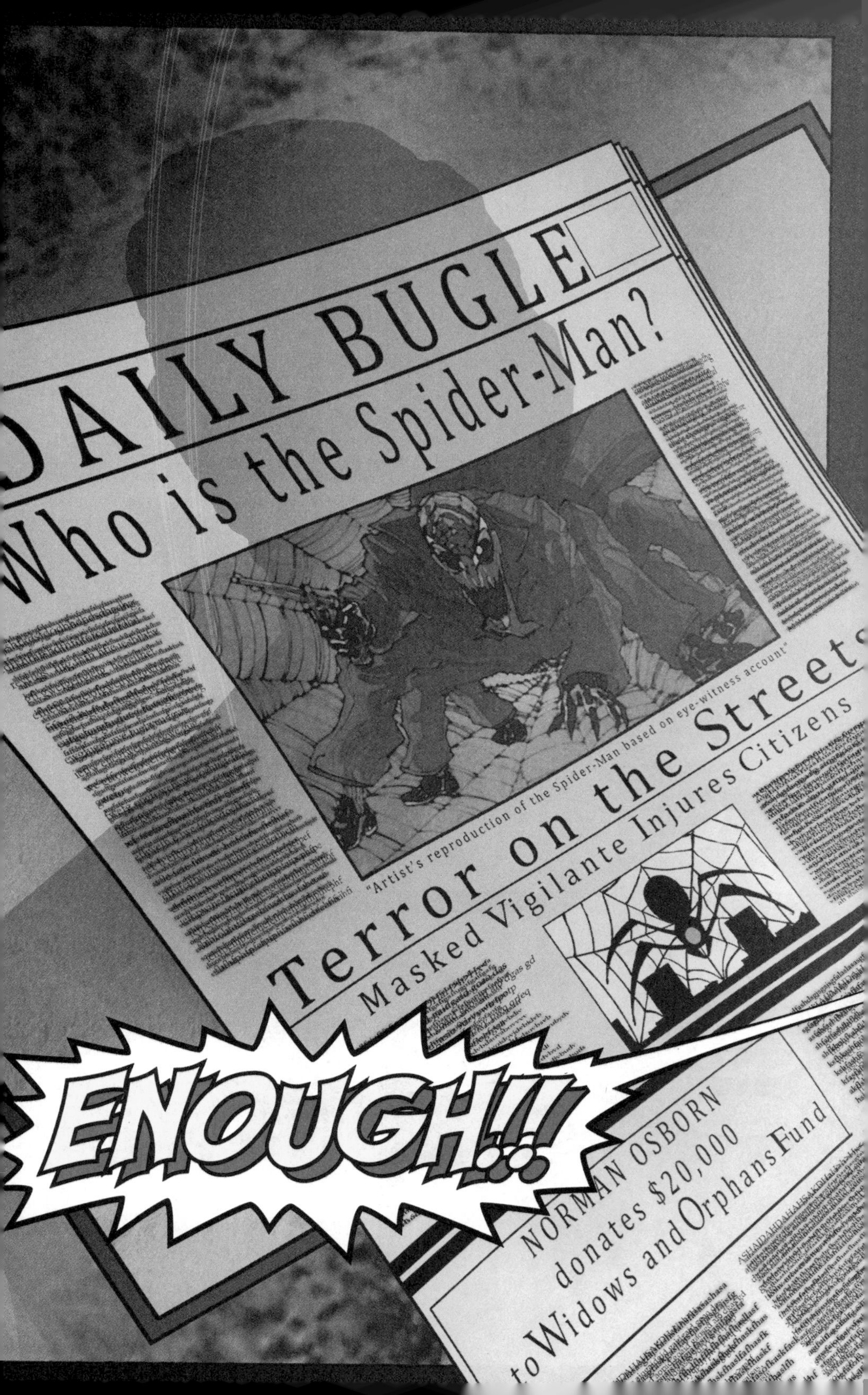
DAILY BUGLE
Who is the Spider-Man?
"Artist's reproduction of the Spider-Man based on eye-witness account"
Terror on the Streets
Masked Vigilante Injures Citizens
NORMAN OSBORN donates $20,000 to Widows and Orphans Fund
ENOUGH!!

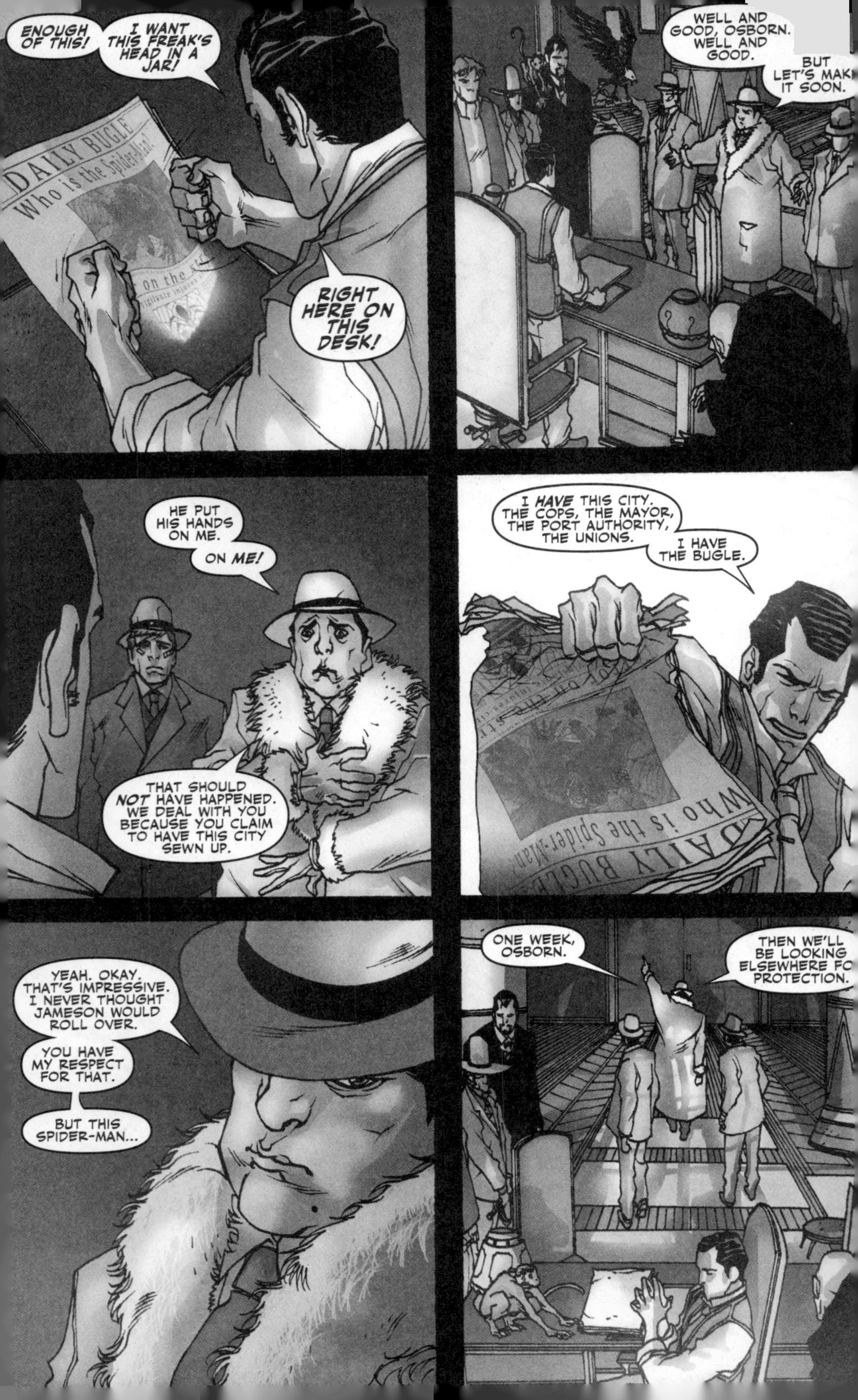

ENOUGH OF THIS!
I WANT THIS FREAK'S HEAD IN A JAR!
DAILY BUGLE
Who is the Spider-Man?
RIGHT HERE ON THIS DESK!
WELL AND GOOD, OSBORN. WELL AND GOOD.
BUT LET'S MAK IT SOON.
HE PUT HIS HANDS ON ME.
ON ME!
THAT SHOULD NOT HAVE HAPPENED. WE DEAL WITH YOU BECAUSE YOU CLAIM TO HAVE THIS CITY SEWN UP.
I HAVE THIS CITY. THE COPS, THE MAYOR, THE PORT AUTHORITY, THE UNIONS.
I HAVE THE BUGLE.
YEAH. OKAY. THAT'S IMPRESSIVE. I NEVER THOUGHT JAMESON WOULD ROLL OVER.
YOU HAVE MY RESPECT FOR THAT.
BUT THIS SPIDER-MAN...
ONE WEEK, OSBORN.
THEN WE'LL BE LOOKING ELSEWHERE FO PROTECTION.

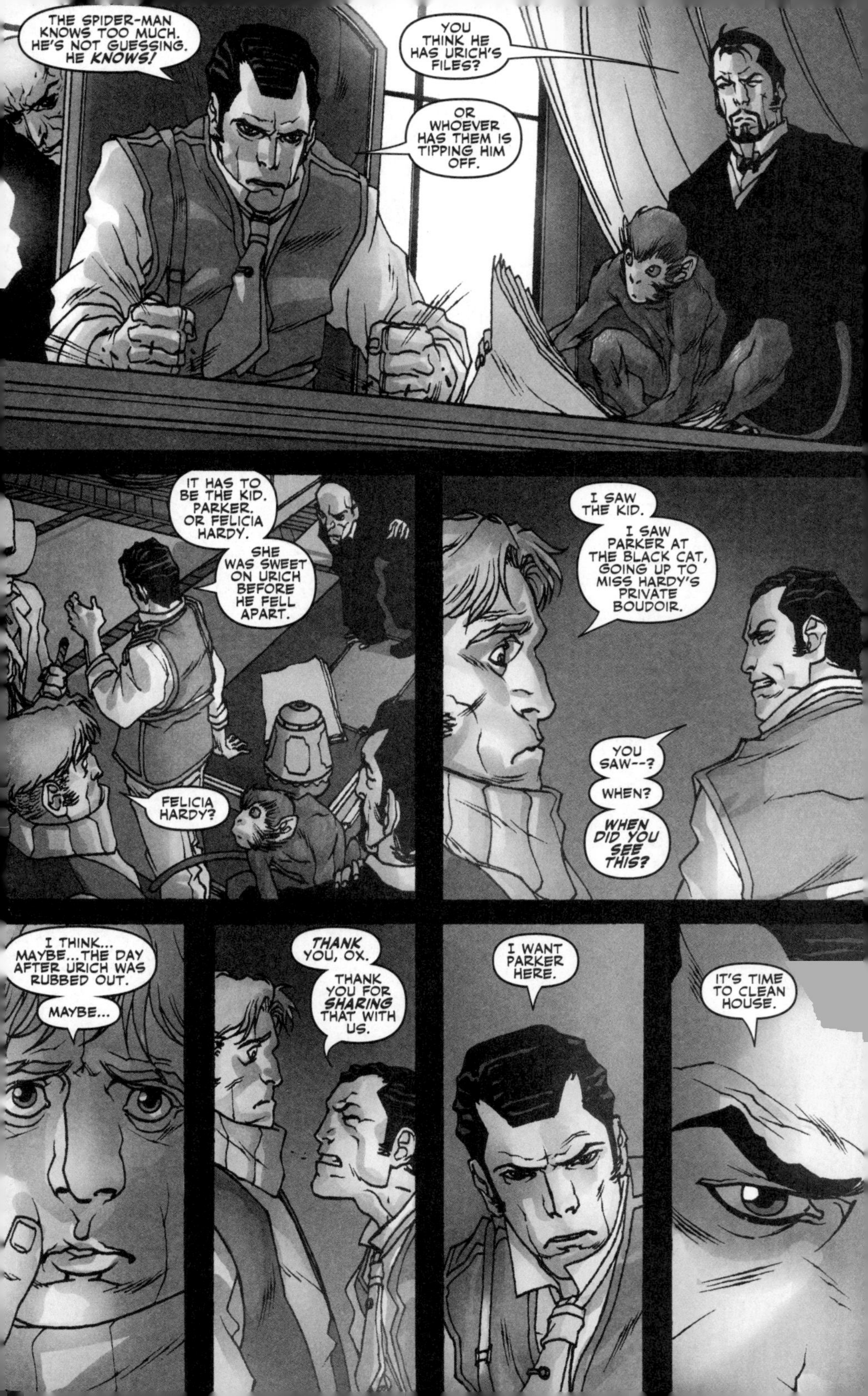
THE SPIDER-MAN KNOWS TOO MUCH. HE'S NOT GUESSING. HE *KNOWS!*
YOU THINK HE HAS URICH'S FILES?
OR WHOEVER HAS THEM IS TIPPING HIM OFF.
IT HAS TO BE THE KID. PARKER. OR FELICIA HARDY.
SHE WAS SWEET ON URICH BEFORE HE FELL APART.
FELICIA HARDY?
I SAW THE KID.
I SAW PARKER AT THE BLACK CAT, GOING UP TO MISS HARDY'S PRIVATE BOUDOIR.
YOU SAW--?
WHEN?
WHEN DID YOU SEE THIS?
I THINK... MAYBE...THE DAY AFTER URICH WAS RUBBED OUT.
MAYBE...
THANK YOU, OX.
THANK YOU FOR *SHARING* THAT WITH US.
I WANT PARKER HERE.
IT'S TIME TO CLEAN HOUSE.

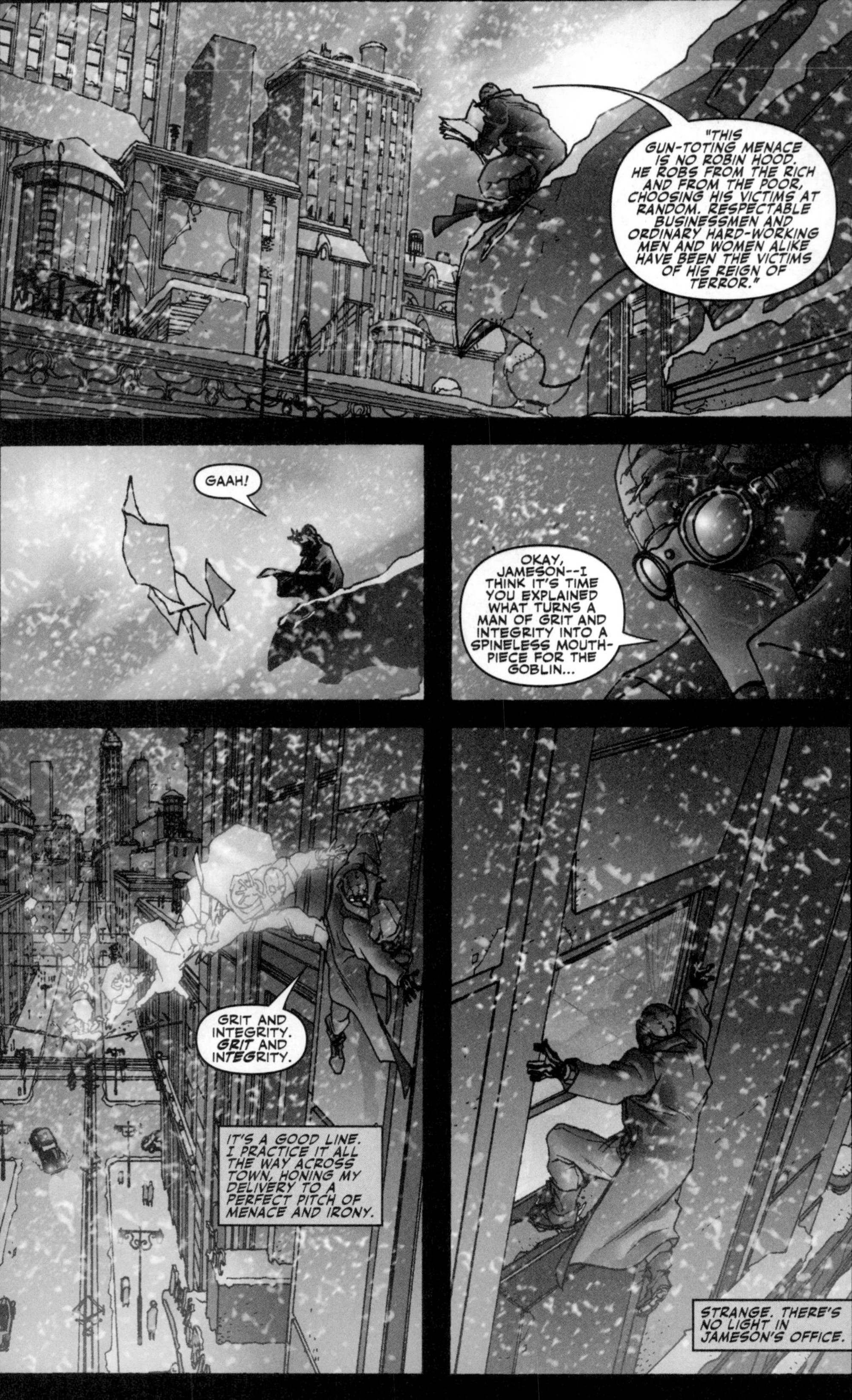
"THIS GUN-TOTING MENACE IS NO ROBIN HOOD. HE ROBS FROM THE RICH AND FROM THE POOR, CHOOSING HIS VICTIMS AT RANDOM. RESPECTABLE BUSINESSMEN AND ORDINARY HARD-WORKING MEN AND WOMEN ALIKE HAVE BEEN THE VICTIMS OF HIS REIGN OF TERROR."
GAAH!
OKAY, JAMESON--I THINK IT'S TIME YOU EXPLAINED WHAT TURNS A MAN OF GRIT AND INTEGRITY INTO A SPINELESS MOUTH-PIECE FOR THE GOBLIN...
GRIT AND INTEGRITY. *GRIT* AND INTEGRITY.
IT'S A GOOD LINE. I PRACTICE IT ALL THE WAY ACROSS TOWN, HONING MY DELIVERY TO A PERFECT PITCH OF MENACE AND IRONY.
STRANGE. THERE'S NO LIGHT IN JAMESON'S OFFICE.

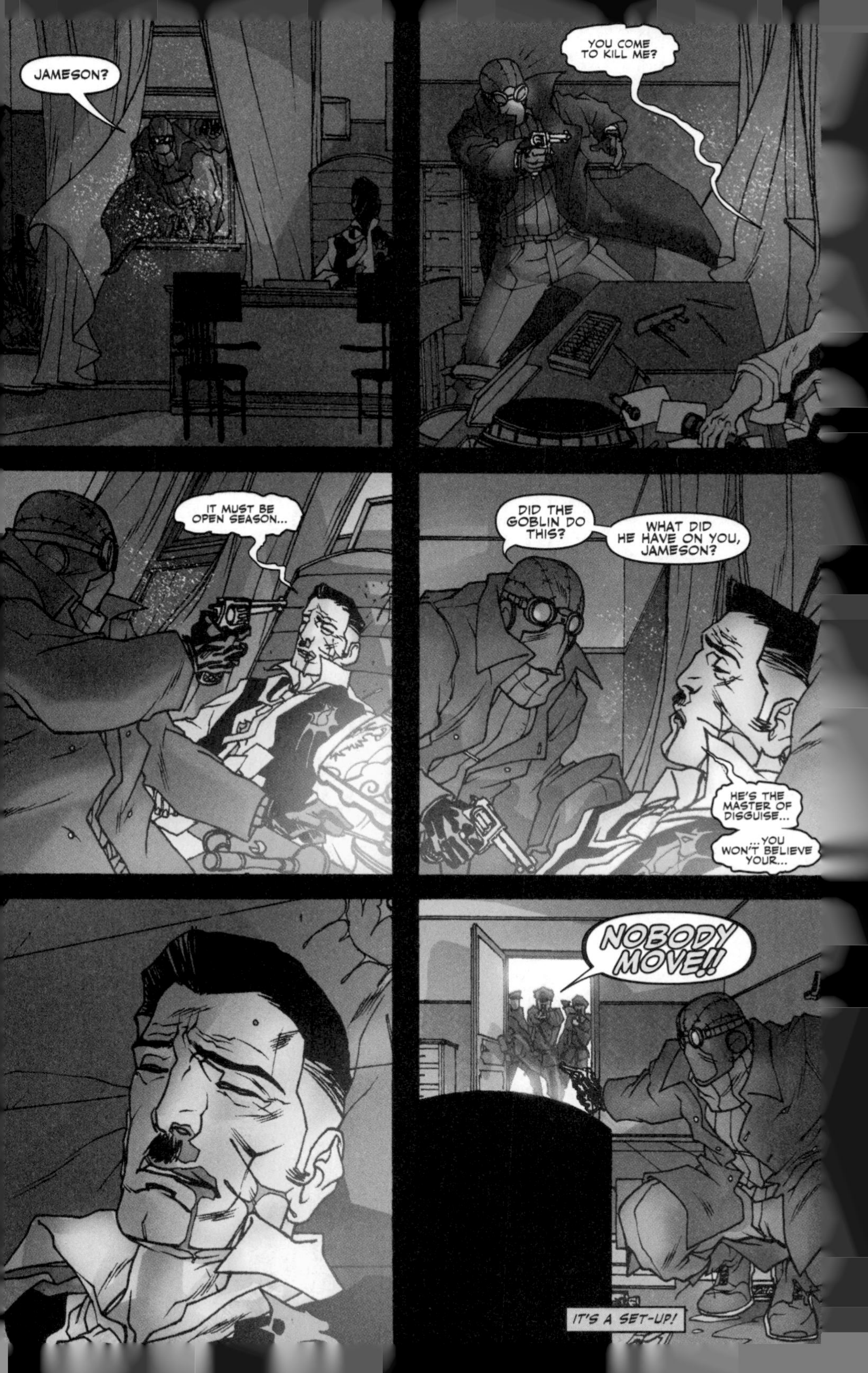
JAMESON?
YOU COME TO KILL ME?
IT MUST BE OPEN SEASON...
DID THE GOBLIN DO THIS?
WHAT DID HE HAVE ON YOU, JAMESON?
HE'S THE MASTER OF DISGUISE...
...YOU WON'T BELIEVE YOUR...
NOBODY MOVE!!
IT'S A SET-UP!

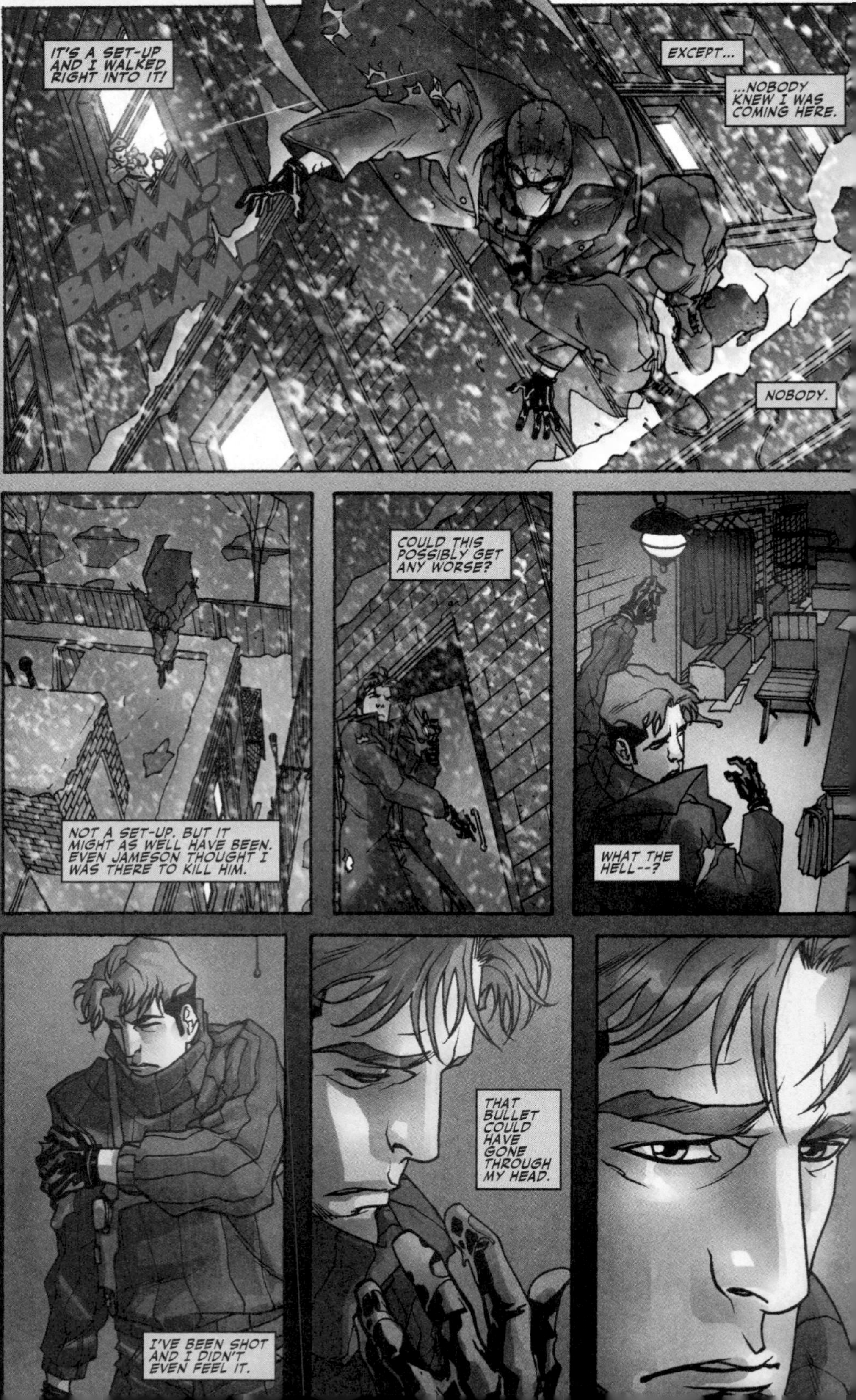
IT'S A SET-UP AND I WALKED RIGHT INTO IT!
BLAM! BLAM! BLAM!
EXCEPT...
...NOBODY KNEW I WAS COMING HERE.
NOBODY.
NOT A SET-UP. BUT IT MIGHT AS WELL HAVE BEEN. EVEN JAMESON THOUGHT I WAS THERE TO KILL HIM.
COULD THIS POSSIBLY GET ANY WORSE?
WHAT THE HELL--?
I'VE BEEN SHOT AND I DIDN'T EVEN FEEL IT.
THAT BULLET COULD HAVE GONE THROUGH MY HEAD.

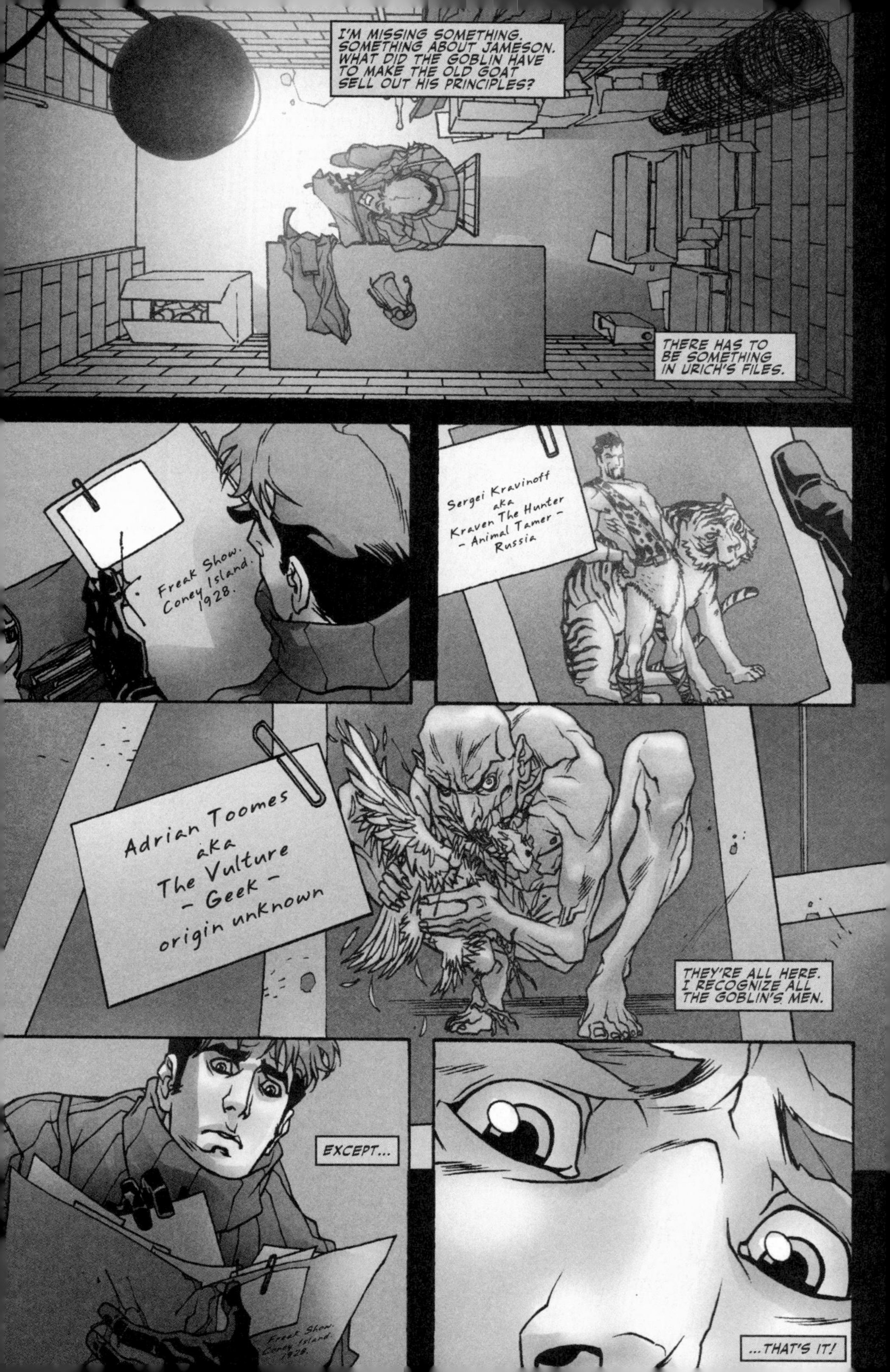
I'M MISSING SOMETHING. SOMETHING ABOUT JAMESON. WHAT DID THE GOBLIN HAVE TO MAKE THE OLD GOAT SELL OUT HIS PRINCIPLES?
THERE HAS TO BE SOMETHING IN URICH'S FILES.
Freak Show. Coney Island. 1928.
Sergei Kravinoff aka Kraven The Hunter - Animal Tamer - Russia
Adrian Toomes aka The Vulture - Geek - origin unknown
THEY'RE ALL HERE. I RECOGNIZE ALL THE GOBLIN'S MEN.
EXCEPT...
Freak Show. Coney Island. 1928.
...THAT'S IT!

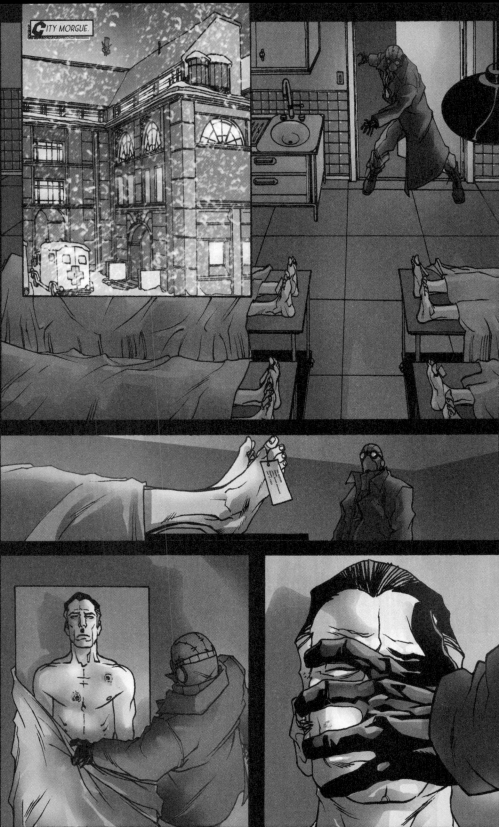

CITY MORGUE.

WHOEVER PERFORMS THE AUTOPSY ON THIS CORPSE IS IN FOR A BIG SURPRISE.

"DMITRI SMERDYAKOV, A.K.A. THE CHAMELEON--RUSSIAN, HALF-BROTHER OF KRAVEN--HAS THE ABILITY TO MOLD HIS FEATURES IN PERFECT IMITATION OF ANY SUBJECT."

THE GOBLIN RECRUITED ALL HIS INNER CIRCLE FROM CIRCUSES AND FREAK SHOWS.

Dmitri Smerdyakov
a.k.a.
The Chameleon

KRAVEN'S HALF-BROTHER HAD TO BE ONE OF THEM.

THE CHAMELEON

HE'S THE MASTER OF DISGUISE YOU WON'T BELIEVE YOUR EYES

THIS MUST HAVE BEEN THE CHAMELEON'S GREATEST PERFORMANCE.

THE QUESTION IS, WHAT HAPPENED TO THE REAL J. JONAH JAMESON?

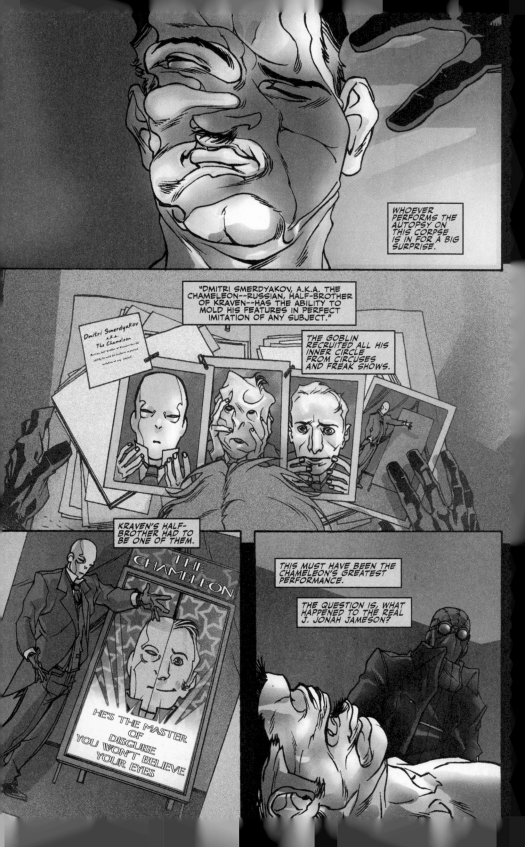

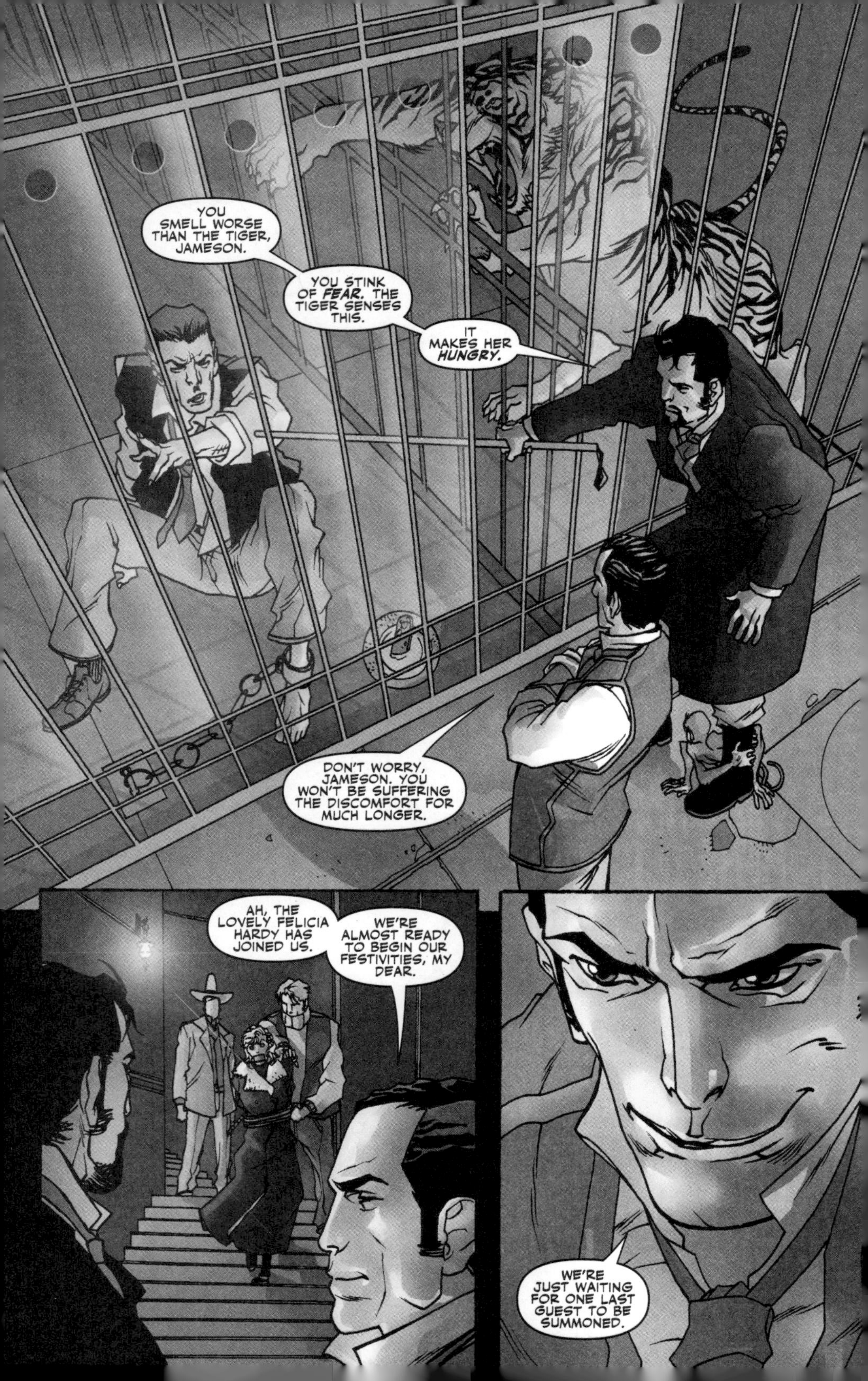
YOU SMELL WORSE THAN THE TIGER, JAMESON.
YOU STINK OF FEAR. THE TIGER SENSES THIS.
IT MAKES HER HUNGRY.
DON'T WORRY, JAMESON. YOU WON'T BE SUFFERING THE DISCOMFORT FOR MUCH LONGER.
AH, THE LOVELY FELICIA HARDY HAS JOINED US.
WE'RE ALMOST READY TO BEGIN OUR FESTIVITIES, MY DEAR.
WE'RE JUST WAITING FOR ONE LAST GUEST TO BE SUMMONED.

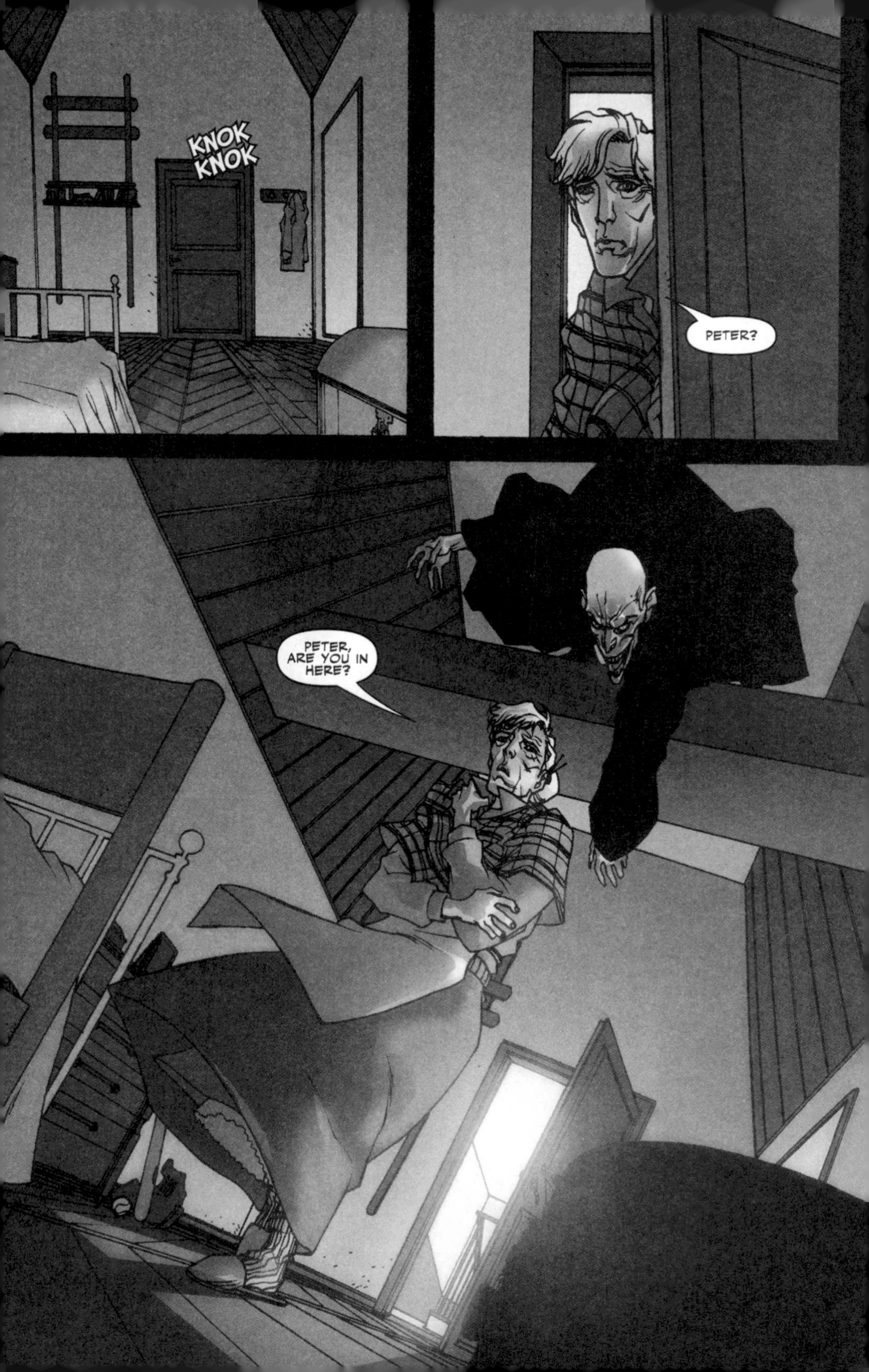
KNOK KNOK
PETER?
PETER, ARE YOU IN HERE?

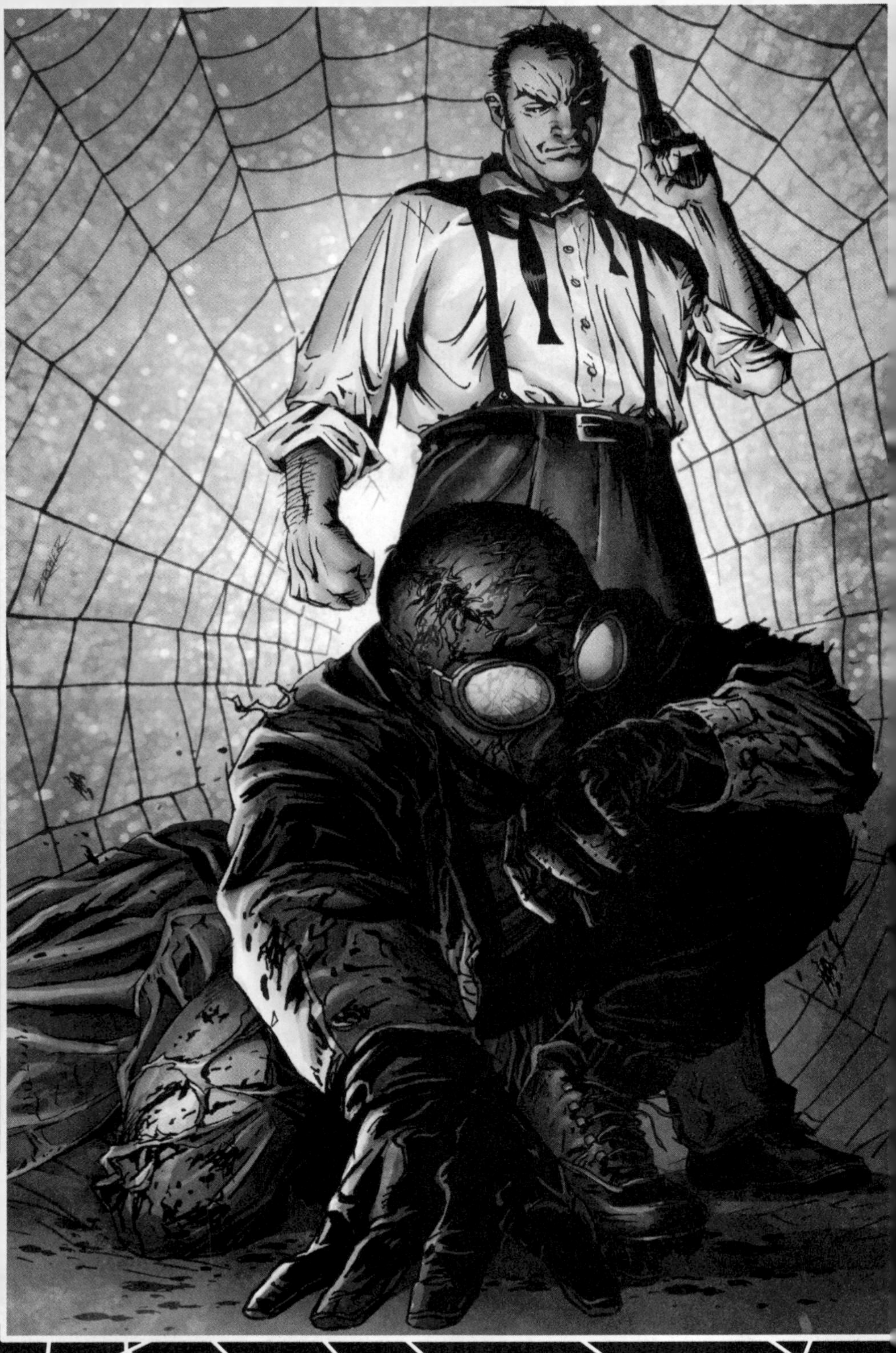

FOUR

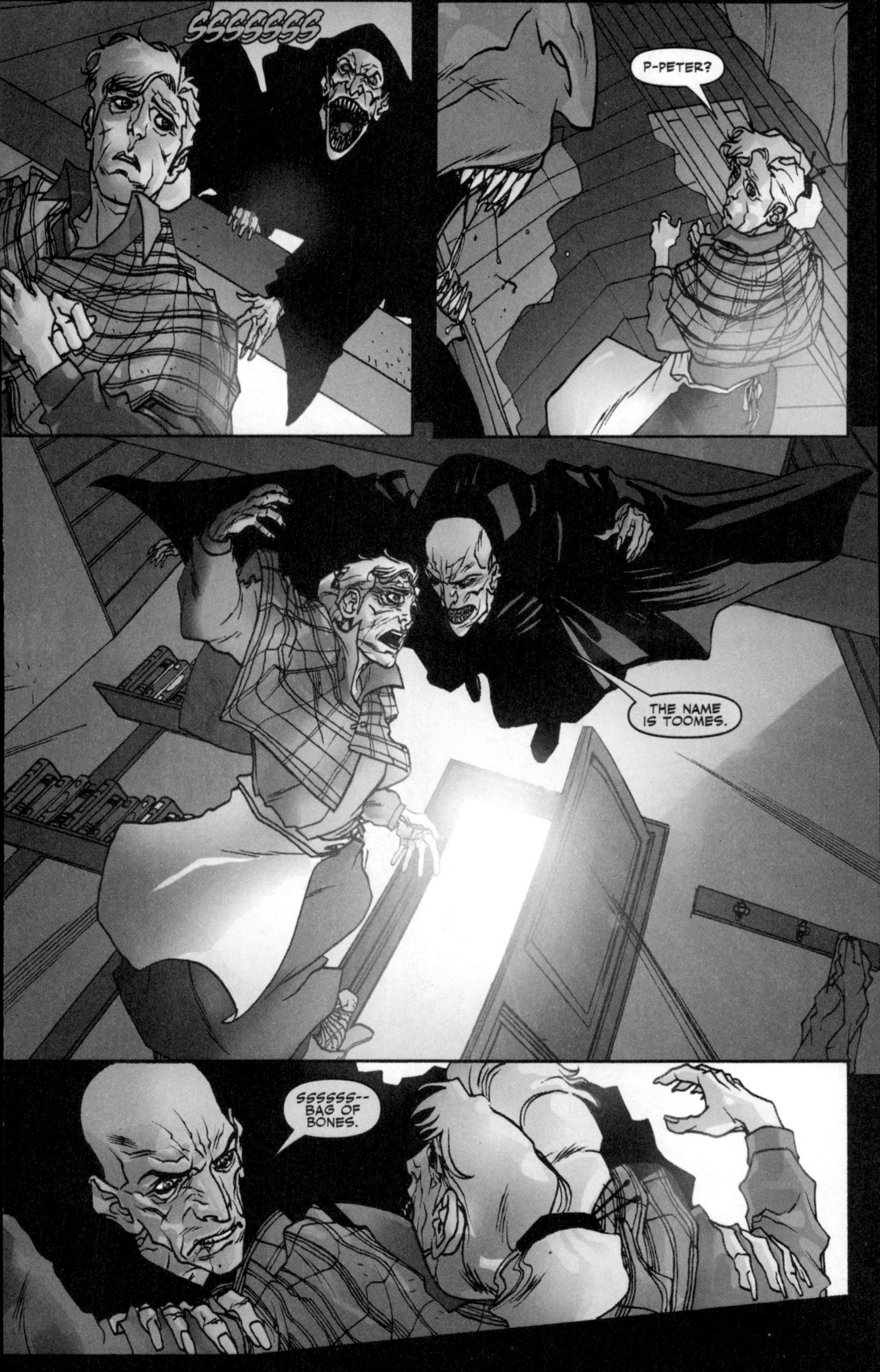
SSSSSSS
P-PETER?
THE NAME IS TOOMES.
SSSSSS-- BAG OF BONES.

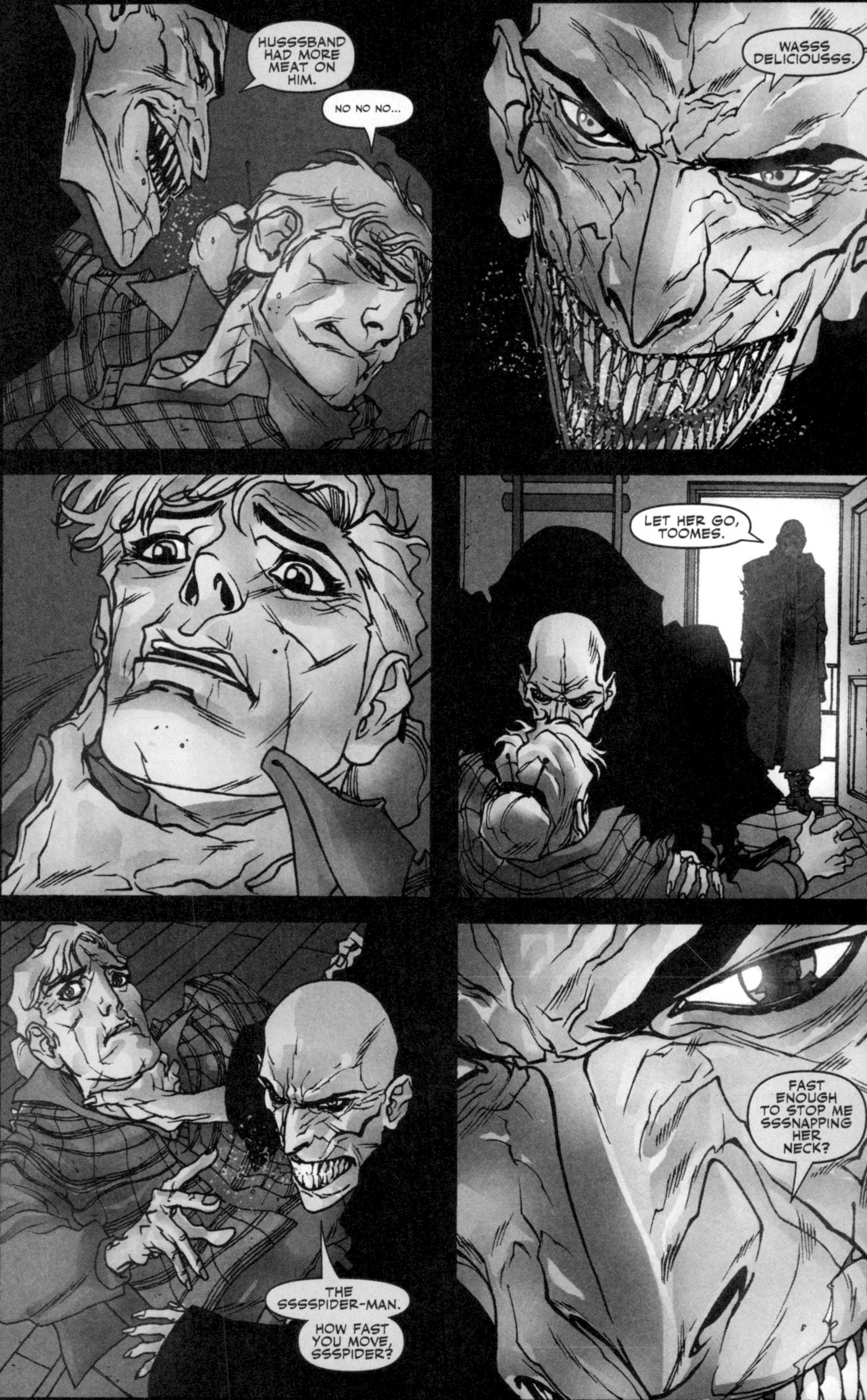
HUSSSBAND HAD MORE MEAT ON HIM.
NO NO NO...
WASSS DELICIOUSSS.
LET HER GO, TOOMES.
THE SSSSPIDER-MAN.
HOW FAST YOU MOVE, SSSPIDER?
FAST ENOUGH TO STOP ME SSSNAPPING HER NECK?

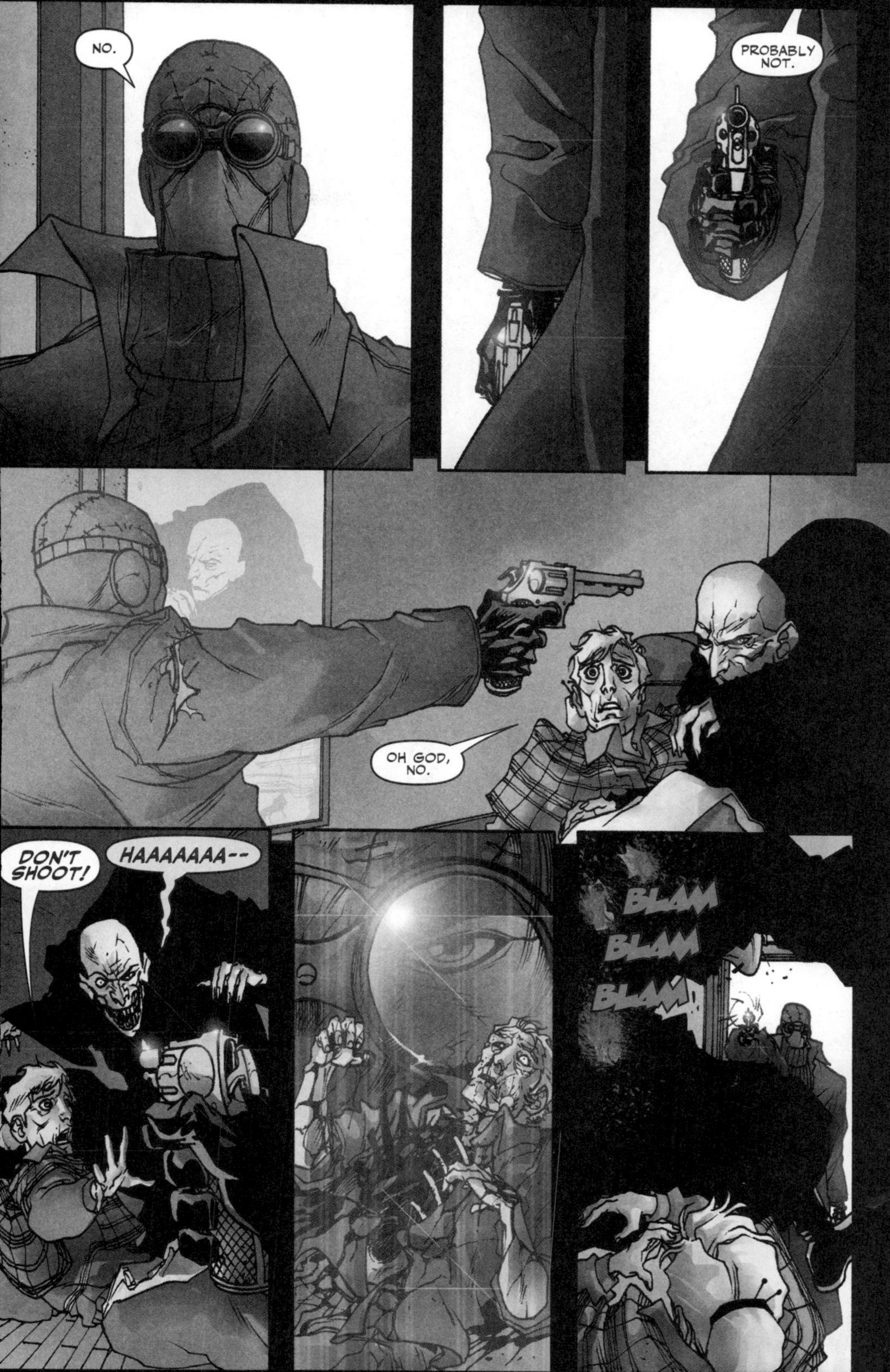

NO.
PROBABLY NOT.
OH GOD, NO.
DON'T SHOOT!
HAAAAAAA--
BLAM
BLAM
BLAM

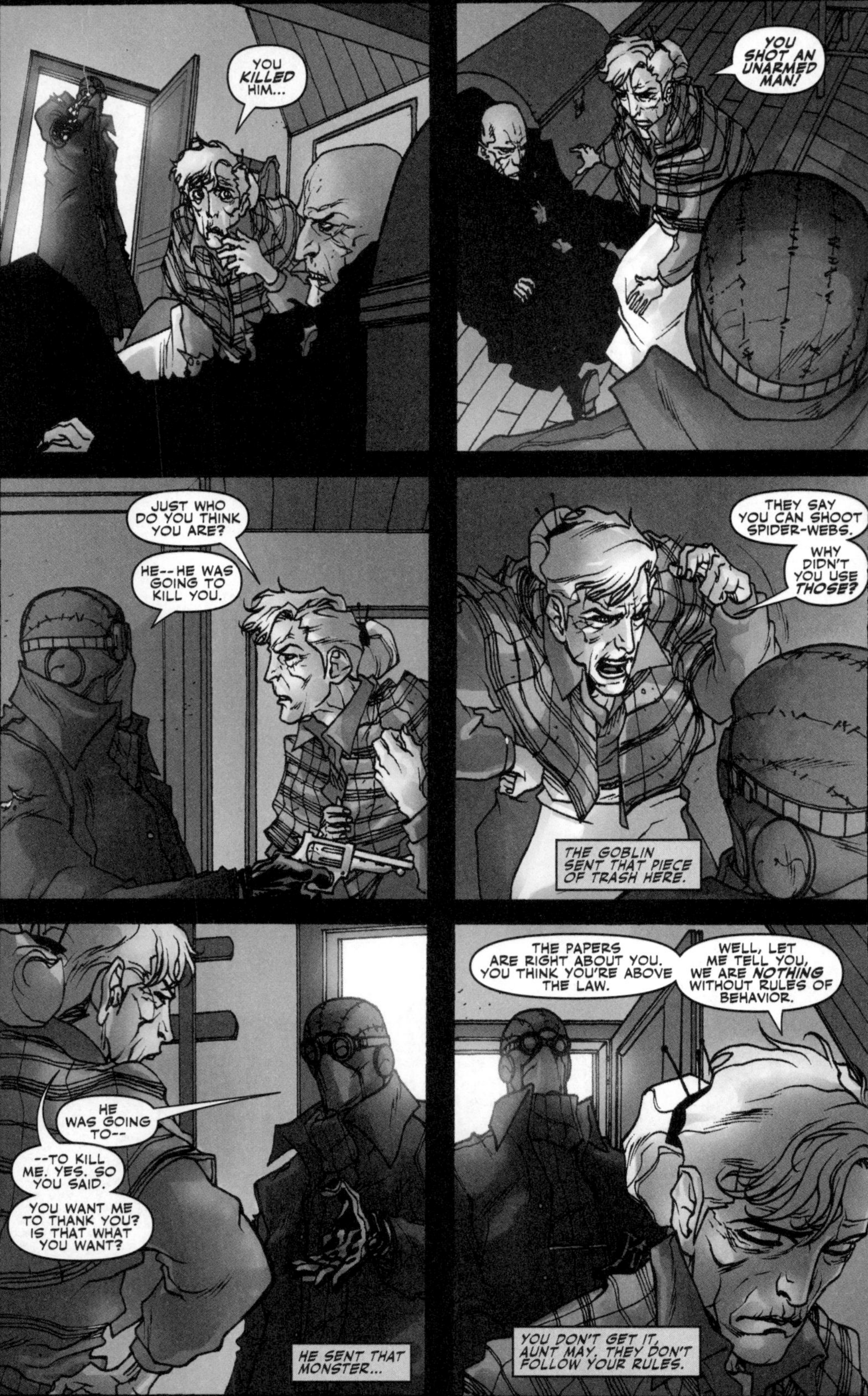
YOU KILLED HIM...
YOU SHOT AN UNARMED MAN!
JUST WHO DO YOU THINK YOU ARE?
HE--HE WAS GOING TO KILL YOU.
THEY SAY YOU CAN SHOOT SPIDER-WEBS.
WHY DIDN'T YOU USE THOSE?
THE GOBLIN SENT THAT PIECE OF TRASH HERE.
HE WAS GOING TO--
--TO KILL ME. YES. SO YOU SAID.
YOU WANT ME TO THANK YOU? IS THAT WHAT YOU WANT?
HE SENT THAT MONSTER...
THE PAPERS ARE RIGHT ABOUT YOU. YOU THINK YOU'RE ABOVE THE LAW.
WELL, LET ME TELL YOU, WE ARE NOTHING WITHOUT RULES OF BEHAVIOR.
YOU DON'T GET IT, AUNT MAY. THEY DON'T FOLLOW YOUR RULES.

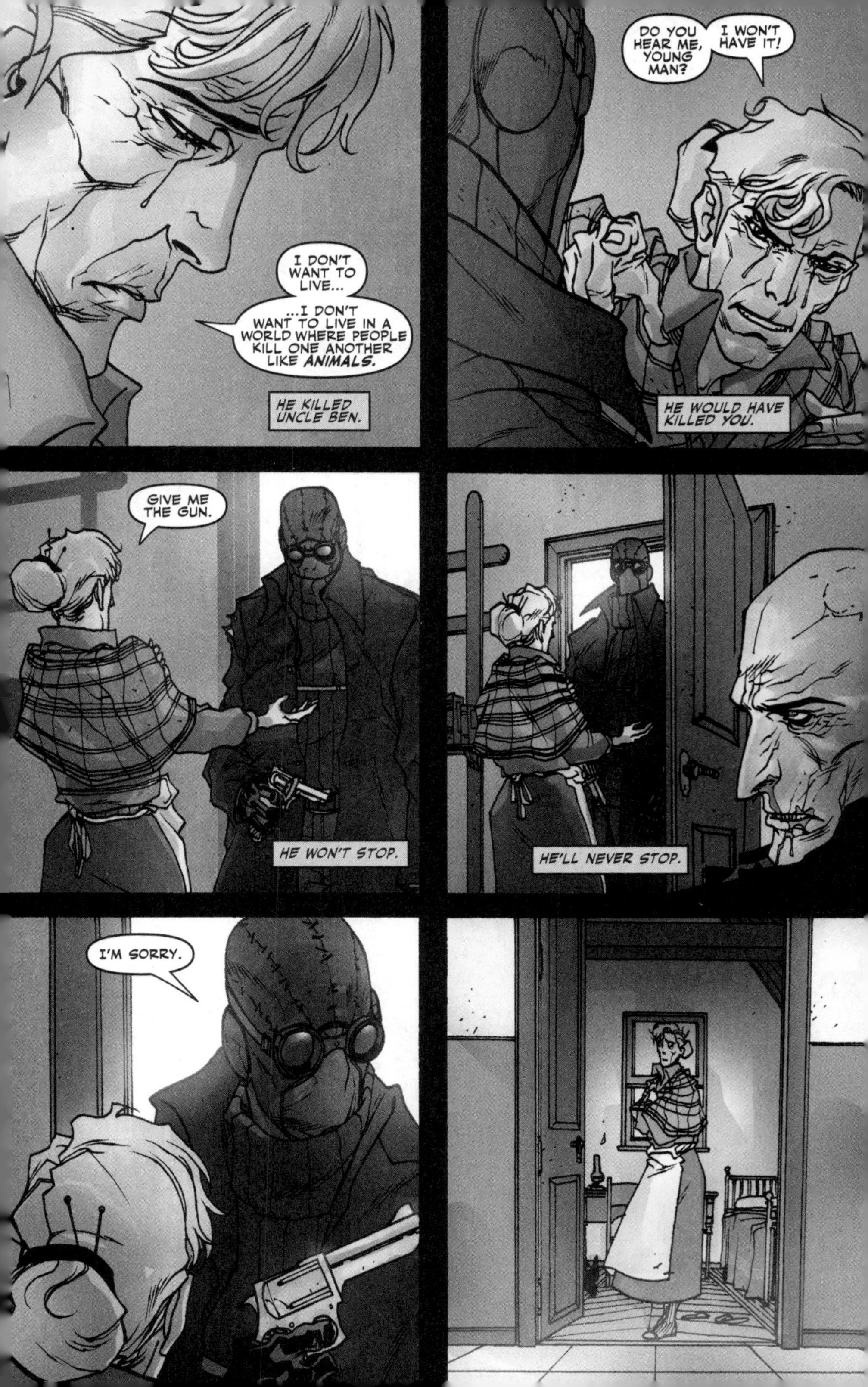
I DON'T WANT TO LIVE...
...I DON'T WANT TO LIVE IN A WORLD WHERE PEOPLE KILL ONE ANOTHER LIKE *ANIMALS.*
HE KILLED UNCLE BEN.
DO YOU HEAR ME, YOUNG MAN?
I WON'T HAVE IT!
HE WOULD HAVE KILLED YOU.
GIVE ME THE GUN.
HE WON'T STOP.
HE'LL NEVER STOP.
I'M SORRY.

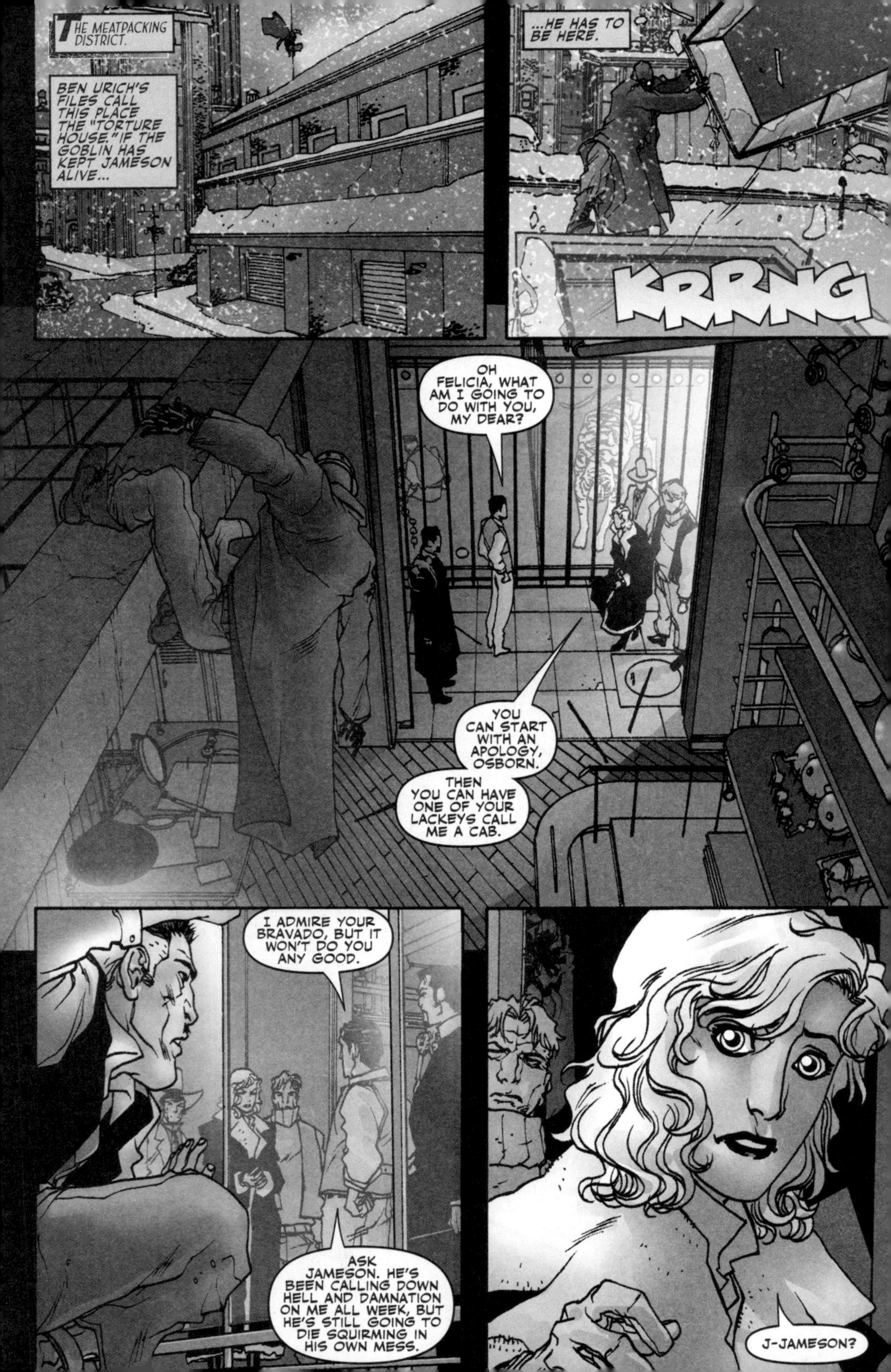
THE MEATPACKING DISTRICT.
BEN URICH'S FILES CALL THIS PLACE THE "TORTURE HOUSE." IF THE GOBLIN HAS KEPT JAMESON ALIVE...
...HE HAS TO BE HERE.
KRRNG
OH FELICIA, WHAT AM I GOING TO DO WITH YOU, MY DEAR?
YOU CAN START WITH AN APOLOGY, OSBORN.
THEN YOU CAN HAVE ONE OF YOUR LACKEYS CALL ME A CAB.
I ADMIRE YOUR BRAVADO, BUT IT WON'T DO YOU ANY GOOD.
ASK JAMESON. HE'S BEEN CALLING DOWN HELL AND DAMNATION ON ME ALL WEEK, BUT HE'S STILL GOING TO DIE SQUIRMING IN HIS OWN MESS.
J-JAMESON?

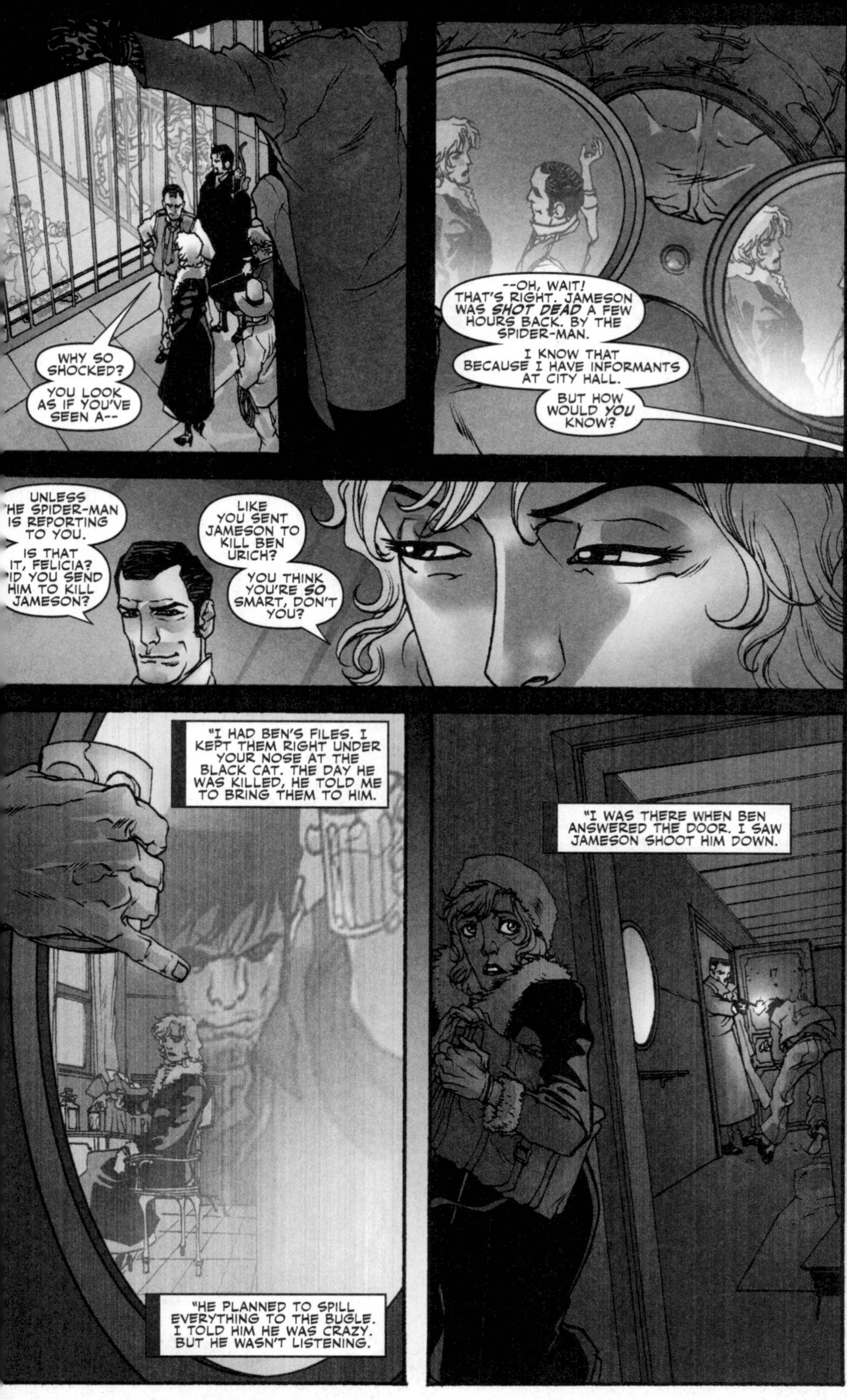

WHY SO SHOCKED?
YOU LOOK AS IF YOU'VE SEEN A--
--OH, WAIT! THAT'S RIGHT. JAMESON WAS SHOT DEAD A FEW HOURS BACK. BY THE SPIDER-MAN.
I KNOW THAT BECAUSE I HAVE INFORMANTS AT CITY HALL.
BUT HOW WOULD YOU KNOW?
UNLESS THE SPIDER-MAN IS REPORTING TO YOU.
IS THAT IT, FELICIA? DID YOU SEND HIM TO KILL JAMESON?
LIKE YOU SENT JAMESON TO KILL BEN URICH?
YOU THINK YOU'RE SO SMART, DON'T YOU?
"I HAD BEN'S FILES. I KEPT THEM RIGHT UNDER YOUR NOSE AT THE BLACK CAT. THE DAY HE WAS KILLED, HE TOLD ME TO BRING THEM TO HIM.
"HE PLANNED TO SPILL EVERYTHING TO THE BUGLE. I TOLD HIM HE WAS CRAZY. BUT HE WASN'T LISTENING.
"I WAS THERE WHEN BEN ANSWERED THE DOOR. I SAW JAMESON SHOOT HIM DOWN.

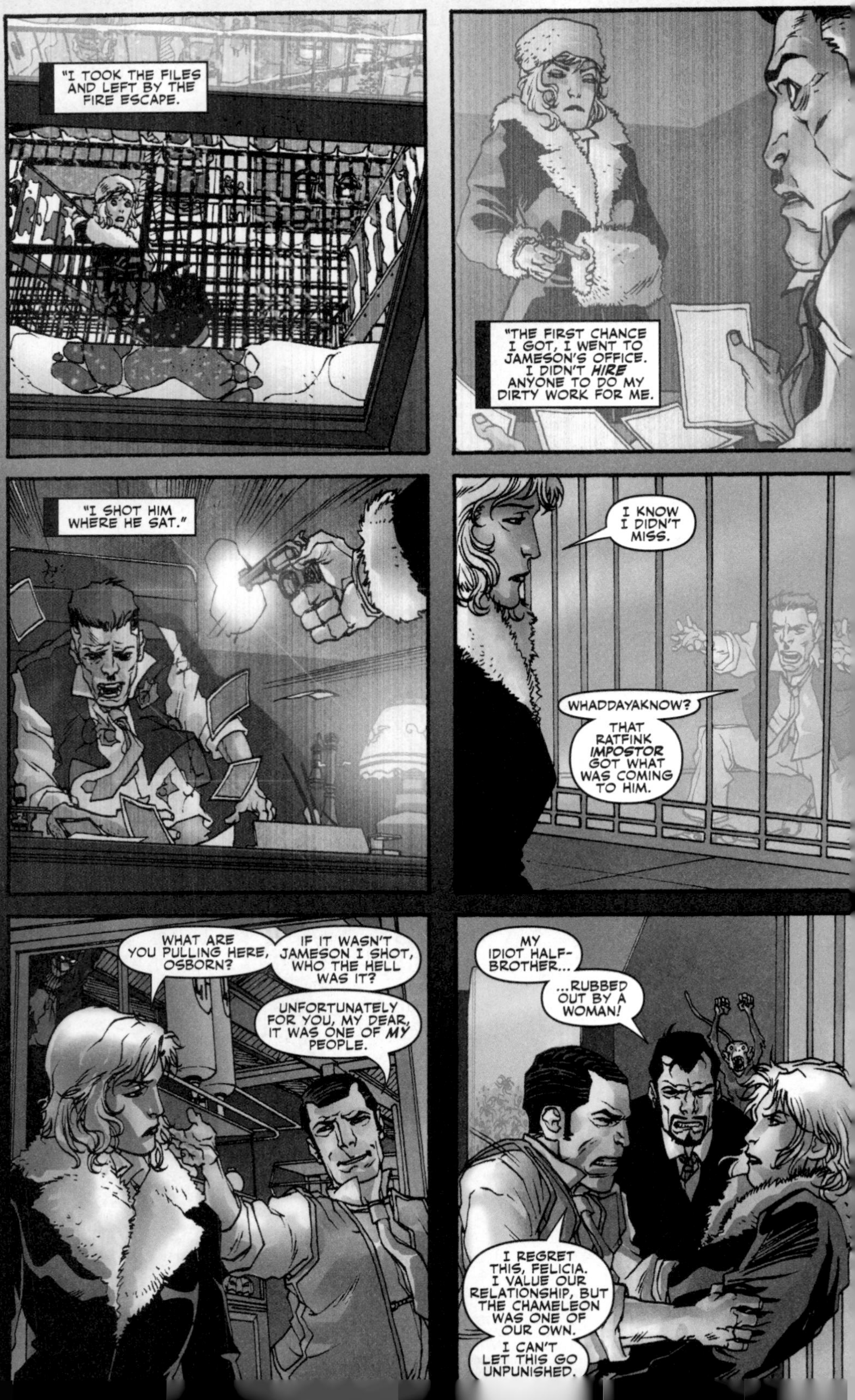
"I TOOK THE FILES AND LEFT BY THE FIRE ESCAPE.
"THE FIRST CHANCE I GOT, I WENT TO JAMESON'S OFFICE. I DIDN'T HIRE ANYONE TO DO MY DIRTY WORK FOR ME.
"I SHOT HIM WHERE HE SAT."
I KNOW I DIDN'T MISS.
WHADDAYAKNOW?
THAT RATFINK IMPOSTOR GOT WHAT WAS COMING TO HIM.
WHAT ARE YOU PULLING HERE, OSBORN?
IF IT WASN'T JAMESON I SHOT, WHO THE HELL WAS IT?
UNFORTUNATELY FOR YOU, MY DEAR, IT WAS ONE OF MY PEOPLE.
MY IDIOT HALF-BROTHER...
...RUBBED OUT BY A WOMAN!
I REGRET THIS, FELICIA. I VALUE OUR RELATIONSHIP, BUT THE CHAMELEON WAS ONE OF OUR OWN.
I CAN'T LET THIS GO UNPUNISHED.

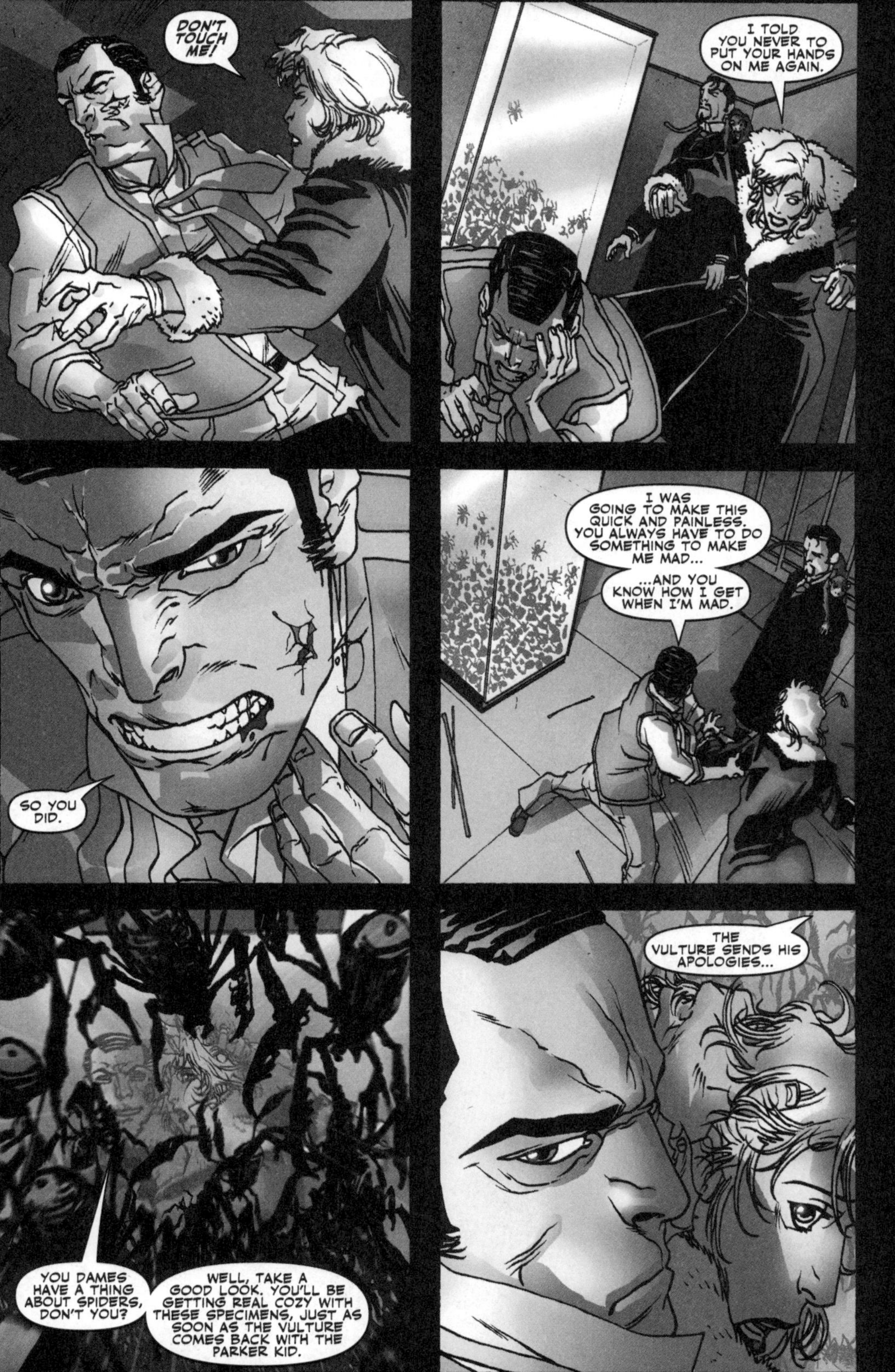
DON'T TOUCH ME!
I TOLD YOU NEVER TO PUT YOUR HANDS ON ME AGAIN.
SO YOU DID.
I WAS GOING TO MAKE THIS QUICK AND PAINLESS. YOU ALWAYS HAVE TO DO SOMETHING TO MAKE ME MAD...
...AND YOU KNOW HOW I GET WHEN I'M MAD.
YOU DAMES HAVE A THING ABOUT SPIDERS, DON'T YOU?
WELL, TAKE A GOOD LOOK. YOU'LL BE GETTING REAL COZY WITH THESE SPECIMENS, JUST AS SOON AS THE VULTURE COMES BACK WITH THE PARKER KID.
THE VULTURE SENDS HIS APOLOGIES...

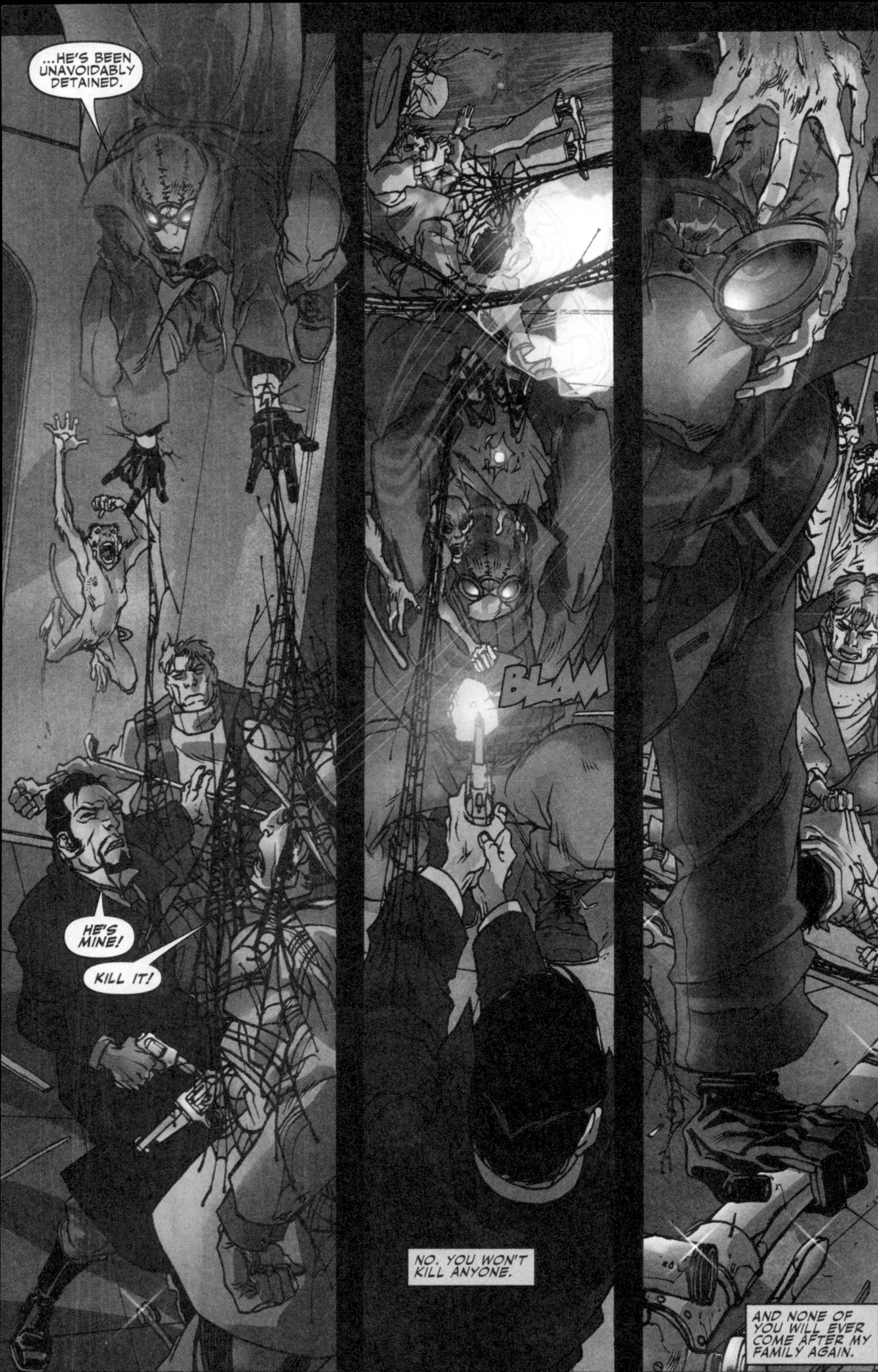
...HE'S BEEN UNAVOIDABLY DETAINED.
HE'S MINE!
KILL IT!
BLAM
NO. YOU WON'T KILL ANYONE.
AND NONE OF YOU WILL EVER COME AFTER MY FAMILY AGAIN.

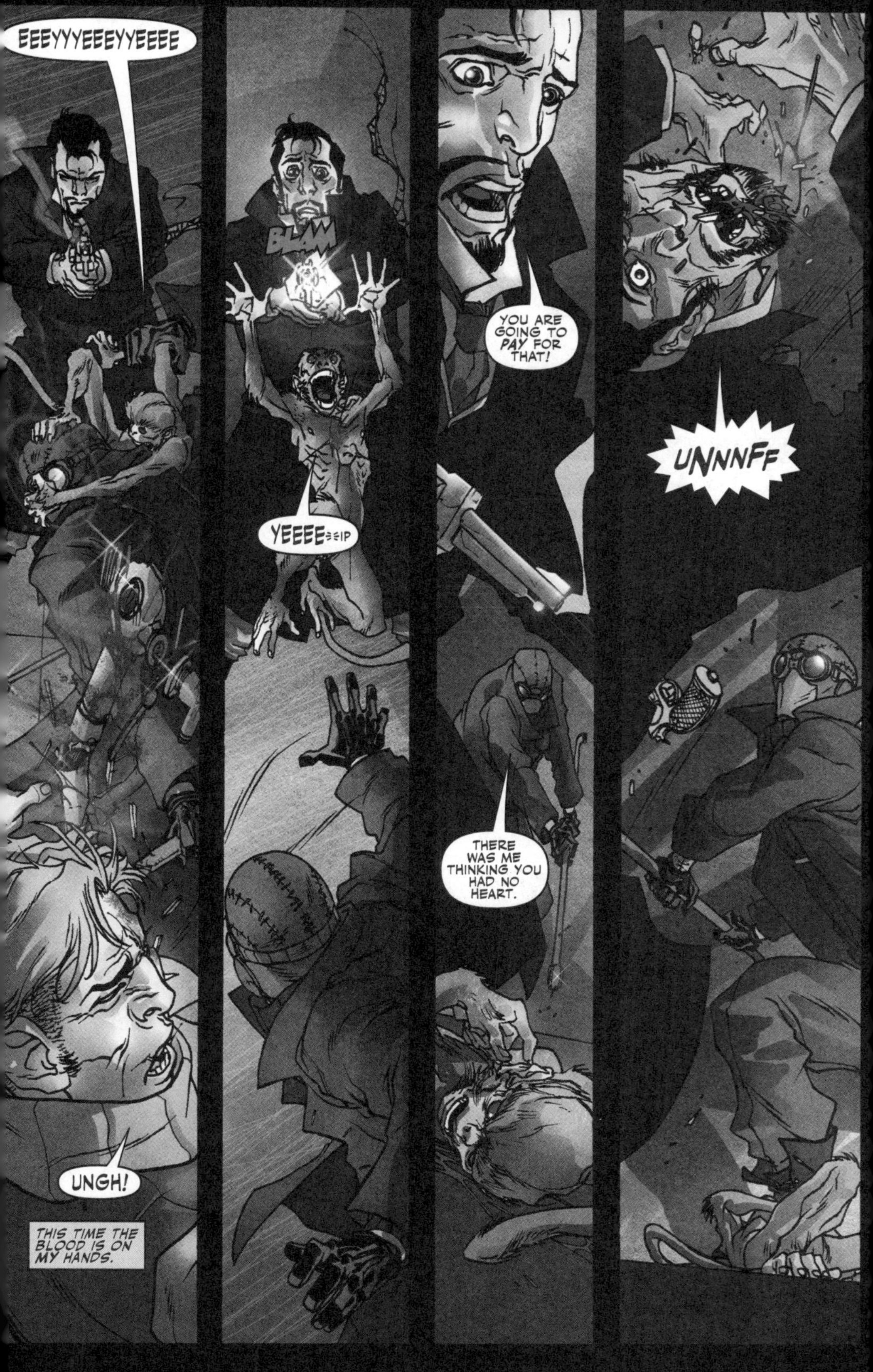
EEEYYYEEEYYEEEE
UNGH!
THIS TIME THE BLOOD IS ON MY HANDS.
BLAM
YEEEE==IP
YOU ARE GOING TO PAY FOR THAT!
THERE WAS ME THINKING YOU HAD NO HEART.
UNNNFF

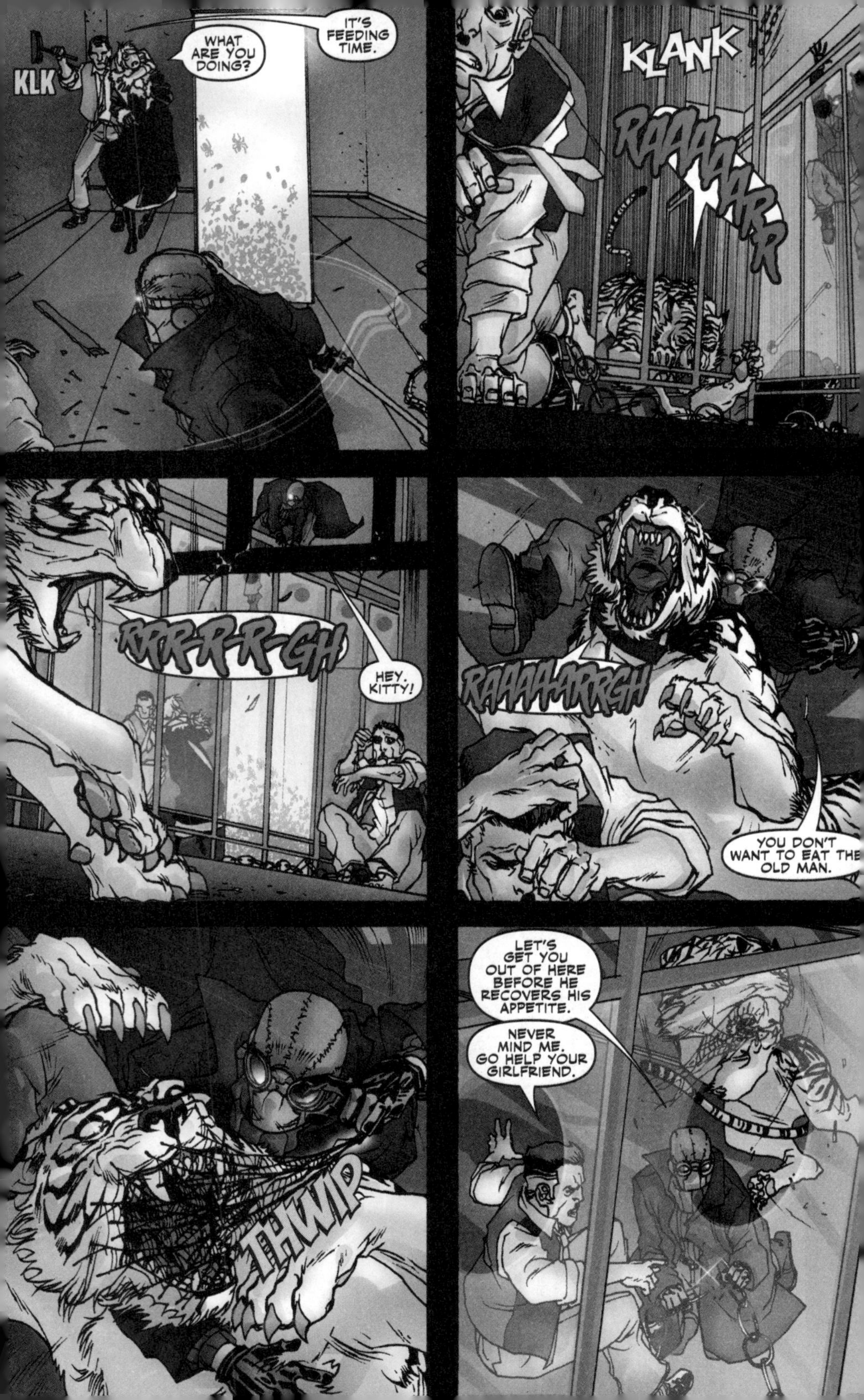
KLK
WHAT ARE YOU DOING?
IT'S FEEDING TIME.
KLANK
RAAAAARRR
RRRR-R-R-GH
HEY. KITTY!
RAAAA-ARRGH
YOU DON'T WANT TO EAT THE OLD MAN.
THWIP
LET'S GET YOU OUT OF HERE BEFORE HE RECOVERS HIS APPETITE.
NEVER MIND ME. GO HELP YOUR GIRLFRIEND.

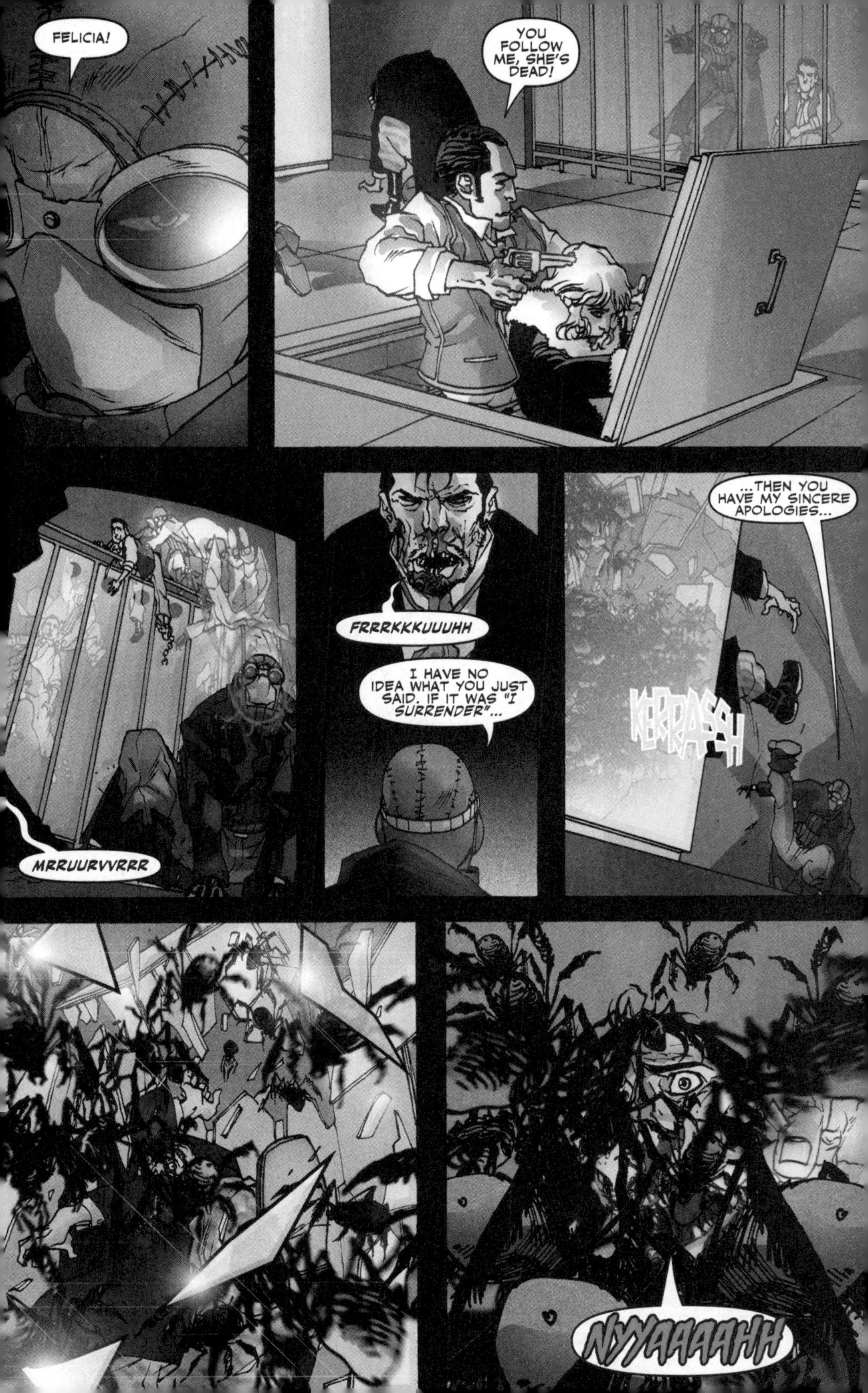
FELICIA!
YOU FOLLOW ME, SHE'S DEAD!
MRRUURVVRRR
FRRRKKKUUUHH
I HAVE NO IDEA WHAT YOU JUST SAID. IF IT WAS "I SURRENDER"...
...THEN YOU HAVE MY SINCERE APOLOGIES...
KERRASSH
NYYAAAAAHH

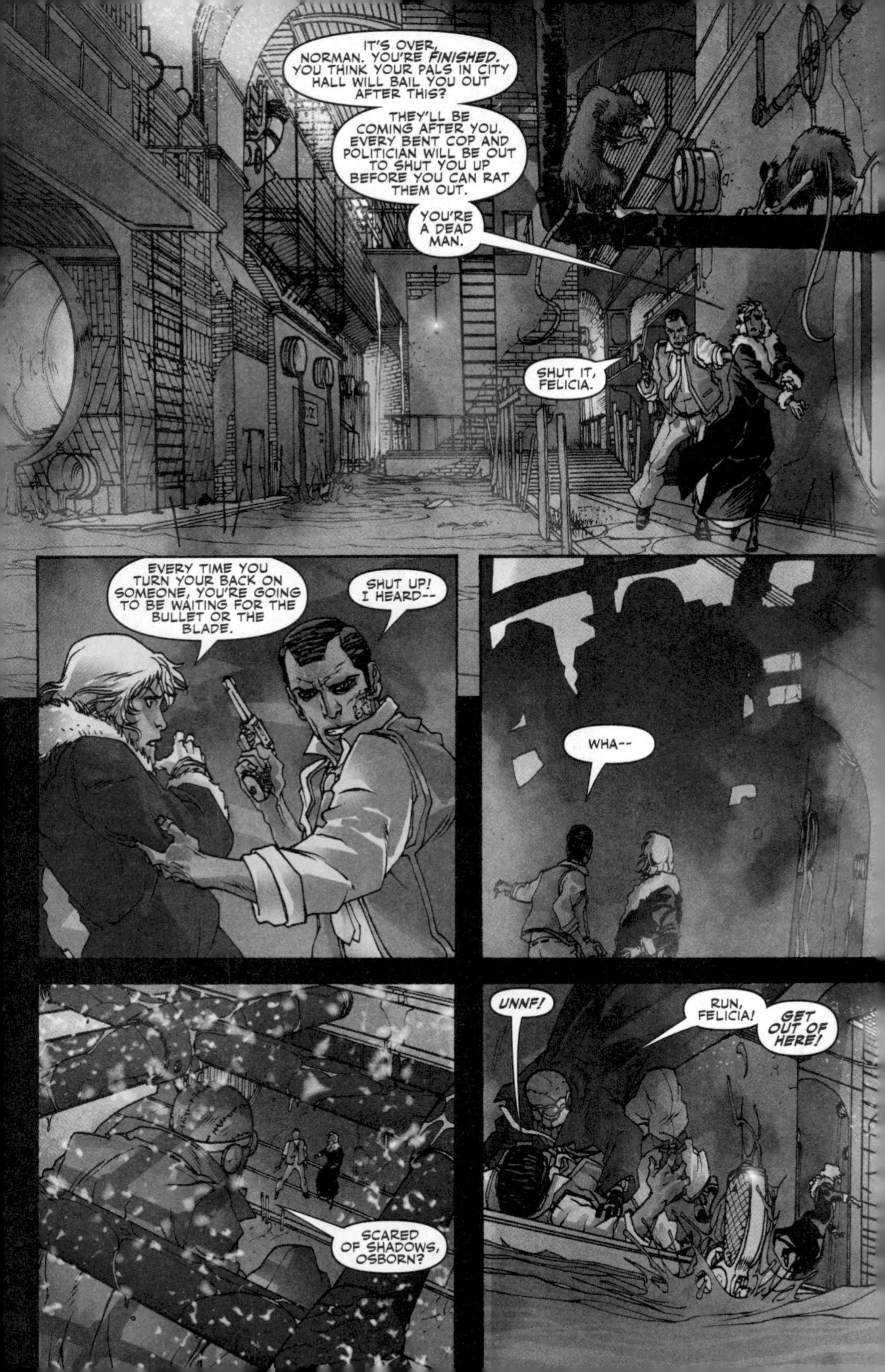

IT'S OVER, NORMAN. YOU'RE *FINISHED.* YOU THINK YOUR PALS IN CITY HALL WILL BAIL YOU OUT AFTER THIS?
THEY'LL BE COMING AFTER YOU. EVERY BENT COP AND POLITICIAN WILL BE OUT TO SHUT YOU UP BEFORE YOU CAN RAT THEM OUT.
YOU'RE A DEAD MAN.
SHUT IT, FELICIA.
EVERY TIME YOU TURN YOUR BACK ON SOMEONE, YOU'RE GOING TO BE WAITING FOR THE BULLET OR THE BLADE.
SHUT UP! I HEARD--
WHA--
SCARED OF SHADOWS, OSBORN?
UNNF!
RUN, FELICIA!
GET OUT OF HERE!

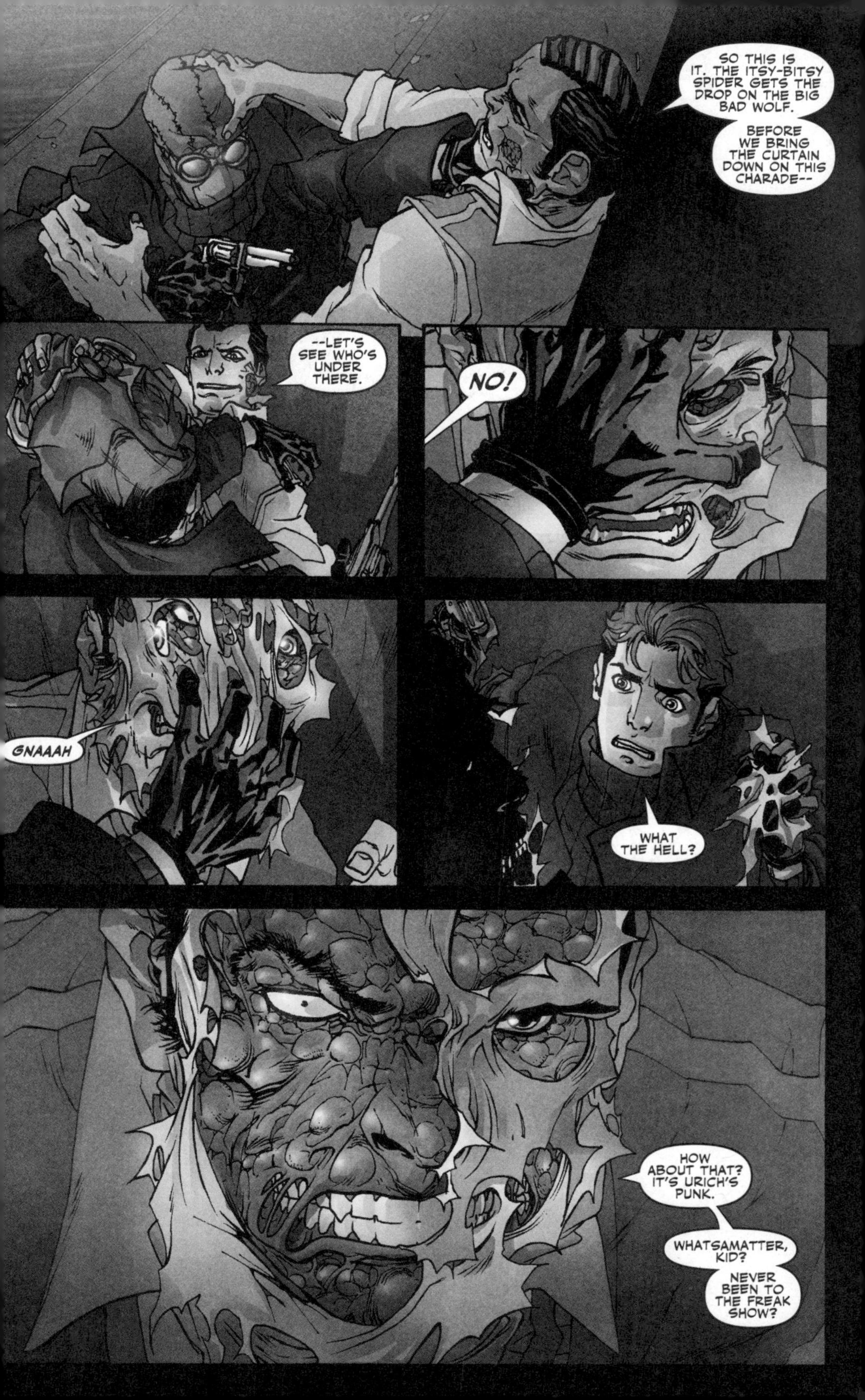
SO THIS IS IT. THE ITSY-BITSY SPIDER GETS THE DROP ON THE BIG BAD WOLF.
BEFORE WE BRING THE CURTAIN DOWN ON THIS CHARADE--
--LET'S SEE WHO'S UNDER THERE.
NO!
GNAAAH
WHAT THE HELL?
HOW ABOUT THAT? IT'S URICH'S PUNK.
WHATSAMATTER, KID?
NEVER BEEN TO THE FREAK SHOW?

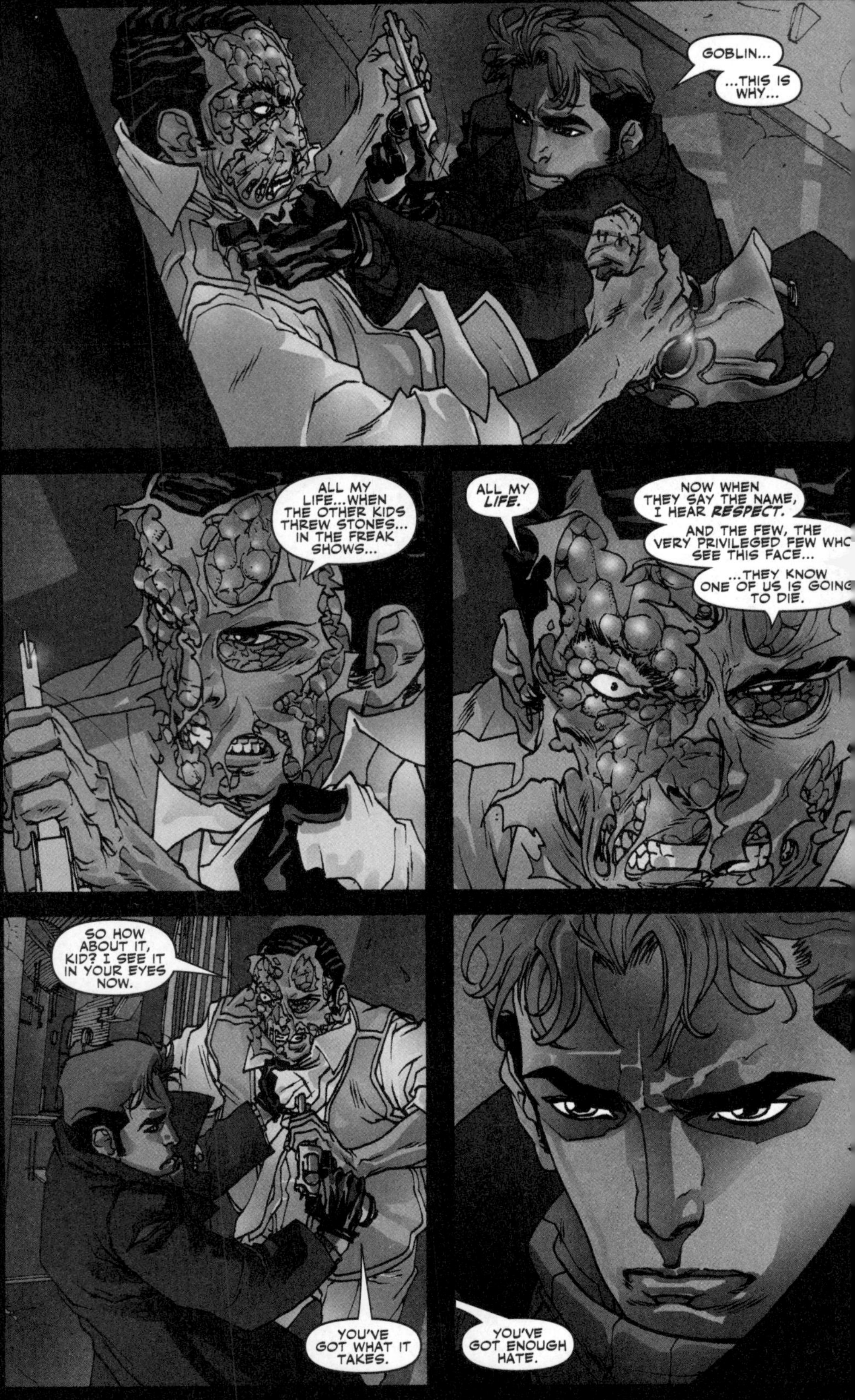
GOBLIN...
...THIS IS WHY...
ALL MY LIFE...WHEN THE OTHER KIDS THREW STONES... IN THE FREAK SHOWS...
ALL MY *LIFE.*
NOW WHEN THEY SAY THE NAME, I HEAR *RESPECT.*
AND THE FEW, THE VERY PRIVILEGED FEW WHO SEE THIS FACE...
...THEY KNOW ONE OF US IS GOING TO DIE.
SO HOW ABOUT IT, KID? I SEE IT IN YOUR EYES NOW.
YOU'VE GOT WHAT IT TAKES.
YOU'VE GOT ENOUGH HATE.

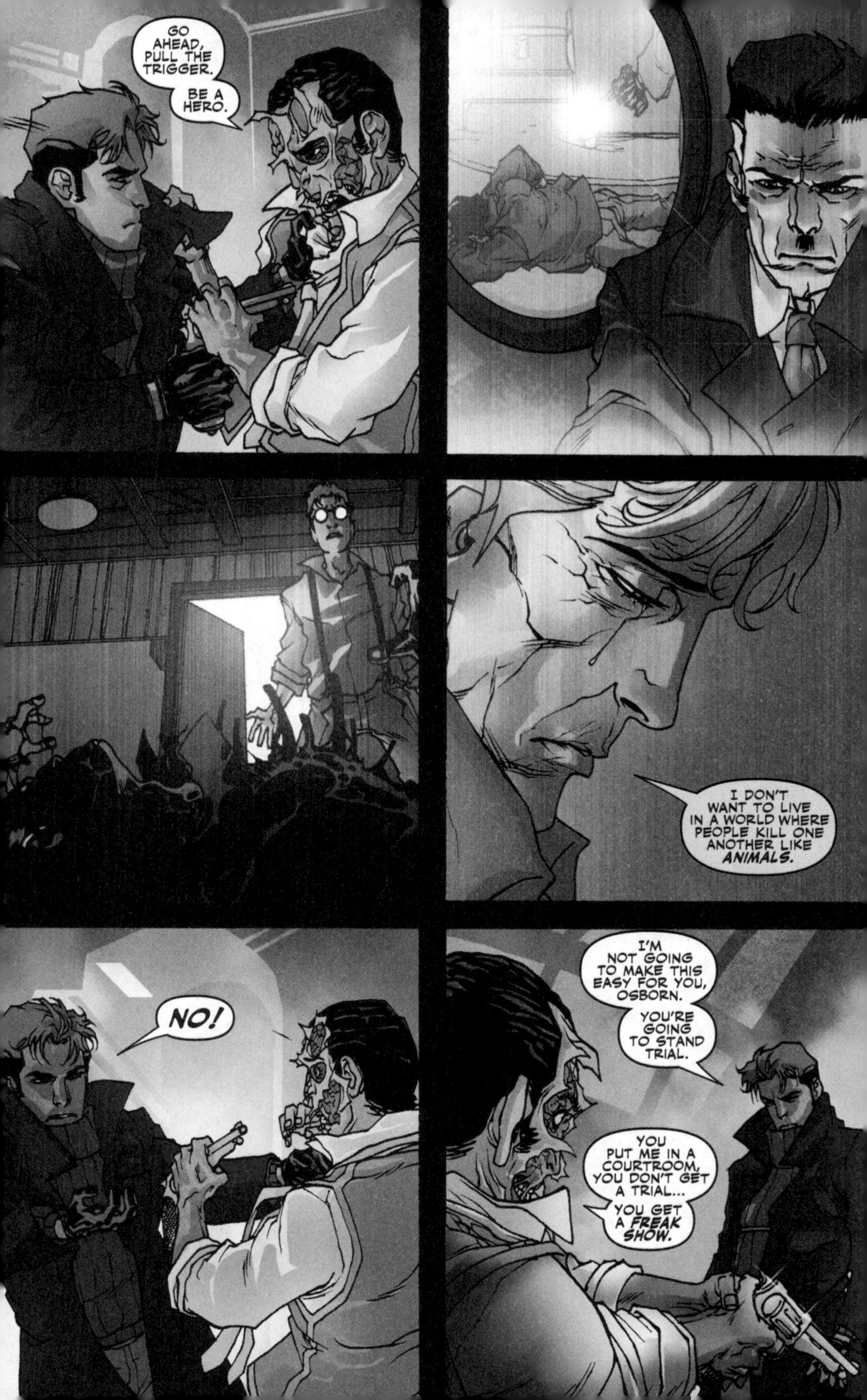
GO AHEAD, PULL THE TRIGGER.
BE A HERO.
I DON'T WANT TO LIVE IN A WORLD WHERE PEOPLE KILL ONE ANOTHER LIKE *ANIMALS.*
NO!
I'M NOT GOING TO MAKE THIS EASY FOR YOU, OSBORN.
YOU'RE GOING TO STAND TRIAL.
YOU PUT ME IN A COURTROOM, YOU DON'T GET A TRIAL...
YOU GET A *FREAK SHOW.*

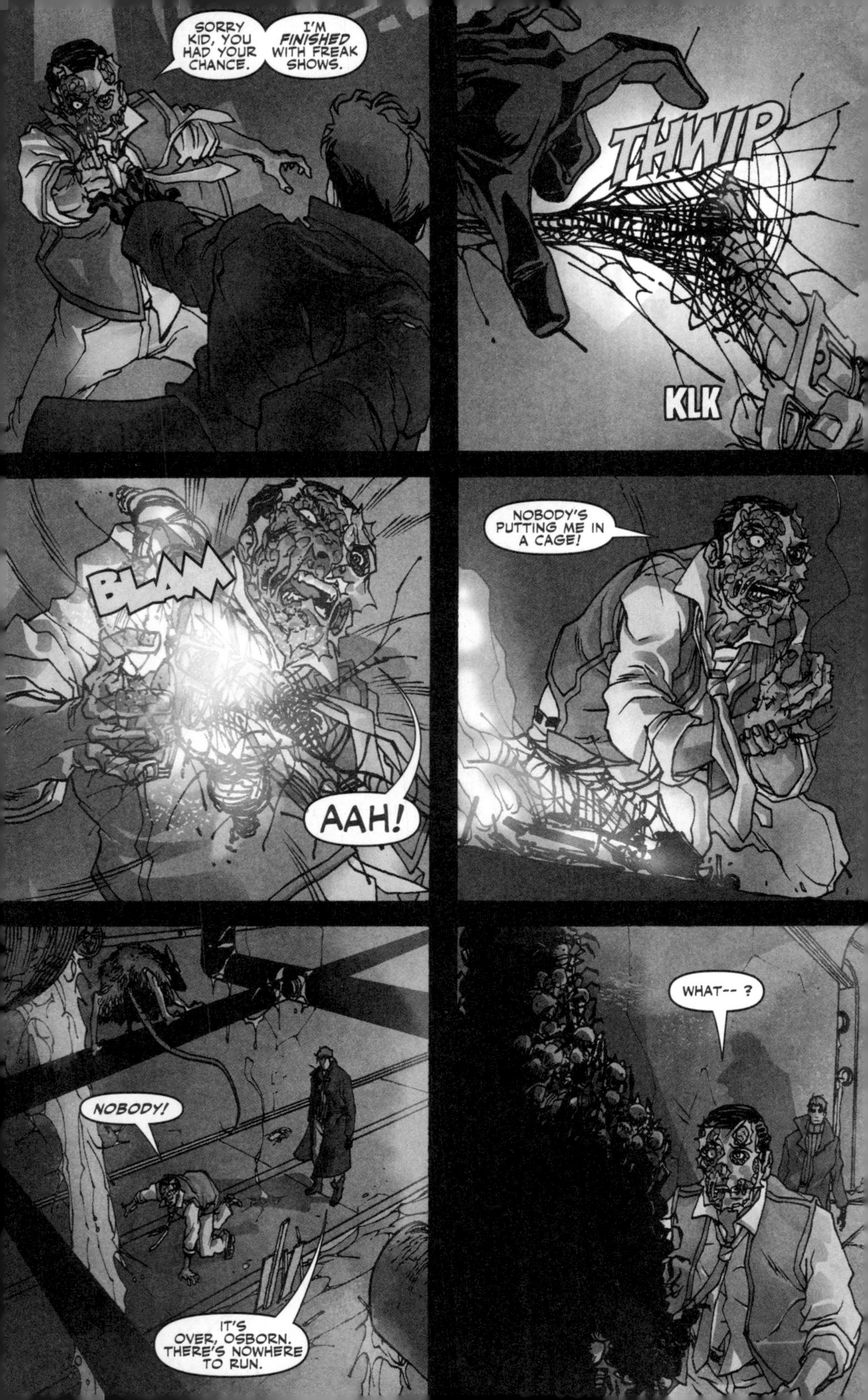
SORRY KID, YOU HAD YOUR CHANCE.
I'M *FINISHED* WITH FREAK SHOWS.
THWIP
KLK
BLAM
AAH!
NOBODY'S PUTTING ME IN A CAGE!
NOBODY!
IT'S OVER, OSBORN. THERE'S NOWHERE TO RUN.
WHAT-- ?

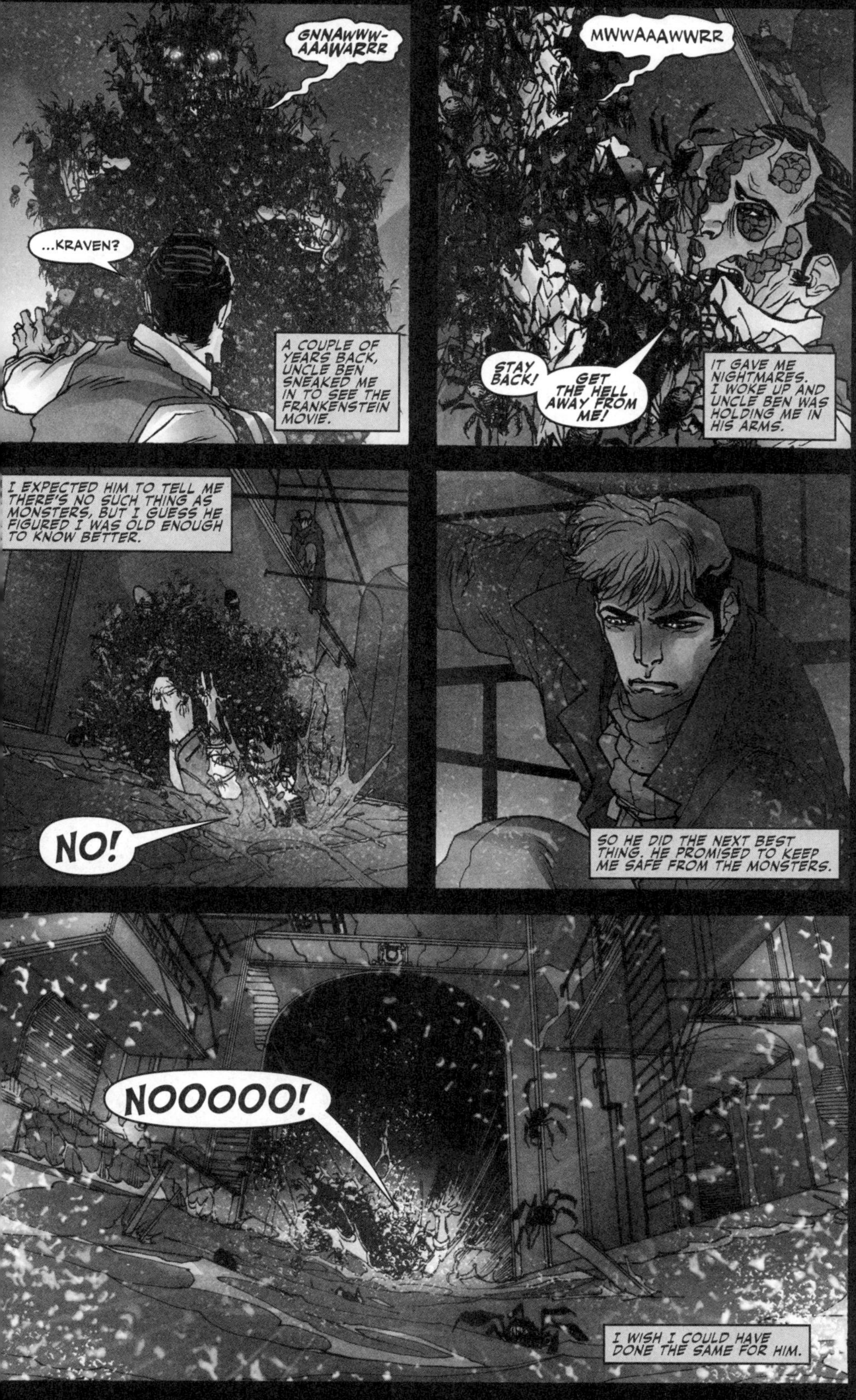
GNNAWWW-AAAWARRR
...KRAVEN?
A COUPLE OF YEARS BACK, UNCLE BEN SNEAKED ME IN TO SEE THE FRANKENSTEIN MOVIE.
MWWAAAWWRR
STAY BACK!
GET THE HELL AWAY FROM ME!
IT GAVE ME NIGHTMARES. I WOKE UP AND UNCLE BEN WAS HOLDING ME IN HIS ARMS.
I EXPECTED HIM TO TELL ME THERE'S NO SUCH THING AS MONSTERS, BUT I GUESS HE FIGURED I WAS OLD ENOUGH TO KNOW BETTER.
NO!
SO HE DID THE NEXT BEST THING. HE PROMISED TO KEEP ME SAFE FROM THE MONSTERS.
NOOOOO!
I WISH I COULD HAVE DONE THE SAME FOR HIM.

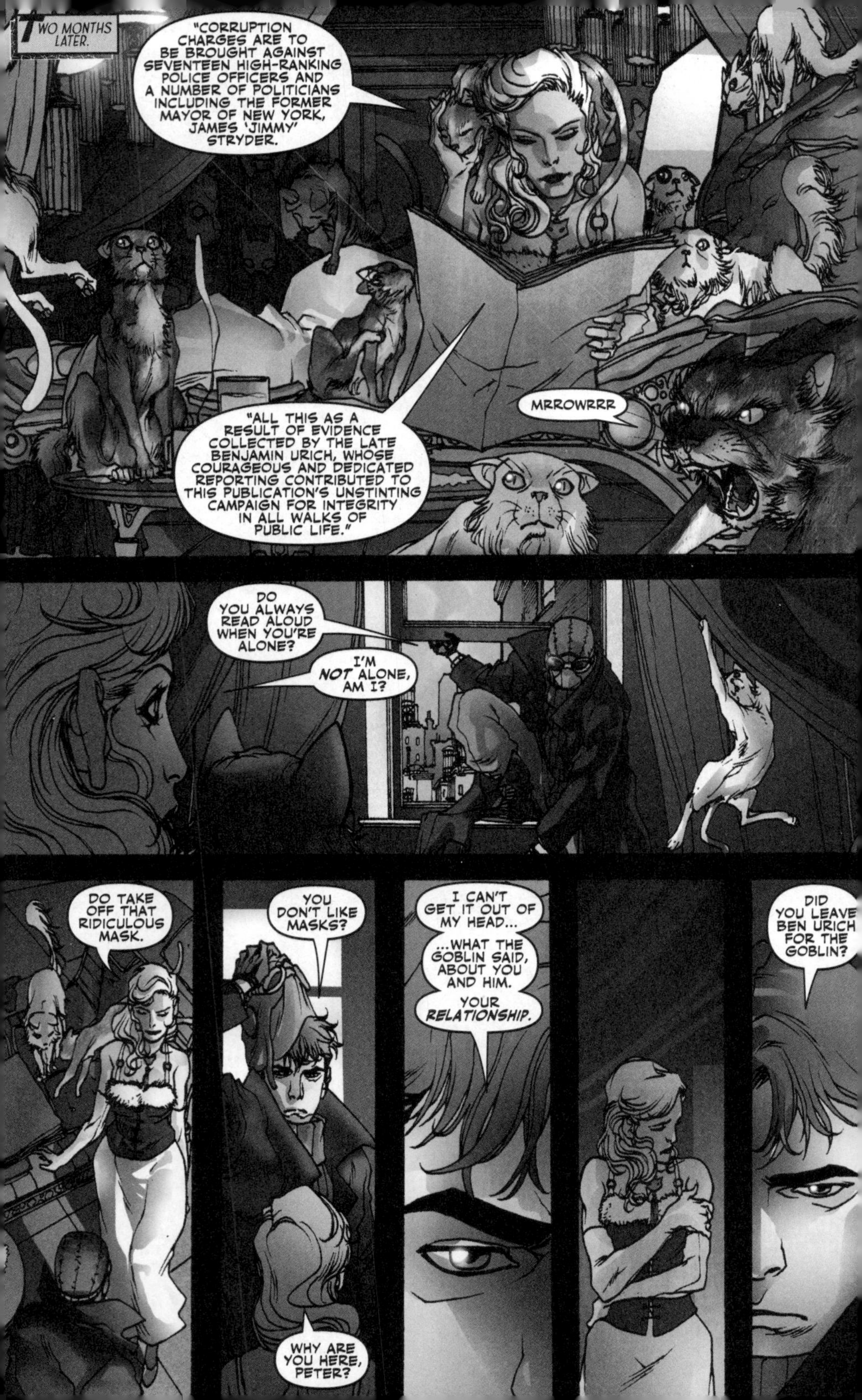
TWO MONTHS LATER.
"CORRUPTION CHARGES ARE TO BE BROUGHT AGAINST SEVENTEEN HIGH-RANKING POLICE OFFICERS AND A NUMBER OF POLITICIANS INCLUDING THE FORMER MAYOR OF NEW YORK, JAMES 'JIMMY' STRYDER.
"ALL THIS AS A RESULT OF EVIDENCE COLLECTED BY THE LATE BENJAMIN URICH, WHOSE COURAGEOUS AND DEDICATED REPORTING CONTRIBUTED TO THIS PUBLICATION'S UNSTINTING CAMPAIGN FOR INTEGRITY IN ALL WALKS OF PUBLIC LIFE."
MRROWRRR
DO YOU ALWAYS READ ALOUD WHEN YOU'RE ALONE?
I'M *NOT* ALONE, AM I?
DO TAKE OFF THAT RIDICULOUS MASK.
YOU DON'T LIKE MASKS?
WHY ARE YOU HERE, PETER?
I CAN'T GET IT OUT OF MY HEAD...
...WHAT THE GOBLIN SAID, ABOUT YOU AND HIM.
YOUR *RELATIONSHIP*.
DID YOU LEAVE BEN URICH FOR THE GOBLIN?

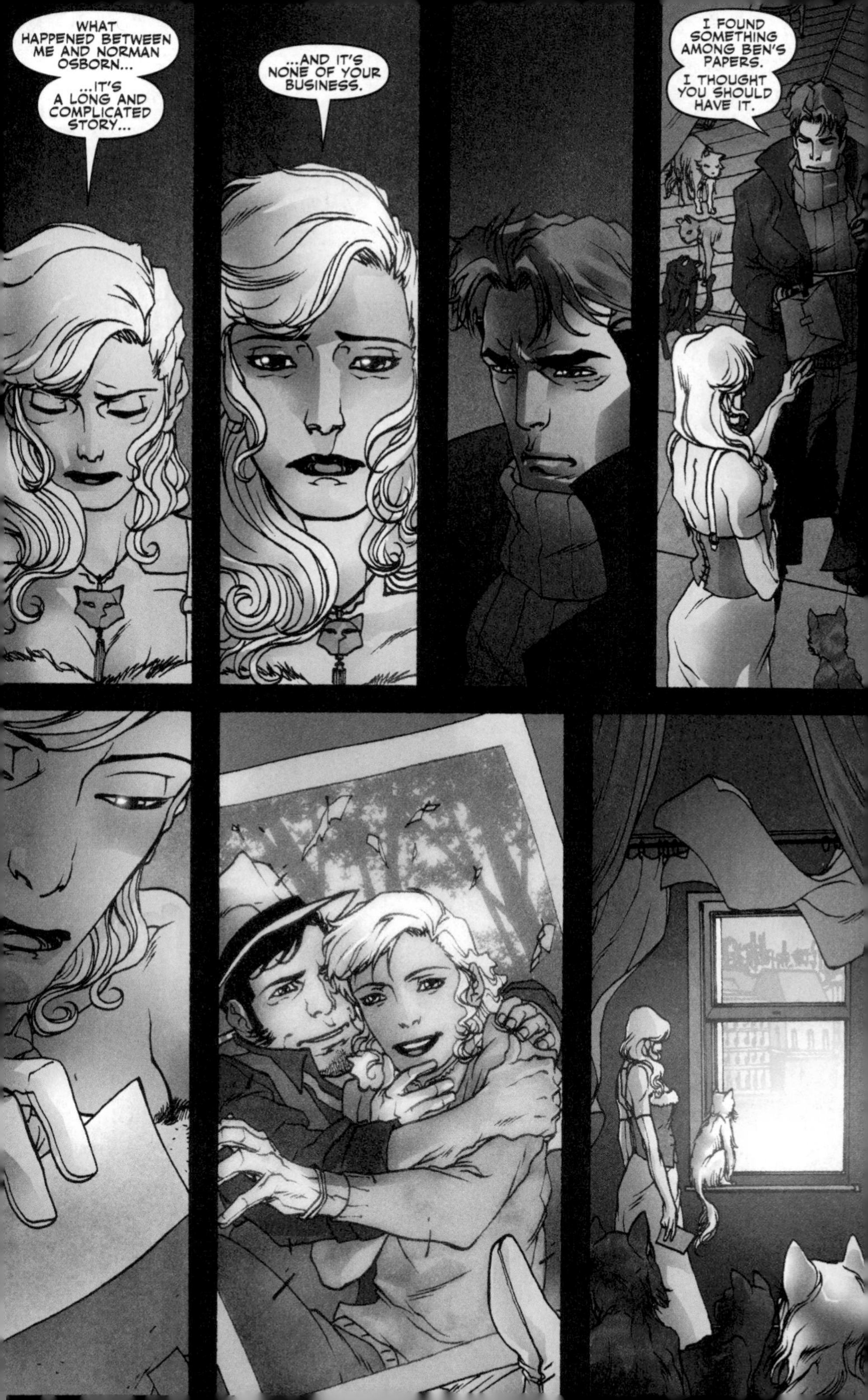
WHAT HAPPENED BETWEEN ME AND NORMAN OSBORN...
...IT'S A LONG AND COMPLICATED STORY...
...AND IT'S NONE OF YOUR BUSINESS.
I FOUND SOMETHING AMONG BEN'S PAPERS.
I THOUGHT YOU SHOULD HAVE IT.

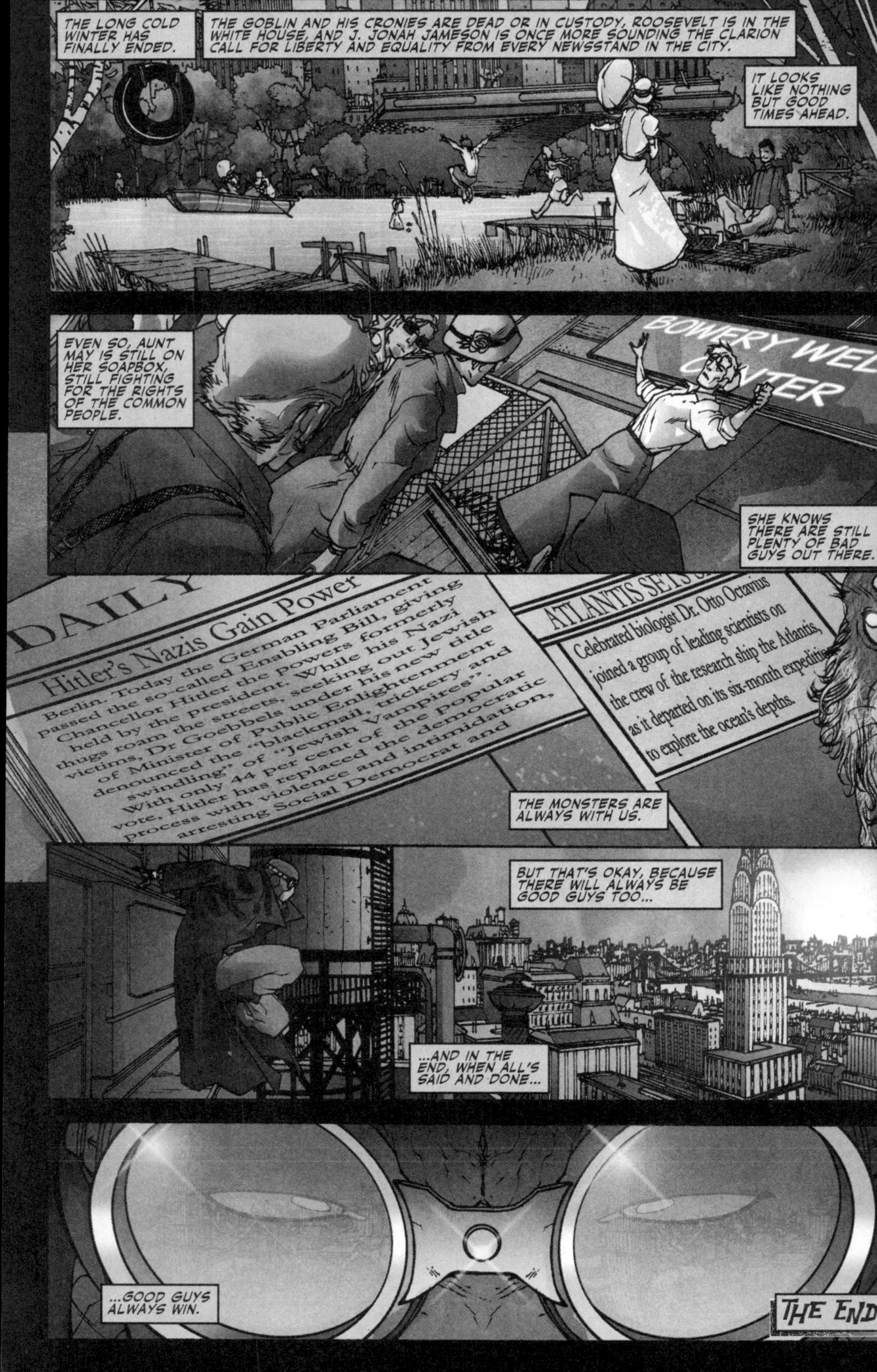

THE LONG COLD WINTER HAS FINALLY ENDED.
THE GOBLIN AND HIS CRONIES ARE DEAD OR IN CUSTODY, ROOSEVELT IS IN THE WHITE HOUSE, AND J. JONAH JAMESON IS ONCE MORE SOUNDING THE CLARION CALL FOR LIBERTY AND EQUALITY FROM EVERY NEWSSTAND IN THE CITY.
IT LOOKS LIKE NOTHING BUT GOOD TIMES AHEAD.
EVEN SO, AUNT MAY IS STILL ON HER SOAPBOX, STILL FIGHTING FOR THE RIGHTS OF THE COMMON PEOPLE.
SHE KNOWS THERE ARE STILL PLENTY OF BAD GUYS OUT THERE.
DAILY
Hitler's Nazis Gain Power
Berlin. Today the German Parliament passed the so-called Enabling Bill, giving Chancellor Hitler the powers formerly held by the president. While his Nazi thugs roam the streets, seeking out Jewish victims, Dr Goebbels under his new title of Minister of Public Enlightenment denounced the "blackmail, trickery and swindling" of "Jewish Vampires". With only 44 per cent of the popular vote, Hitler has replaced the democratic process with violence and intimidation, arresting Social Democrat and
Celebrated biologist Dr. Otto Octavius joined a group of leading scientists on the crew of the research ship the Atlantis, as it departed on its six-month expediti
to explore the ocean's depths.
THE MONSTERS ARE ALWAYS WITH US.
BUT THAT'S OKAY, BECAUSE THERE WILL ALWAYS BE GOOD GUYS TOO...
...AND IN THE END, WHEN ALL'S SAID AND DONE...
...GOOD GUYS ALWAYS WIN.
THE END

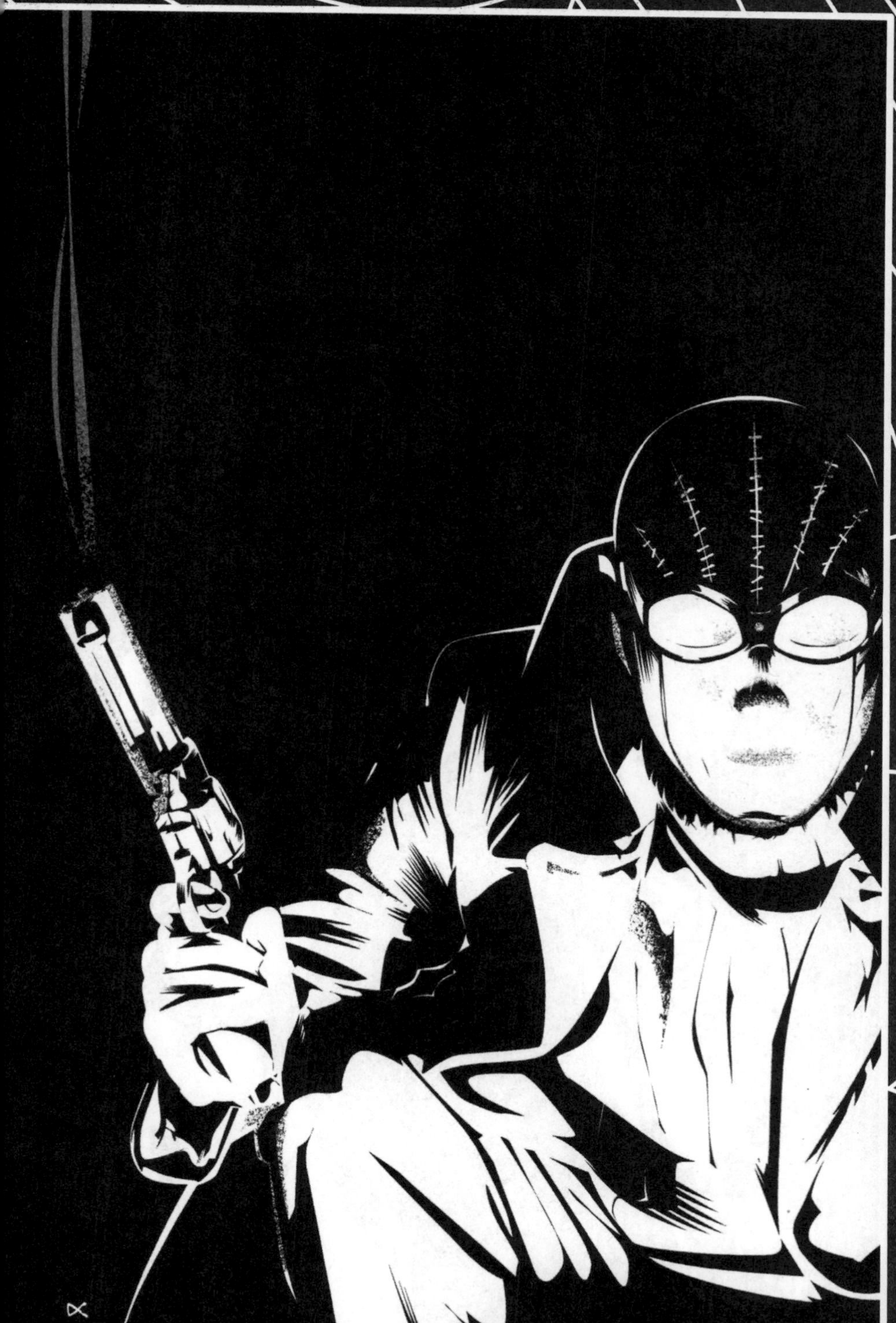

#1 VARIANT BY DENNIS CALERO

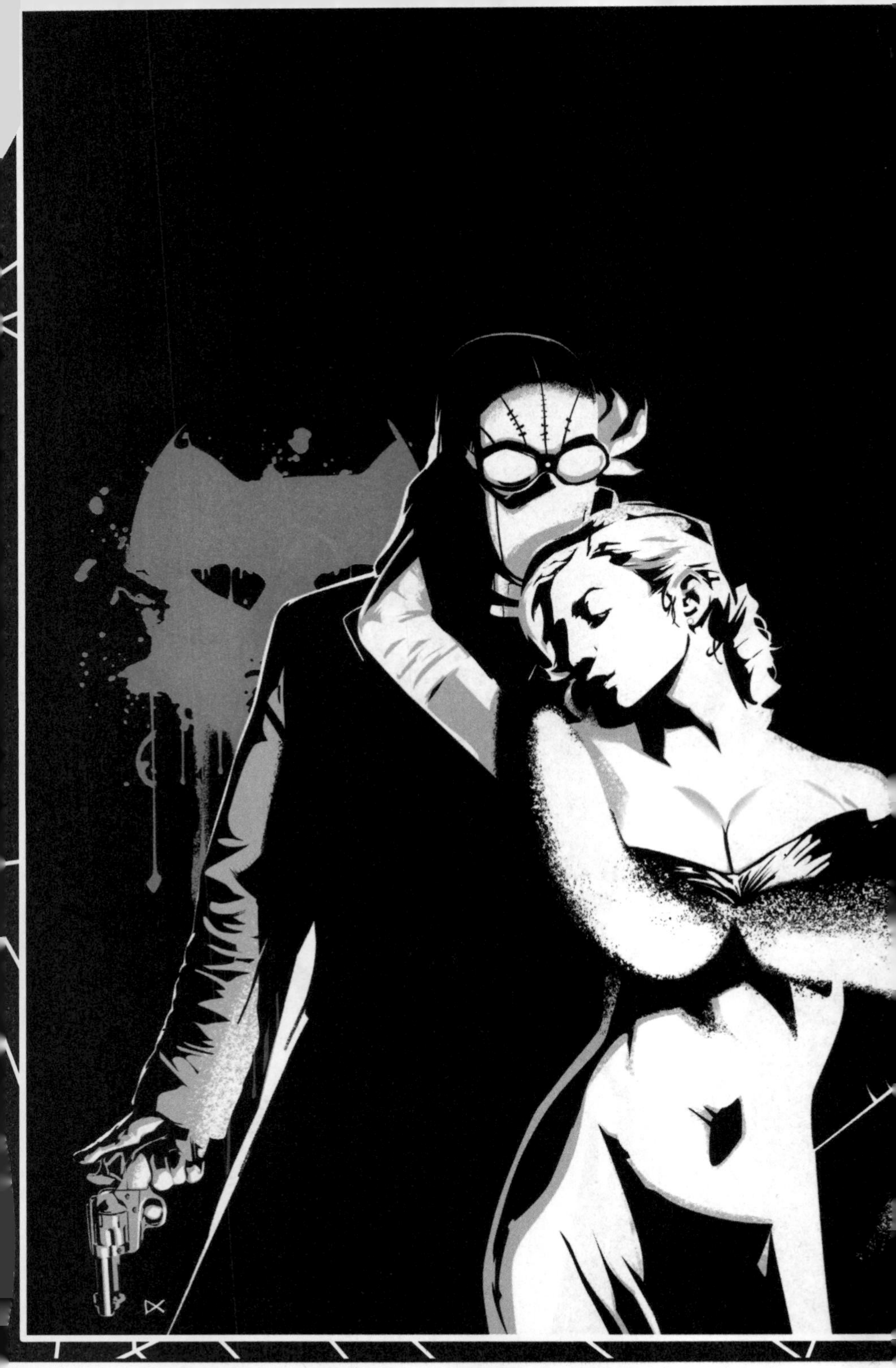

#2 VARIANT BY DENNIS CALERO

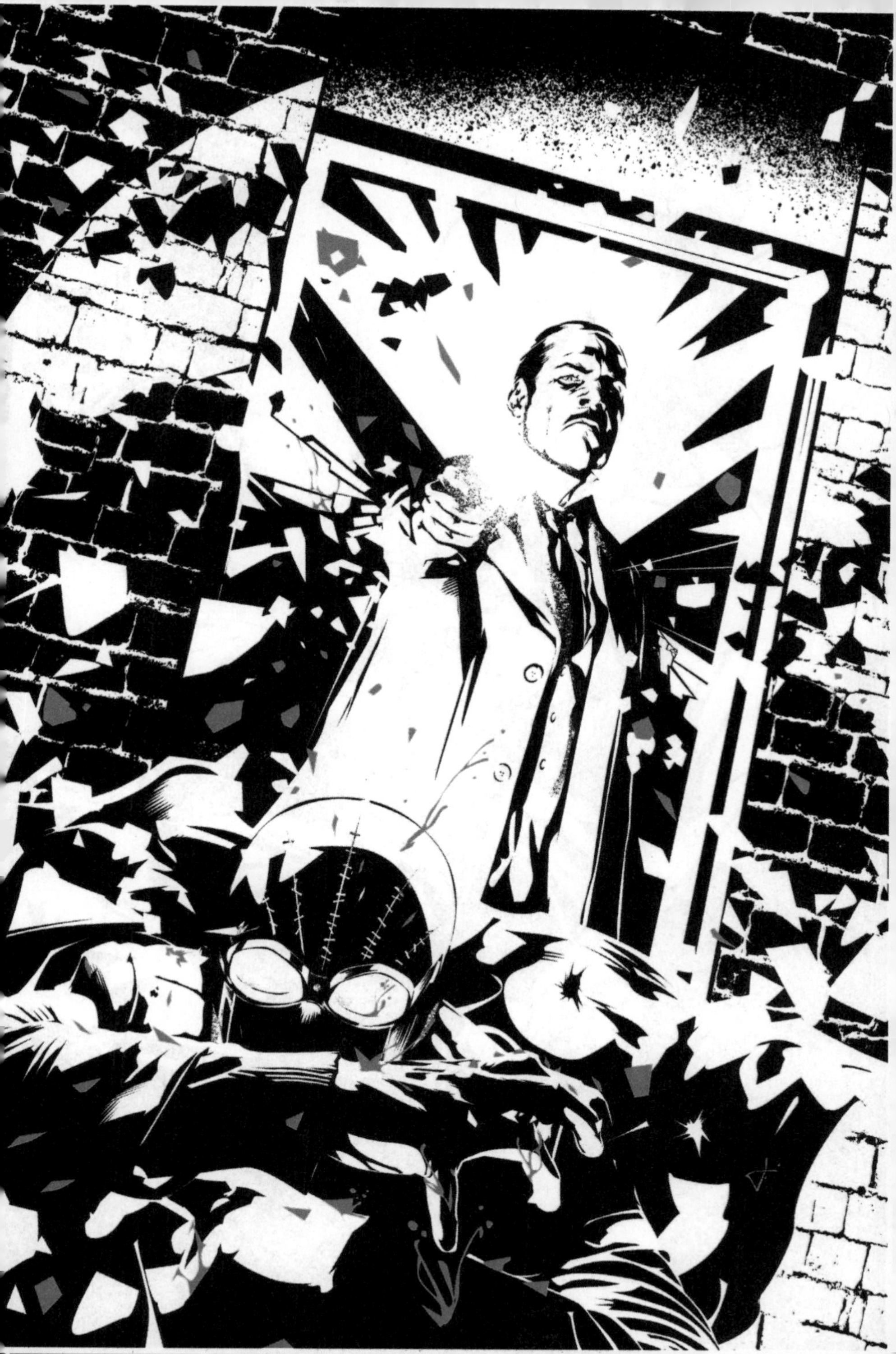

#3 VARIANT BY DENNIS CALERO

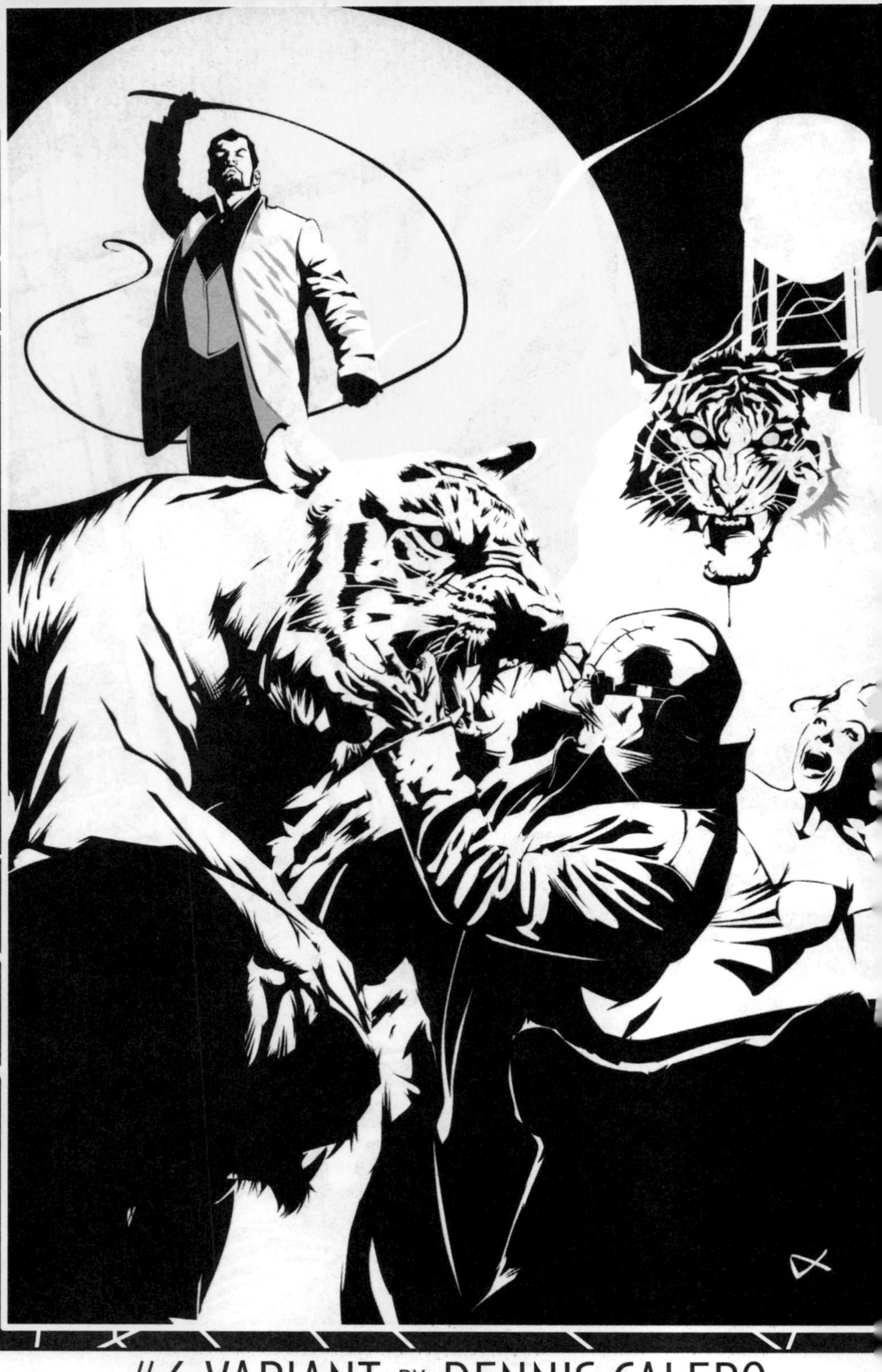

#4 VARIANT BY DENNIS CALERO

SPIDERMAN NOIR

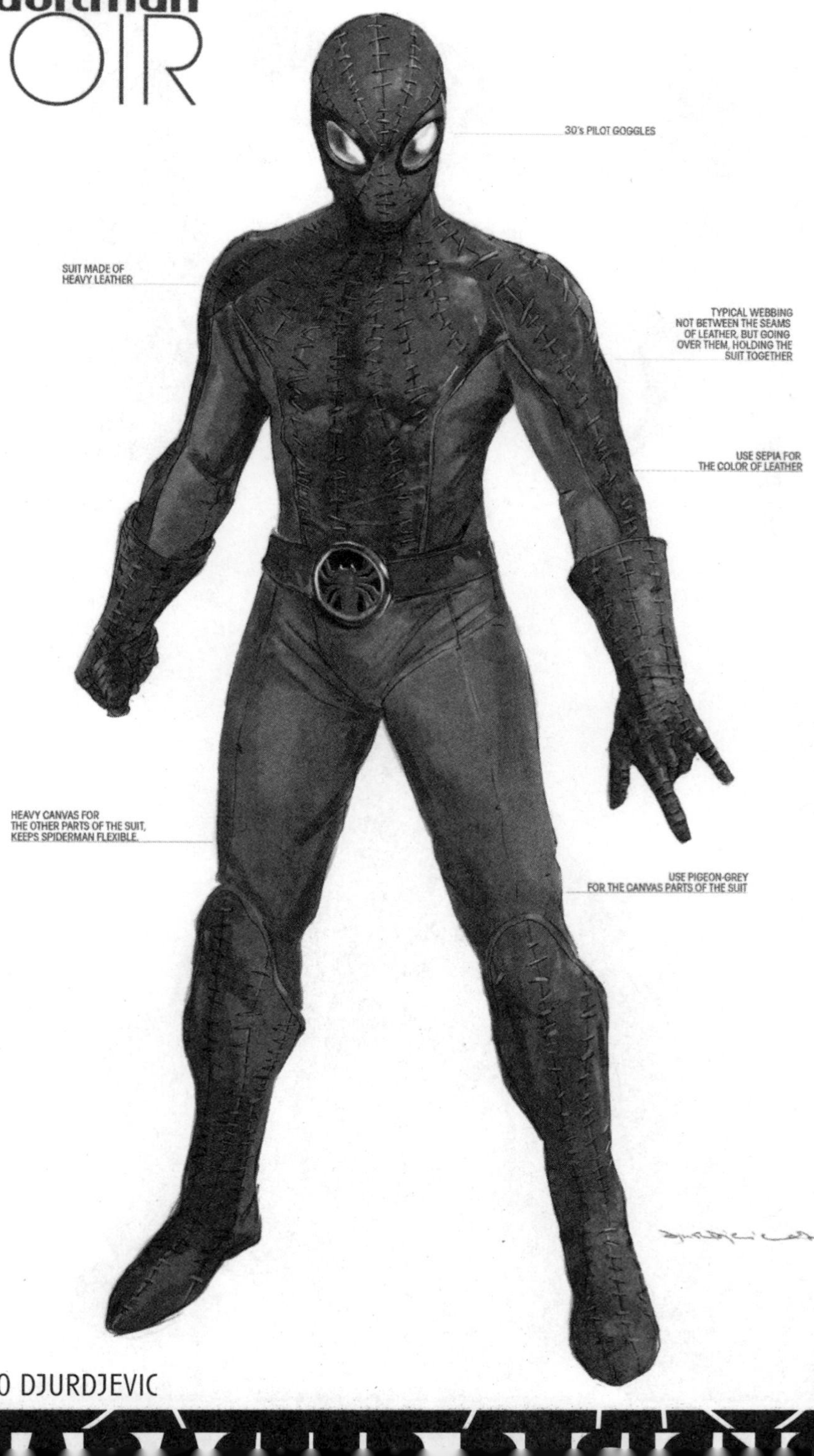
30's PILOT GOGGLES
SUIT MADE OF HEAVY LEATHER
TYPICAL WEBBING NOT BETWEEN THE SEAMS OF LEATHER, BUT GOING OVER THEM, HOLDING THE SUIT TOGETHER
USE SEPIA FOR THE COLOR OF LEATHER
HEAVY CANVAS FOR THE OTHER PARTS OF THE SUIT, KEEPS SPIDERMAN FLEXIBLE.
USE PIGEON-GREY FOR THE CANVAS PARTS OF THE SUIT

BY MARKO DJURDJEVIC

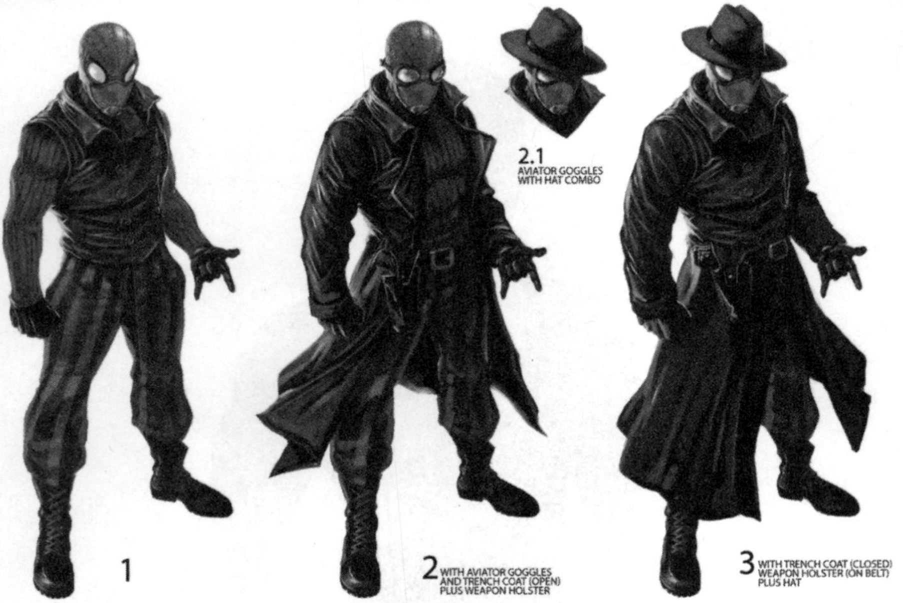

2.1
AVIATOR GOGGLES WITH HAT COMBO
1
2 WITH AVIATOR GOGGLES AND TRENCH COAT (OPEN) PLUS WEAPON HOLSTER
3 WITH TRENCH COAT (CLOSED) WEAPON HOLSTER (ON BELT) PLUS HAT

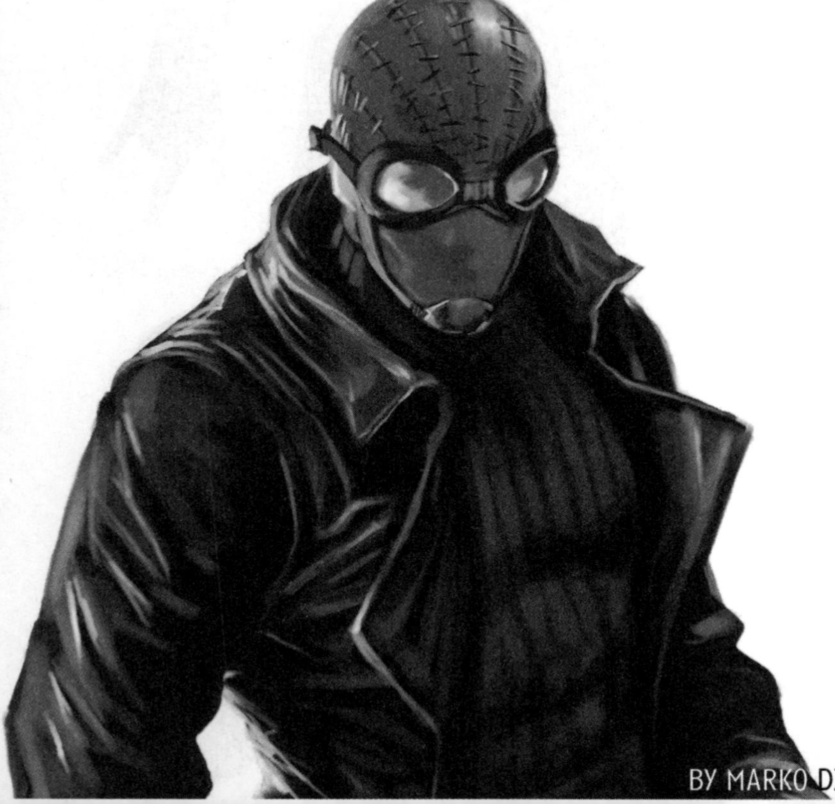

BY MARKO DJURDJEVIC

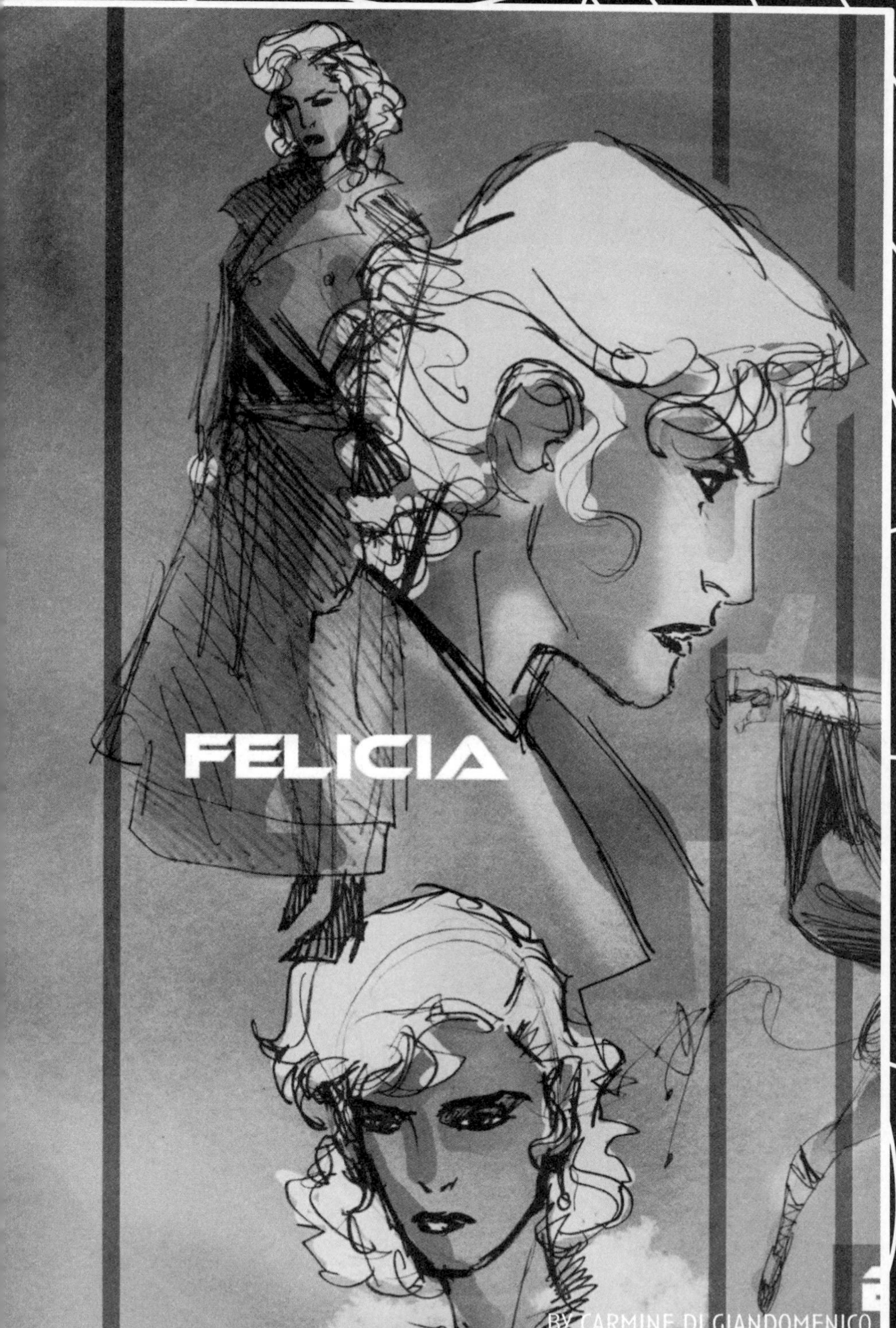
FELICIA
BY CARMINE DI GIANDOMENICO

CHARACTER DESIGNS

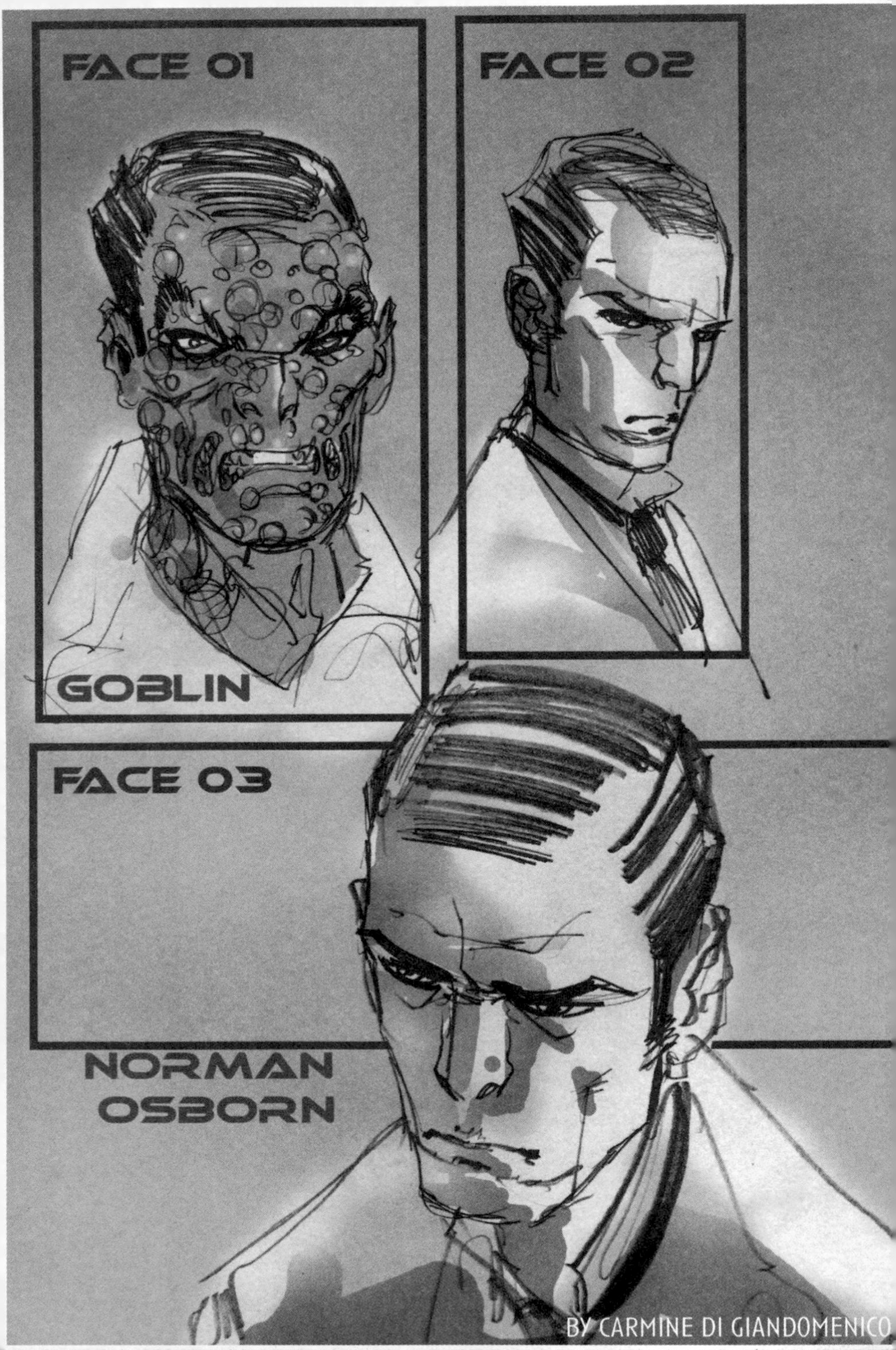
FACE 01
FACE 02
GOBLIN
FACE 03
NORMAN OSBORN
BY CARMINE DI GIANDOMENICO

CHARACTER DESIGNS

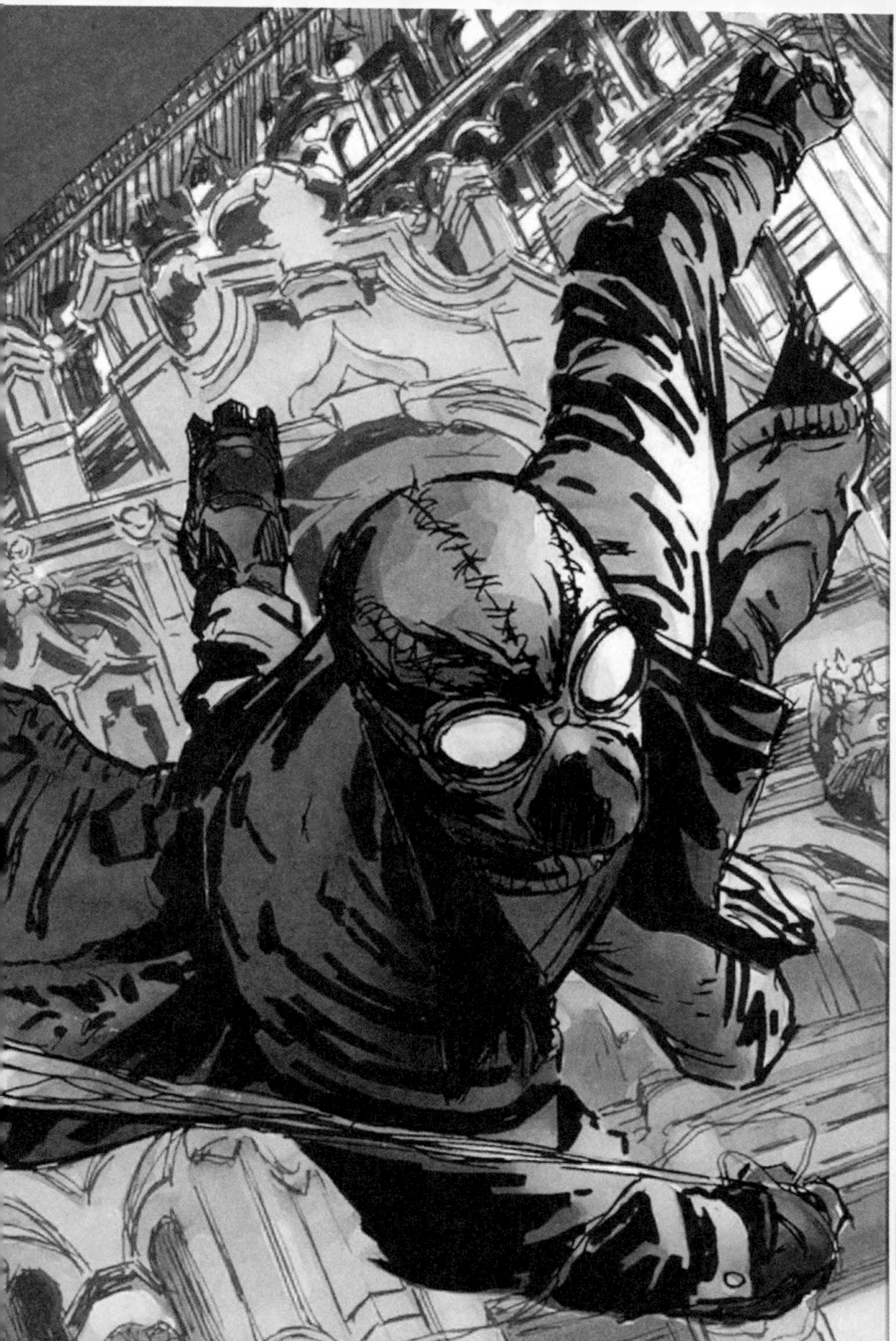

COVER SKETCHES

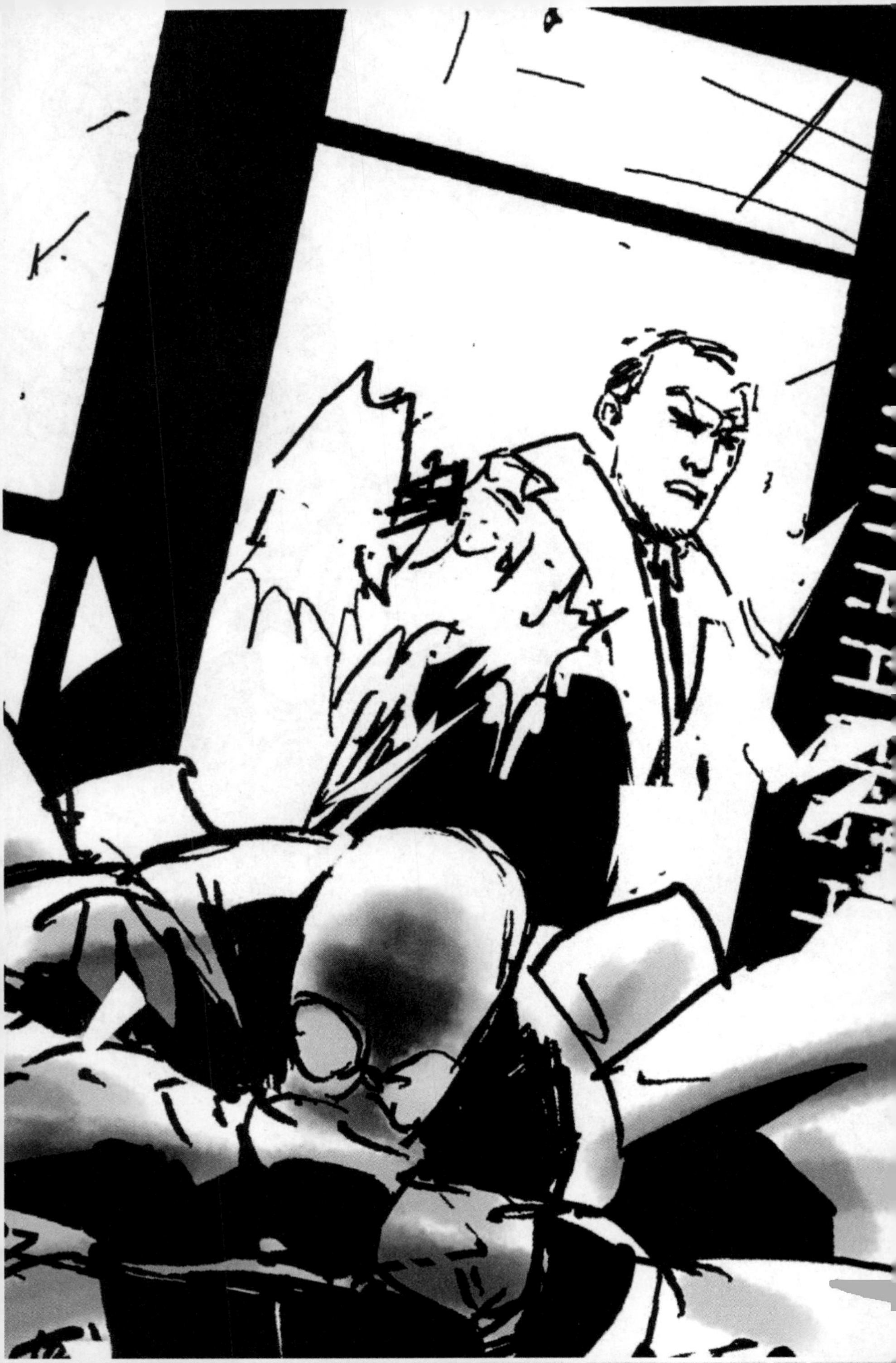

COVER SKETCHES

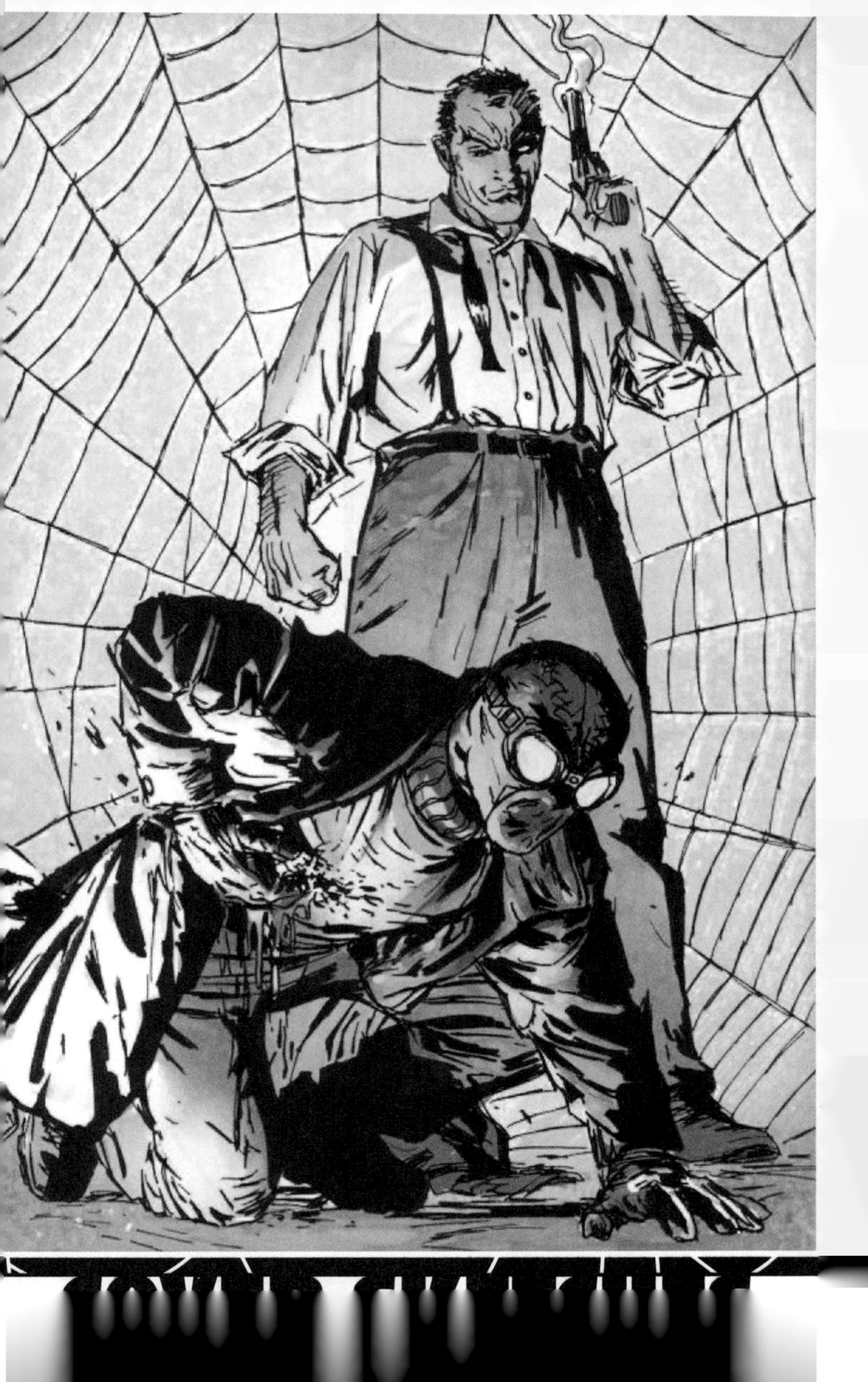

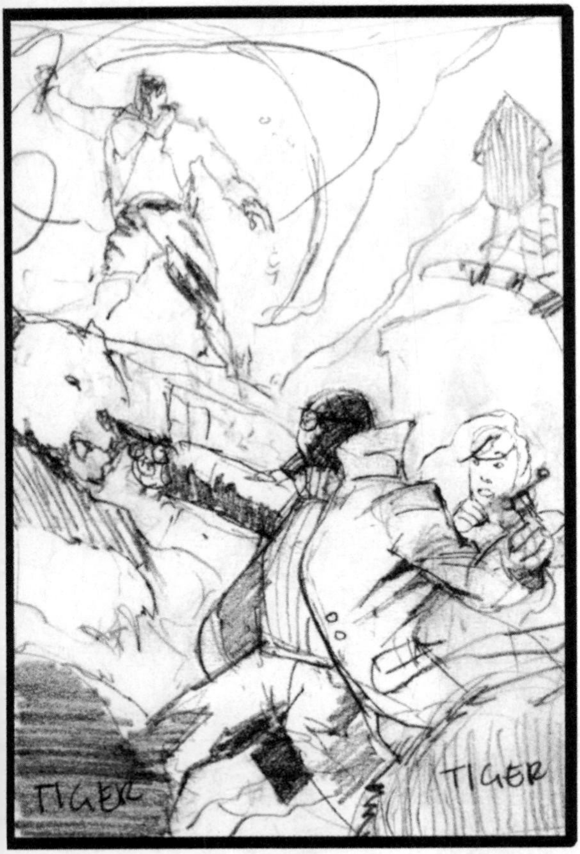
TIGER
TIGER

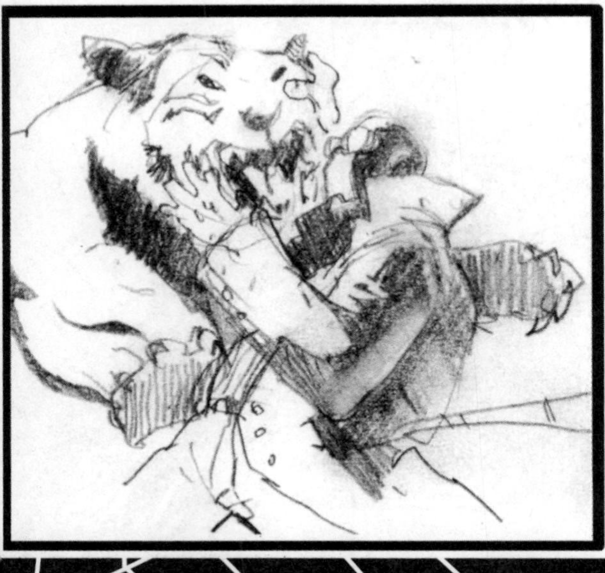

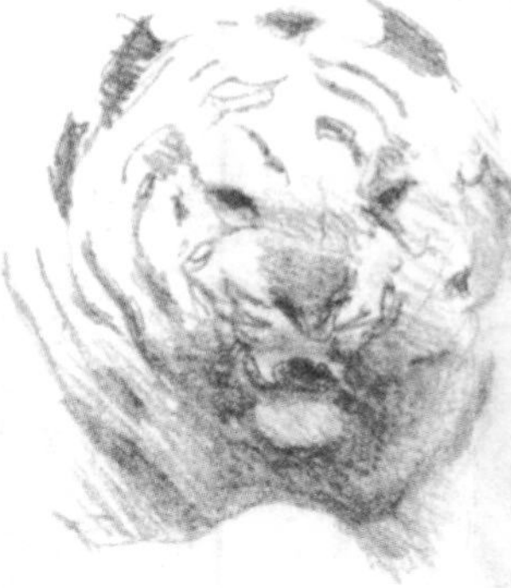

COVER SKETCHES

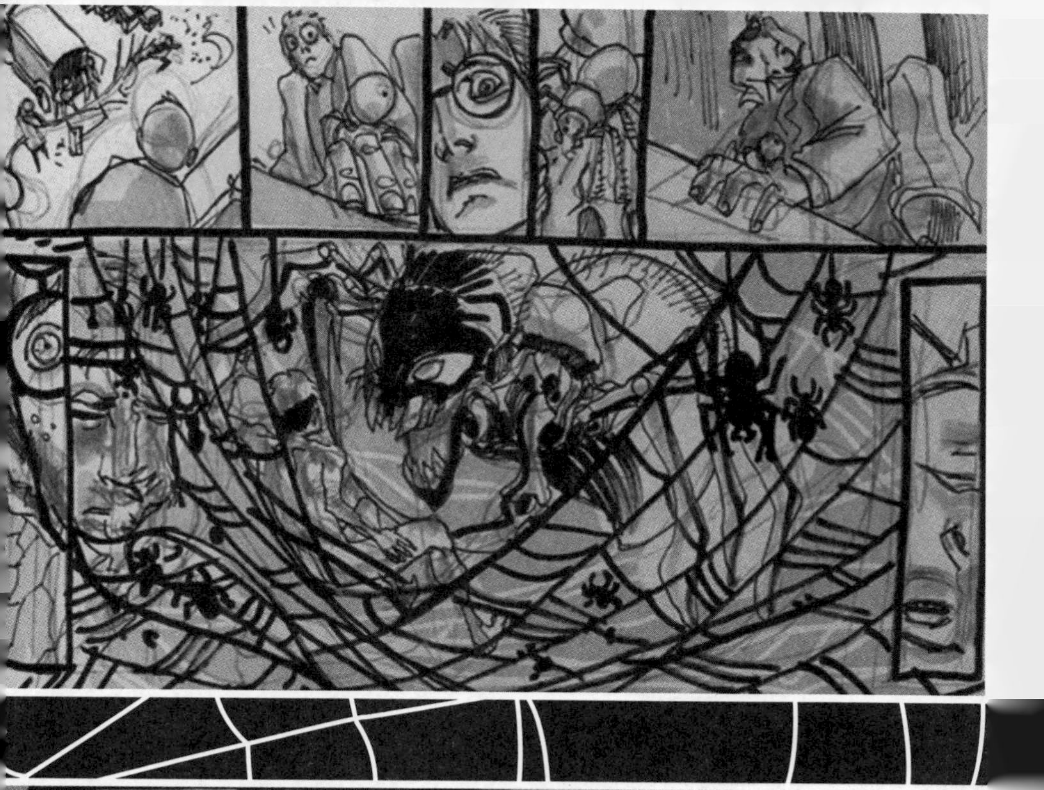

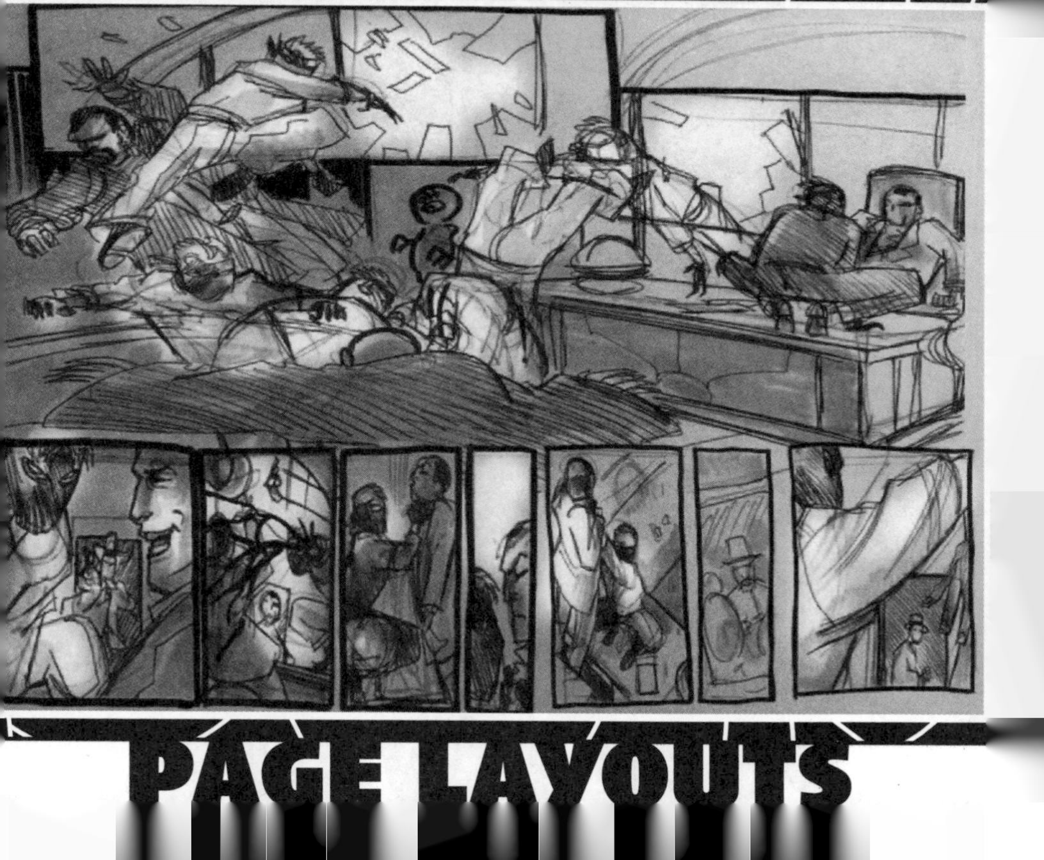

PAGE LAYOUTS

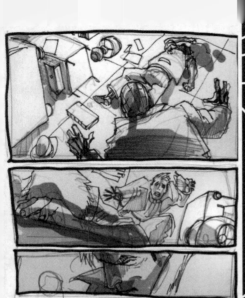

"Even in these very early, very rough layouts, Carmine Di Giandomenico's art communicates tremendous animation— action moves fluidly, locations are atmospheric, and the characters' faces convey expressiveness and emotion. It's art full of life."

—Alejandro Arbona, Editor

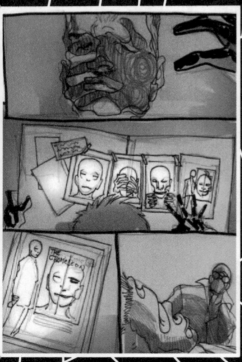

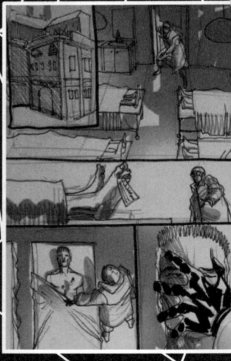

PAGE LAYOUTS

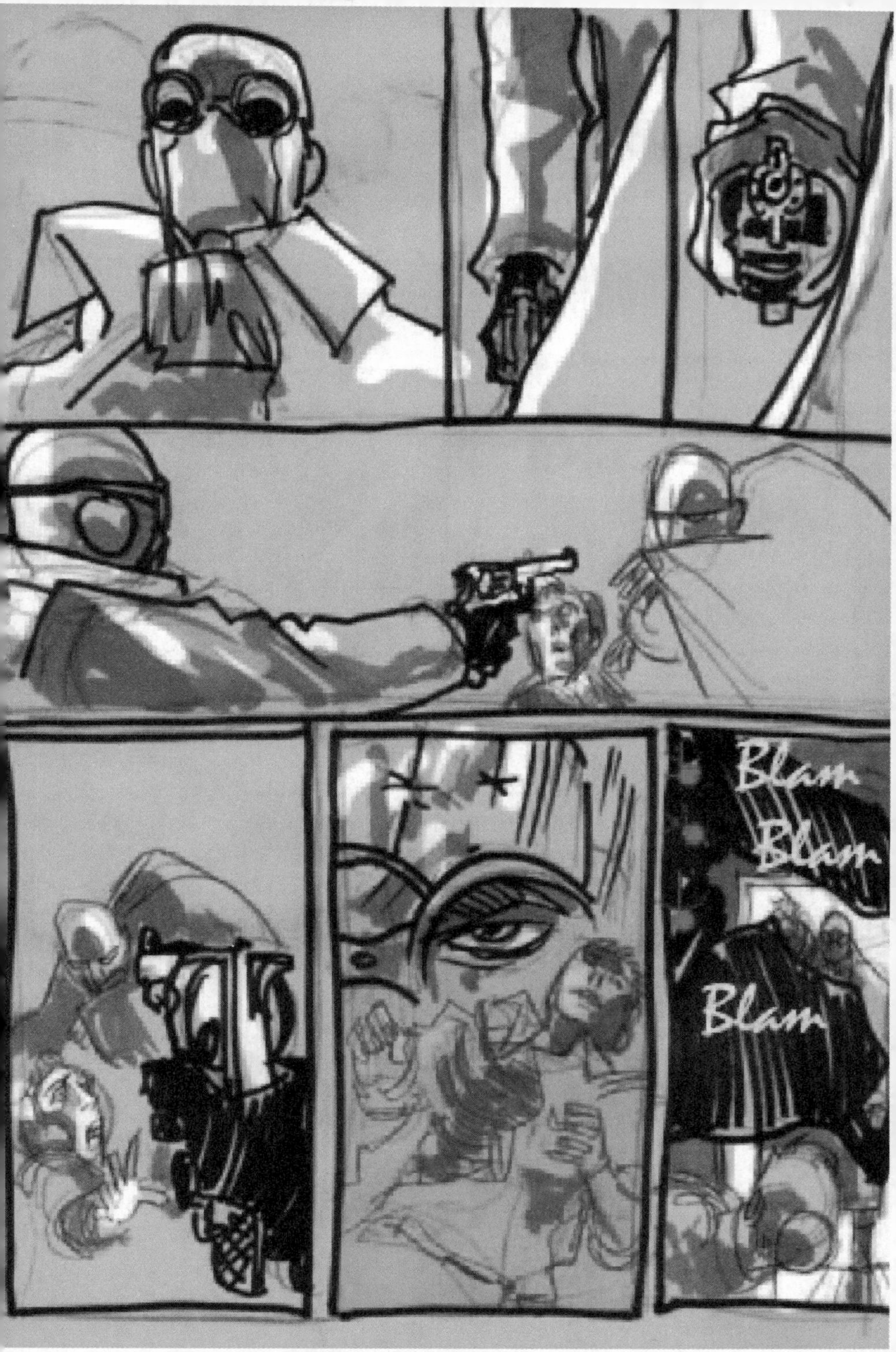
Blam
Blam
Blam

PAGE LAYOUTS

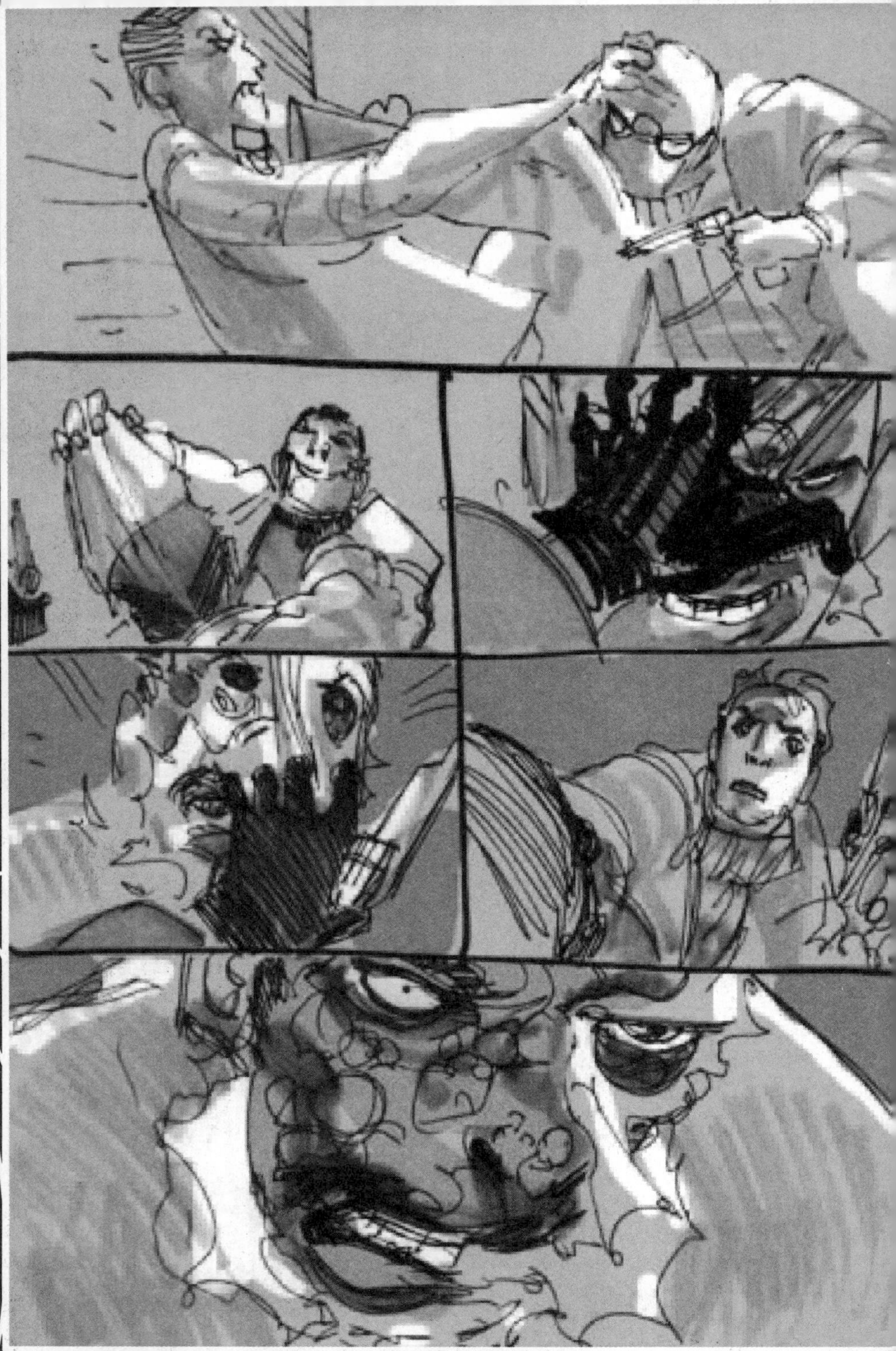

PAGE LAYOUTS